D0773026

WHY DOES LITERATURE MATTER?

WHY DOES
LITERATURE MATTER?

FRANK B. FARRELL

CORNELL UNIVERSITY PRESS

Ithaca and London

First published 2004 by Cornell University Press

Printed in the United States of America

Design by Scott Levine

Library of Cogress Cataloging-in-Publication Data

Farrell, Frank B.
  Why does literature matter? / Frank B. Farrell.
    p. cm.
Includes bibliographical references (p.   ) and index.
  ISBN 0-8014-4180-3 (cloth : alk. paper)
    1. American literature—20th century—History and criticism—Theory, etc. 2. English literature—20th century—History and criticism—Theory, etc. 3. Literature—Philosophy. I. Title.
  PS221.F37 2004
  801—dc22
                              2003019239

Cornell University Press strives to use environmentally responsible suppliers and materials to the fullest extent possible in the publishing of its books. Such materials include vegetable-based, low-VOC inks and acid-free papers that are recycled, totally chlorine-free, or partly composed of nonwood fibers. For further information, visit our website at www.cornellpress.cornell.edu.

Cloth printing   10 9 8 7 6 5 4 3 2 1

In loving memory of Kazuma Suzuki

CONTENTS

ACKNOWLEDGMENTS

I want first of all to express my gratitude for permission to quote from the following sources:

From *Collected Poems* by James Merrill, edited by J. D. McClatchy and Stephen Yenser, copyright 2001 by the Literary Estate of James Merrill at Washington University. Used by permission of Alfred A. Knopf, a division of Random House, Inc.

From *Houseboat Days* by John Ashbery, copyright 1975, 1976, 1977 by John Ashbery. Reprinted by permission of Georges Borchardt, Inc. and Carcanet Press Limited, Manchester, U.K.

From *Self-Portrait in a Convex Mirror* by John Ashbery, copyright 1972, 1973, 1974, 1975 by John Ashbery. Used by permission of Viking Penguin, a division of Penguin Putnam Inc. and Carcanet Press Limited, Manchester, U.K.

From *All the Pretty Horses* by Cormac McCarthy, copyright 1992 by Cormac McCarthy. Reprinted by permission of International Creative Management, Inc.

From *Blood Meridian* by Cormac McCarthy, copyright 1985 by Cormac McCarthy. Reprinted by permission of International Creative Management, Inc.

Various excerpts from *The Emigrants* by W. G. Sebald, translated by Michael Hulse, copyright 1992 by Vito von Eichborn GmbH & Co Verlag KG; translation copyright 1999 by the Harvill Press. Used by permission of New Directions Publishing Corporation.

Various excerpts from *The Rings of Saturn* by W. G. Sebald, translated by Michael Hulse, copyright 1995 by Vito von Eichborn GmbH & Co Verlag KG; translation copyright 1998 by the Harvill Press. Used by permission of New Directions Publishing Corporation.

From *Seeing Calvin Coolidge in a Dream* by John Derbyshire, copyright 1997 by John Derbyshire. Reprinted by permission of St. Martin's Press, LLC.

From *Gravity's Rainbow* by Thomas Pynchon, copyright 1973, 2001 by Thomas Pynchon. Used by permission of Viking Penguin, a division of Penguin Putnam Inc. and Melanie Jackson Agency, LLC.

From *The Heather Blazing* by Colm Tóibín, copyright 1992 by Colm Tóibín. Reprinted by permission of Macmillan, London, U.K., and Viking Penguin, a division of Penguin Putnam Inc.

From *Molloy* by Samuel Beckett, copyright 1955 by Grove/Atlantic, Inc. Reprinted by permission of Grove/Atlantic, Inc. and Calder Publications, London, U.K.

From *How It Is* by Samuel Beckett, copyright 1964 by Grove/Atlantic, Inc. Reprinted by permission of Grove/Atlantic, Ltd. and Calder Publications, London, U.K.

From *Freedom Song* by Amit Chaudhuri, copyright 1998 by Amit Chaudhuri. *Afternoon Raag* copyright 1993 by Amit Chaudhuri. *A Strange and Sublime Address* copyright 1991 by Amit Chaudhuri. Reprinted by permission of A. P. Watt Ltd. on behalf of Amit Chaudhuri and Alfred A. Knopf, a division of Random House, Inc.

From *The Centaur* by John Updike, copyright 1962, 1963 by John Updike. Used by permission of Alfred A. Knopf, a division of Random House, Inc.

From *Pigeon Feathers and Other Stories* by John Updike, copyright 1962 and renewed 1990 by John Updike. Used by permission of Alfred A. Knopf, a division of Random House, Inc. and Penguin U.K. (copyright 1965).

From *Museums and Women and Other Stories* by John Updike, copyright 1972 by John Updike. Used by permission of Alfred A. Knopf, a division of Random House, Inc., and Penguin U.K. (copyright 1975).

From *The Afterlife and Other Stories* by John Updike, copyright 1994 by John Updike. Used by permission of Alfred A. Knopf, a division of Random House, Inc.

I also want to thank two of my colleagues, Gary Waller and Gari La-Guardia, who read through an earlier draft of the book and gave me useful comments on it. Bernie Kendler and Ange Romeo-Hall at Cornell University Press have been unusually helpful, and an anonymous outside reader for Cornell gave a thorough review that produced significant improvements in the final version. Stephen Yenser, J. D. McClatchy, and Deborah Garrison helped in getting permission to quote extensively from James Merrill's poetry. This may also be a good place to thank Richard Rorty. After I used an earlier book to attack his views quite strongly, he turned around and helped me very generously at two points in my career. I mention him in this book briefly but still, I must confess, critically.

One theme that holds together much of what I write here is that of literature and loss. I began to have the ideas for this book not long after the death of James Merrill, who is perhaps my central figure, and I was working on the final draft when W. G. Sebald, another figure important to my narrative, died. The philosopher Bernard Williams, a strong influence on this book and on my general take on philosophy, died while the book was being edited. I hope my treatment of their work is, at some level, a proper memorial to writers who have enriched my life and an argument as to why we have to keep on reading them and authors like them. If that theme of literature and loss is dominant here, then the principal loss behind the book is that of my partner of thirteen years, Kazuma Suzuki, who died a decade ago. In one of his poems Merrill says that someone apparently absent from a text may be there "in the breath drawn after every line." That is true, I think, in the present case.

WHY DOES LITERATURE MATTER?

THE SPACE OF LITERATURE

To read widely in academic literary criticism of recent decades (that written from 1970 to 2000) is to wonder why literature matters at all. An impoverishment of literary space has occurred, or at least of our accounts of
it, in the way that thinkers such as Nietzsche and Bernard Williams have
found an impoverishing of modern ethical space.[1] The literary text appears as one more site, no more privileged than others, where cultural
codes linked with issues of power reveal themselves; or it is a site where
language seems an impersonal machinery generating meanings on its own,
in a manner that confounds the human writer's attempts to speak about
the world or to express intentional states. The result of either of these conceptions is that the arrangements of the literary text itself, the precise way
the author has placed particular words in a particular order, seem to lose
their importance. Authority passes to the critic, who is able to read the
hidden cultural codes or will set the textual machinery in motion to generate effects that have little to do with the context of production or the
work's specific arrangements. With the text having so little integrity of its
own, judgments that one work has greater literary worth than another
must appear as disguised projections of power and interest. It is not just
that these ways of reading are preferred; there is also a portrayal of earlier
ways of reading as philosophically naive about reference, truth, and subjectivity; as theoretically unsophisticated about the working of language;
and as politically ignorant of the machineries of social power. I want to
examine whether or not the older ways of reading can be defended, and I
hope to reverse the impoverishment of literary space.

First I will consider reasons that one might be tempted to think of literature in ways I will be opposing. Over much of the past century there was a widespread movement in philosophy, literature, and elsewhere that is often called "the linguistic turn": a recognition that large issues in metaphysics and aesthetics, for example, might be usefully studied through greater sophistication about linguistic theory and about the functioning of language in general.[2] In some respects that movement has now been rejected; in philosophy it led to arguments that undermined its own pretensions, and in literary theory it has been replaced by cultural studies and a politically oriented social history. Nevertheless the linguistic turn still has strong effects on literary theory, and we must work through some of its arguments to understand how we have arrived at the present state of criticism.

There might be weaker and stronger versions of such a turn to language. Certain related tendencies of thought may encourage a stronger version and may lead one astray in thinking about literature. The first tendency might be labeled *theological*. To understand it we need to take a brief look at intellectual history, beginning with how the Aristotelian world was undermined by the medieval notion that God's willing could have no limits.[3] Aquinas tried to balance the independent metaphysical integrity of things, through their Aristotelian natures, and the all-powerful status of the divine activity. He claimed that God, in knowing or willing any of these independent natures, was really engaged in a self-knowing or self-willing. Additionally, God had to be both creator and conserver of each existence, so that if his support of any existent should stop for even an instant that existent would fall into nothingness. Since this Thomist compromise could not remain stable it was not surprising to see, in the late medieval era, an increasing erosion of the metaphysical integrity of individual things, as the power and possible arbitrariness of God's will were emphasized.

That model of theological voluntarism casts a long shadow over later intellectual history. Its key feature is a radical thinning out of the world over against a determining other. In modern philosophy it was the thinking and willing subject that took over that role of determination; more recently it has been language or culture. In works by Richard Rorty and Stanley Fish, among many others, we find accounts in which a way of speaking is said to generate its own objects rather than being measured against something external to itself.[4] The more radical the turn to language, that is, the more it resembles the stance of theological voluntarism, then the thinner and emptier the world becomes. This pattern of thought is important even for those who now do cultural studies instead of letting textual machineries perform their deconstructive feats. In practicing that form of criticism one is simply replacing language in the theological position with what are known, after Foucault, as social regimes of discourse/power; these then engage in a social construction of both world and selves.

The second tendency of thought is close to the first but not quite the same; its ubiquity across different areas of discourse is impressive. It concerns what might be called a change of direction away from energies and relationships that appear to move between self and other, language and world, subject and object. Preference is instead given to energies that move in a lateral or sideways direction: from some linguistic utterances to other ones or from some beliefs to other beliefs, so that the truth-revealing character of texts seems to resolve itself into their intertextual references. The philosopher Willard Quine argues, for example, that language faces the world holistically, and that the way an individual word links up to the world is in principle mediated by its relations with all the other words of the language.[5] Reference becomes so inscrutable with that intralinguistic resonance that it seems too weak a notion to do much work. Rorty argues that in asking about the truth of sentences we have to give up any notion of language confronting the world and getting matters right, in favor of a notion of conversation among members of a speaking community.[6] Habermas says that the key mistake made in earlier German philosophy was to emphasize a model of subjectivity, of subjects setting themselves in relation to objects, instead of the model of a linguistic community that aims at communication and noncoercive agreement.[7] In other thinkers as well we see a turn to a lateral movement connecting some linguistic utterances with other ones, instead of a truth-determining confrontation with how matters stand. Wittgenstein shows that the rule now being followed, when one means to follow it, depends on what is a following of the rule in cases now absent, cases that help to fix what is a continuing of the rule-following in the same way as before.[8] But no pointing, whether to the world or to a linguistic or mental expression, can fix a unique path for that process of continuation as the same. Again any attempt to pin down meaning by linking it to a portion of the world or to a mental state becomes, instead, a sideways movement linking any particular use to past and future uses and repetitions.

A reinforcement of that directional shift was due to work in formal languages and grammars. Whether through structuralism in Europe or the model of formal logic in Anglo-American philosophy, it seemed that determinacy was fixed primarily by internal relations within something like a formal system. The meaning of a certain bit of language was owed to the rules determining what moves could be made with it as a counter in a game, what positions it could take up and what transformations it would allow and warrant. These models, we might say, were *grammatical,* using that term in a wide sense, whereas earlier philosophical models had been *phenomenological,* that is, more concerned with how the world appeared to the conscious experiencer, with the character of the self's intentional relations to the world and to itself. As the grammatical model becomes more dominant, it may lead to the third tendency of thought I am now surveying. This is a tendency to favor accounts for which the most significant patterns, whether in culture or in literature, are due to anonymous pattern-generating machineries that operate beneath or external to the realm of the self and its experiences. The notion of the grammatical is used in a broad sense here. It will include matters, for example, for which there may not be clear rules, as there normally are in grammar, for demarcating arrangements of items into those that are well formed and those that are not. It will also include the ways languages operate to destabilize their grammars as well as to express them. The level of the grammatical, as a term of art, may then be taken to include not only syntactic forms but any properties that are due to pattern-generating machineries of language itself, insofar as these transcend the work of referring to or displaying the world or of expressing psychological states. These patterns seem artifacts of a more autonomous operation of the linguistic or conceptual system; as in a formal language, there are internal capacities for generating arrangements that seem to position themselves on their own, or with which world and self must then match up. This notion may be expanded to include cultural grammars more generally, where there are rules or power grids for determining how various cultural units, whether representations or individual selves, may combine and circulate.

This notion of the grammatical is not at all precise; it cannot be, since I want to include in it, for the purposes of this book, rather different phenomena. What I call the grammatical tries to press together the notion of grammar in structuralism and formal languages; the working of the deconstructive and rhetorical machineries of language that undermine stable meanings; the way patterns of words may keep generating novel connections beyond what a speaker or writer intended; the way systems of concepts may become more free floating and be defined by their internal relations more than by concept-to-world linkages; the claim by linguistic philosophers such as Rudolf Carnap that the metaphysical is a projection of the grammatical;[9] the notion of discursive regimes of power as defining cultural grammars; and the game-theory sense of seeing a conceptual field in terms of moves and positions, of strategic conceptual moves against other ones, rather than in terms of truth and representation. Surely that is a diverse set, but certain oppositions serve to give the notion of the grammatical a relatively stable usage that will prove helpful later. It will be consistently opposed to all of the following: to a phenomenological space of conscious experiencing, of self-to-other relations; to features that are fundamentally referential or world revealing or expressive of psychological states; to kinds of ordering that are identificational or metaphorical, or that depend on similarities of iconic and spatial patterns across different items; and to what might be thought of as dyadic, oscillating, pre-Oedipal patterns of relationship. There will be consistency as well in that, throughout, I will be attacking what I see as a hypertrophy of the grammatical, in its various forms, in the ways literature has come to be read. (A crucial question in both philosophy and literature is the degree to which what I have just opposed to the grammatical can be explained in terms of it. Can one's conscious experience of something in the world be explained as the running of a computer program? Can a literary text be explained in terms of the hidden grammars that determine how representations circulate through it? Are standard logics rich enough to express a theory of meaning for a language or is linguistic meaning built on a scaffolding of earlier ways of ordering? There are many similar issues.)

I will use the notions of a theological stance, a turn to the sideways energies of language, and a grammatical level in order to address aspects of literary theory. First I wish to set these notions within a broader schema that underlies the overall argument, a schema that, while far too neat to account properly for a complex intellectual history, will prove useful. The passage from modern thought to the present might be described in terms of three great reductions: first, modern thinkers dissolve the world into mind or subjectivity; second, the subjective or psychological, as expressed in a phenomenology of the conscious self and its self-to-world relations, is dissolved into language; and third, that level of the linguistic or grammatical may be dissolved into social practices, into patterns of social power.

It is important that in each of the three cases the reduction may be either more or less radical. One may, for example, agree that what we mean by truth and reality will be due in part to how we as selves light up the world and make it significant; or one may, more radically, believe that reality is no more than a construction out of individual or communal subjectivity. On another level, one may agree that our psychological lives are strongly shaped by language or culture; or one may believe, more radically, that psychological states are in some sense constructed out of the anonymous grammatical machineries of language. Finally, one may agree that truth and meaning, and the properly linguistic power of texts, are implicated in various ways in social practices; or one may believe, more radically, that these phenomena are nothing more than a projection of systems of social power and the rules they determine for how representations can circulate and take on value. This third reduction in its radical form would yield a strong version of social constructionism, with even the truth of scientific statements determined by distributions of social power that favor some speakers and not others. In each of the three cases the radical reduction opens up what I described above as a theological position: that is, it allows whatever level the different phenomena are being reduced to, whether subjectivity, language, or social power, to generate the features of other levels out of its self-relational activity. Note that there is a certain dependence of the later reductions on the earlier ones, as with the folding back in of the sections of a telescope. It is only because the world has been radically dissolved into subjectivity that both world and subjectivity can be radically dissolved into language. And only that radical linguistic turn allows later on for world, subject, and language to be dissolved into practices of social power.

Literary theory of the past three decades can perhaps be characterized in terms of those reductions. On the one hand, I will examine how critics represent, in their theorizing about literature and their reading of texts, a radical reduction of the psychological to the linguistic or grammatical. On the other hand, I will consider how the cultural studies model of criticism performs a radical reduction of both the psychological and the literary-linguistic to sociology and social history and to a politics of power. The argument throughout will be that in every case these three reductions in their radical forms are in error. They are not merely unjustified; they involve serious misunderstandings of how it is that linguistic utterances or social power moves are meaningful in the first place. Arguments for that claim will be examined in chapter 3 and elsewhere. The result of these arguments will be that meaning cannot be accounted for, whether in epistemic space or literary space, without a commitment to richer versions of the world and of subjectivity than these radical turns can allow for. The world will turn out to have substantial metaphysical depth of its own; and a rich phenomenology of self-to-world relations must also be in play in our forms of engagement with reality. To reduce these to projections of language or social power is to lose hold of the context that is needed to prevent the level of language or of social power from itself being emptied out. Instead of the model of levels collapsing into other ones, as in the image of the telescope, we are forced to develop more sophisticated notions of truth and representation and selfhood, without supposing that these notions have been deconstructed into the operations of language or social power.

In making these arguments I run the risk of appearing to some as nostalgic about thought patterns I do not quite wish to give up. But I will attempt to show that my opponents here are the ones who are not being radical enough. Consider different possible versions of the historical process of disenchantment. The world is no longer seen as a place magically invested with meaning. But modern thinkers, in acknowledging that point, continued to invest subjectivity with a divinized power to determine meaning, without its own meaningfulness being explained. The linguistic turn then disenchants subjectivity but grants the theological role to language, and one does not go on to question in a rigorous manner how language itself gets to be meaningful. Finally the linguistic level is disenchanted, losing its autonomous (and magical) power to generate and project reference schemes. It dissolves into a set of circulating representations caught in the flows, negotiations, and contestations of social power. Of course those regimes of social power now take over the theological role.

The pattern should be clear. Put oversimply, these matters can be pictured as involving successive levels: the world, subjectivity, language, and machineries of social power. In each case one tries to accomplish the move of disenchantment by divinizing the position one move farther up the line. Over against that newly determined theological position, everything farther down becomes emptied out and loses any integrity and character it might have on its own, so that it can be nothing but the mirroring effect of the theological position above it. But that pattern of thought is itself the naive strategy. Once we understand that disenchantment goes all the way up, as it were, then it is clear that none of these stopping points can play the theological role assigned to it; none has the ability to determine its own character from within its own self-relational powers.

A more sophisticated conception, in allowing full disenchantment and thus in assigning no such theological position, destroys the basis of the more radical turns described. Instead, even as we understand the shaping role of each level higher up, the prior levels retain an irreducible richness of content. To disenchant the world but not subjectivity, for example, seems to lead to an emptied-out world. A more sophisticated double disenchantment of world and subjectivity shows that one's conscious states could have no meaning whatever unless they varied in regular ways with well-articulated worldly states that cast their shadows on the operations of mind. (This argument will be examined in greater detail in chapter 3.) The entire network of meaningful relations could not get going at all without the granting of a more independent status to those features that the more radical reductions would thin out. (There is a relation of mutual dependence among these phenomena that this picture of different levels perhaps does not properly express. An account of what the world truly is depends on how we talk about it, just as linguistic items could not be meaningful unless they varied in regular ways with a world independent of them. The determining goes in both directions.)

This schema is useful as well in developing a response to the claims in literary theory that notions of truth, representation, and subjectivity, to take just three examples, have been destabilized and deconstructed. They would be so only if the more radical turns spoken of were accomplished. The correct analysis is that such notions become more complicated rather than destabilized. Take the notion of representation and consider it in the context of this four-level schema. On a naive reading one may suppose that the world simply stamps itself on mental states or bits of language, thus producing accurate representations of itself. But then one discovers the role of subjectivity, of our processes of *taking* the world to be such and such, in what we count as real. One recognizes as well how the field of language, with all its sideways connections and repetitions, comes into play to complicate how any thought or utterance can count as referring to the world. Finally one sees how configurations of social power serve as machineries for circulating representations into and out of various power networks. In all these ways one must accept more complicated conceptions of how thoughts or words are about the world. But provided we do not make the error of allowing a radical reduction of one level to another, the notion of representation becomes more sophisticated rather than destabilized. We may retain notions of the world and of subjectivity that are rich enough for making sense of an engagement with the world in which thoughts and words can track the truth, can roughly get matters right. So we end with a relatively stable, even if philosophically much more subtle, notion of representation.

It may appear that such a schema is too abstract to be useful in the reading of literary texts, but I will put it into play in the reading of works by John Ashbery and James Merrill, among many others. My general account of literary space, of what makes literature powerful, will focus precisely on those aspects of that space that depend on our *not* making the radical turns this schema describes. I will focus, then, on how the space of literature is constituted such that the metaphysical does not fold back into the moves of subjectivity; how the phenomenological, the psychological, the perceptual do not fold back into the conceptual or linguistic; and how linguistic power does not fold back into social power. In each case the less radical turn makes literary space more complex and interesting.

In many areas of experience there is often a double move of both holding on to and letting go. In Merrill's poem "Lost in Translation," for example, various translations are shown: from childhood to adulthood; from iconically powerful scenes to the grammatical setting into position of language; from metaphorical identification to cooler metonymic arrangements. The power of the poem depends on a complex continuing relationship to what is being translated from and not just on the translation. Such activities of identification and attachment, of separation and loss can occur both personally and culturally, as when, for example, we must leave behind premodern or archaic or less transparent modes of experience in order to become more fully modern selves. It will be important to my various readings here that these are not straightforward transitions. Rather there are usefully complicated ways of retaining weaker attachments to, and identifications with, what is thus let go of. In several different ways this investigation will favor transitions where that which one turns away from must still remain in play, if in a more sophisticated manner.

In marking out the features of literary space in order to show why literature matters, I am trying to pick out features that help articulate an account deliberately set against standard accounts in the field. I do not pretend, then, to be giving a general theory of literature, whatever that would be. My purposes are narrower and somewhat polemical, so that I give more attention precisely to those features that other critics may have been happy to leave behind as outdated or naive or regressive. The second criterion for choosing the aspects here is that they are concerned with a more internalist account of literary space, that is, one that supposes it to be a privileged space whose power depends more on its particular arrangements than on the social context.

Let me present here, then, those features that I will be looking for in my readings of poems and works of fiction. The first of these is one already briefly mentioned. Literary space as I will characterize it is *phenomenological;* I intend to capture several ideas through describing this feature. Recall how Hegel in his *Phenomenology* articulates different shapes of subjectivity, different overall ways, that is, in which the self may be implicitly self-engaged in taking a stance toward a world of objects. While I will not commit myself to the particular features of Hegel's account, I will argue that those self-to-world patterns, and the intentional investments of the self they assume, are necessary both to an adequate philosophical picture of experience and meaning and to uncovering how literary texts function. Those patterns are evident in Sartre's *Nausea* in the sections where Roquentin is trying under emotional pressure to work out his stance toward a world of objects. I will argue that in many other literary works there is an implicit phenomenological stance, a general way of taking the world to be meaningful that is expressed in the sequence and rhythms of words, in the descriptions of physical space, in the overall style of engagement with the objects brought into view for the narrator, in the character and cadence of a protagonist's movements through space, in a kind of mood that seems a feature both of the world and of one's attitude toward it. The space of the literary text remains one where that life of the self, its fundamental way of setting itself in relation to the universe, its relations to fate and chance, to grief, death, and loss, are being enacted in a particular fashion, not only in the lives of the characters but also in the very processes of writing and reading.

A related feature of literary space is that it can be *metaphysical.* (There is overlap among the dozen or so features I am investigating here, but each brings out a somewhat different aspect.) I have in mind a particular use of this term, a use owed especially to the philosopher Heidegger. While he was at times a moral cripple and an intellectual charlatan, he was also capable of profound reflection on the character of our engagement with the world.[10] Consider the difference between the objects that appear on the stage of a theater and the way they are lit up by the lighting director, so that there is a background mood or space that makes them appear as having a certain style of being real. In some philosophers and poets, Heidegger believed, there is a way of making visible what might be called the metaphysical lighting itself, a deeper space against which things appear as having a certain feel, a certain texture and manner of being real. With a more radically linguistic or postmodern space, in contrast, there is a shrinkage of that space inward, so that we have little sense of a field emptying out beyond our words into a depth that is more than we take it to be, and against which the objects of our experience have the overall character they do. In many powerful works of literature there is an implicit appearing of such a space or clearing, a coming into view of the way things are metaphysically lit up, so that a deeper sense of the universe, and of our place within it, seems to be at stake. (It has been said that in Akira Kurosawa's and Werner Herzog's films the landscape and weather readily become metaphysical, while in most American films they can only be psychological or cinematic.) I will study several texts regarding this feature, but consider one brief literary example, Hemingway's well-known opening to *A Farewell to Arms:*

> In the late summer of that year we lived in a house in a village that looked across the river and the plain to the mountains. In the bed of the river there were pebbles and boulders, dry and white in the sun, and the water was clear and swiftly moving and blue in the channels. Troops went by the house and down the road and the dust they raised powdered the leaves of the trees. The trunks of the trees too were dusty and the leaves fell early that year and we saw the troops marching along the road and the dust rising and leaves, stirred by the breeze, falling and the soldiers marching and afterward the road bare and white except for the leaves.[11]

The soldiers are seen coming into view along the road and then disappearing, in the manner of the leaves, so that there is a clear suggestion of existence as an emerging into individual form and then dissolving. The very line of prose seems to be enacting such a metaphysical vision and our own attitude of acceptance. If literary texts are performing that function, then it is not surprising that writers give much attention, for metaphorical purposes, to descriptions of physical space and light, to a style combining rising and falling, determinacy and loss.

Besides that very specific sense of the metaphysical, literary space is also *truth-revealing*. Someone trained in a postmodern self-consciousness about the circulation of signs may suppose that the notion of truth can be used only ironically or in quotation marks. But I believe that in a straightforward manner literature can make visible significant patterns of how the world is arranged that cannot be had by other means. As clever as we may become about recognizing how our sayings are shaped by other sayings and express hidden discursive codes, it remains the case that in our fundamental orientation toward the world we are sophisticated pattern-recognizers, adept filterers of patterns from the world's noise. We would not have made it this far if we were not generally truth-tropic in exercising this ability. If this is our typical mode of operation, works of literature may stand out as letting us see patterns that are only faintly emergent, that cut across different semantic registers in unexpected ways, and that are not visible elsewhere or otherwise. Take a casual remark, the mood of an afternoon, a scene observed by chance through the window of a store, a quotation memorized long ago in school, an umbrella blown awry, a memory of fixing a car. There may be no apparent logic that joins these, but the writer finds a barely appearing field in which somehow they belong together. Such an emergent belonging-together, in its faint and inchoate form, may become possible only through a kind of attention, as in literature, that employs resources across several registers of the psyche. Literature can then satisfy a certain definition of philosophy: a study of how things, in the widest sense of the term, hang together, in the widest sense of the term. Philosophy shows that we can refer to the truth-revealing function of literature without being theoretically naive.

Referring to literature as truth-revealing includes those moments when we do not simply gather information but have some fundamental character of being human, and especially of human relationships, brought intensely into view. In reading authors such as Shakespeare and George Eliot, Edward Albee and Henry James, we may have the experience not merely of adding more to what we know, as journalism might do, but of having some truth about human interaction emerge from shadows into light, so that we seem to understand it clearly for the first time. It is true that such experiences cannot justify themselves simply by that feeling of emergence. Most of us will recall earlier reading experiences that seemed to give the truth of something, and then later we came to see that particular "truth" as artificial, as an unconvincingly made fiction. But as with science, the experience of shedding earlier convictions should not make us deny that some literary works do a better job than others do, however difficult it may be to specify this, of displaying the subtle and hard-to-grasp patterns that make human relationships what they are. Even as children we find a certain pleasure, perhaps compensating for other ones, when what becomes visible for us seems to express a sense of the world as such, apart from how we might take it to be. With some literary works we may feel that the world, including the human psychological world, is presenting itself not only as true but also as showing its truth-character as such in a more evident manner, so that the experience of seeing what is there is more intensely felt (as a scientist may have in a moment of discovery the experience of a pattern suddenly clicking into shape and becoming visible). It might be useful to consider here the simple four-level schema mentioned earlier of world, subjectivity, language, and social power. As each level colonizes the earlier ones more visibly, there can be special literary power in moments that let those earlier levels emerge with a special intensity. As one feels immersed, for example, in a self-conscious linguistic play, with all its sideways linkages and energies, one can feel moved by having a vista seem to open up suddenly on the world in its character as such, or on the patterns of the psyche's investments in the world, its attachments and losses.

An additional feature of the space of literature is that it is *psychological*. Again, this is meant in a specific sense, one that owes a great deal to work in object-relations theory but is not dependent on any particular version of that theory. D. W. Winnicott and others suppose that in producing literature or art one has access to a transitional or potential space that formed an earlier stage in the process of self-formation.[12] In this early childhood stage one had to accomplish the work of separation and individuation, of determining the boundaries of the self against what is other, of setting oneself in relation to a world of stable objects, of establishing a secure sense of selfhood over against forces that would threaten to blur or dissolve it. The young child may be seen as a metaphysician and epistemologist in miniature, trying to establish a recognition of, and a characteristic style of engagement with, the surrounding world, through a certain implicit self-understanding. One hypothesis is that in writing, one is often handling difficult experiences that trigger anxieties about those earlier accomplishments. One has a kind of attenuated access to the earlier transitional space where so much was at stake in setting oneself reliably in relation to things. That is why the writer's working out of a relationship to objects, through the handling of the line of prose and other textual features, can generate a space of heightened significance for whatever enters into it. (Even the power of a philosopher such as Wittgenstein might be due in part to his access, through mental states that were vaguely regressive, to a space where the most basic issues of how one is engaged with a meaningful world were still in play.)

Another aspect of literary space as I will characterize it is that it is *ritualized*. In the life of cultures there are opportunities to enter a ritual space where a controlled sequence of activities, an already set scheme of performance, is enjoined on one. The goal is to produce, ultimately, a more satisfying sense of one's relationship to the forces of the cosmos and to one's community. Nietzsche famously argued that the strongest art has in it certain elements found in Greek tragedy. Against our consciousness of existence as blind, driven, and meaningless we raise up an Apollonian world of beautiful forms that makes us delight in the ongoing play of appearances. We also come for a while to forge a revitalizing identification with the Dionysian forces that put forth these phenomenal individuals and endlessly dissolve them. In art or literature one may both accept a disenchanted, more mature stance and hold on ritually to faint, attenuated forms of an earlier psychological or cultural pattern, in the way that the tragic chorus was a weakened leftover of Dionysian ceremonies. Through examining different literary works I will argue that literature often provides such a ritual space. Making this claim goes against a tendency of recent criticism: the tendency toward an externalism regarding significant features of the text. Critics, in other words, see those features as resulting less from the specific arrangements of words and images in a text than from structures imposed from without, by cultural grammars or by interpreters.

To speak of the literary text as a ritual space is to give, in contrast, a more internalist account of a text's power, through seeing the writer as offering a controlled sequence of verbal experiences, of patterns of investment and identification. By giving oneself over to these ceremonial patterns, the reader enters slightly hypnotic states determined by the rhythms and sounds as well as by the scenes and images of the text. In these states, as in older rituals, there may be a tension between maintaining individuation, as expressed in the ongoing energy and well-orderedness of the sequence of words, and connecting with less individuating forces and patterns. Beneath the line, as in Nietzsche on tragedy, may be the traces of a distant music, a more archaic pattern of psychological investments. As one comes through the ritual successfully, with its various risks and appeals, one finds a restored sense of vitality in living out one's life. That is why even profoundly sad or despairing novels and poems can give readers a sense of exhilaration. This ritual power is present not just in works such as *King Lear* and *Moby-Dick*; also in popular novels such as Anne Tyler's *The Accidental Tourist* and *Saint Maybe* one finds that terrible experiences of loss, grief, and guilt are gradually internalized and accepted, and the reader's vicarious acceptance of these resolutions depends on the ritual sequences designed by the author.

The claim is sometimes made that earlier reading practices emphasized absorption in the sequences of the text while the reading practices favored by critics today are antiabsorptive. One uses critical and deconstructive and politically sensitive habits to resist the identifications the text would entice us into. Instead one reads the text against its grain, from a more reflective and skeptical stance. I do not deny the value of that critical skepticism, but its efforts to deny the virtues of absorptive reading practices should be resisted. As selves we remain not merely critical of beliefs but also in need of ceremonies that test our anxieties about individuation and loss. (To speak as I have of distant music is to connect the cadences of literature with psychological states that were at one time more strongly encouraged, in a more archaic tribal life, by music, dance, and religious ritual. It is likely that research in cognitive science will be able at some point to tell us about brain states triggered by these activities and about their functions. One point of such activity must be to join us through rhythm in coordinated psychological states that can ground communal feeling and action. Literature, even when written or read alone, can perhaps through its rhythms give us a weaker connection to such feelings and actions, and so may offer a sense of support as the pressures of individuation and self-consciousness increase.)

A corollary of the last feature is that literary space can also be characterized as a *regressive-disenchanted* one. It is important that there is often a certain doubleness in the space of literary texts. We live within a stance of disenchantment from which certain archaic investments are no longer possible. Yet those earlier worlds are not simply left behind; they remain as scaffoldings that support our more advanced structures of thought. The earlier world or style of engagement is held in view and often returned to symbolically, even while we cannot believe in the possibility or the value of an actual return. A good example of this structure can be seen in "The House Fly," a poem by James Merrill.[13] In it the poet is sitting in a room and sharing a communion ritual with a fly that is buzzing around him, as the sun becomes the "mist-white wafer she and I partake of / Alone this afternoon." The fly, he assumes, is descended from one that, "founding the cult" in that very room, alit one evening on the bare chest of the poet's former lover. The very weakness of the metonymic connection is suggested in the tone of the final stanza, where the earlier scene is "brought back on every autumn feebler wings." The final lines state that the rite now available is "distinct from both the blessing and the blight." It is not a return of the immediacy of the remembered experience but retains that earlier world in a weakened manner, in a way that prevents the present world from being one of emptiness and blight. Another example is a well-known passage in James Joyce's "The Dead" in which Gabriel sees his wife on the staircase listening to a traditional ballad being sung invisibly in an upper room. He thinks that a painting of the scene would call it "Distant Music," and distant music has been a theme throughout the story—the cadence of an earlier form of Irish life and the cadence of the universe itself whose processes will soon annihilate all in the room as the annihilating snow becomes general over Ireland, and as a rhythm that has been faint throughout becomes much stronger in the final passages.[14]

The claim here that literary space is a regressive-disenchanted one, a space of doubleness, also goes against the typical thinking of recent criticism. That thinking would have it that any turn to a linguistic, postmodern, discursive space ought to be a more radical one, and so ought to leave behind the outdated patterns of earlier cultural paradigms and of more regressive sorts of engagement with the world. One might favor the more radical turn for theoretical reasons, as the earlier patterns will seem to depend on magical thinking and on identifications that a deconstructive critic can no longer accept; or for political reasons, as any regression may seem to favor premodern or patriarchal or even fascist modes of organization. Or one might speak of cultural ideas as like fashions, for which earlier forms of discourse bog down and become uninteresting and are replaced by others. Thus one might argue that culture has gone through a long stage in which matters of separation and individuation, of the ritual enactment of our relations to the cosmos, were of great importance. But now we have taken up new forms of discourse for which those issues, and the psychological patterns they encourage, no longer matter. (Perhaps, for example, we now engage in strategic maneuvers within cultural grammars and systems of representation, instead of focusing on pre-Oedipal worries about dissolution, loss, and the feel of reality over against us. Artists, for example, may seem less adept now at picking out faintly emergent patterns of the world and more skilled at a sideways glance that allows a placing of various moves in the art game in relation to other such moves.) It will be up to me, in my individual readings, to show that talk of this double space of regression and disenchantment accounts for literary work better than does a more radical linguistic-postmodern colonizing of earlier spaces. I will argue that various models of experience and meaning that might appear as regressive are in fact necessary background conditions that prevent the supposedly more sophisticated stance from becoming shallow and empty.

A related feature of literary space is that it is *translational.* By this I mean that what is of interest generally, and of special interest to the writer, is the process of experience *becoming* language, rather than movements within a space already constituted as linguistic or discursive. One does not shrink the space of what is represented into having the character of the space of representation. There is instead the satisfaction of bringing difficult experience, and the hard-to-grasp patterns of reality, into the ordering architecture of language. But one has a proper sense of the gains and losses in that translation only if that which was translated *from* still remains in view as such, only if one is sensitive to what resists colonizing by language even as that colonizing occurs. The more typical account today has the representational space becoming more autonomous, as a field of lightly moving items that are already discursive, that are circulating cultural signs whose referential and world-revealing functions have become so insubstantial as to be mere projections of language or social power. To think of literary space as translational is, instead, to think of it as intimately connected to the many familiar processes of separation and loss, of finding compensating forms for what we give up, of using linguistic energies both to capture and to replace other ones. It is important for this account that literary language becomes interesting and powerful in the translation from one space to another. Perhaps one might read *The Waste Land,* for example, as offering a space where items of cultural discourse, from different areas, happen to be circulating; since the self is only a thinned-out construct of those discursive patterns it is not necessary to focus also on a psychological reading of the poem. But that attitude is one more unfortunate outcome of the hypertrophy of language and discourse in the radical linguistic turn. The discursive layers of that poem are built on nondiscursive layers having to do with pre-Oedipal anxieties, with obsessive images and fantasies, with fears of dissolution and of the blurring of gender identity. The self's attempts to use language in handling these anxieties, to accomplish a necessary translation, belong not to a merely discursive regime but to the shaping of an individual life out of a rich set of resources for structuring its engagement with the world. One finds in such writing, perhaps, a faint repetition of the long-ago movement of the human species into the world of language, with all that this translation meant.

The space of literature is also *metaphorical* in the following specific sense. Here I extend a point suggested above in speaking of literary space as ritualized. The qualities of the linguistic sequences, their sound patterns and rhythms, can metaphorically enact a staging of the psyche. The advancing line of prose, in its self-sustaining life and rightness of pattern, can suggest the life of the individual self as it also takes in external, difficult-to-absorb material and finds itself capable of keeping its self-sustaining rhythms going, its self-maintaining integrity. The deeper cadences of the line can express the natural and archaic forces over which the life of the individual has been raised up, and into which it will eventually dissolve. Often a literary text will show a character moving across a landscape, whether walking or driving a car, moving in a train or rowing a boat. That steady movement across the terrain matches the rhythmic linguistic advance and also the life of the self as it maintains itself through its ongoing rhythms. The writer may hope that the prose is good enough to take on an air of inevitability and perhaps may hope that, again through the power of metaphor, his own life, in the way its patterns unfold, may come to have a rightness and inevitability about it.

That metaphorical staging of the psyche may involve as well a playing out, in the literary space that emerges, of relations between form and matter, of a field of dispersed, resistant materials and the energies that organize them, of the incarnation of the lighter, more fluent movements of self-consciousness in the material stuff of language and the world. Such lightness and mastery, over against the thickness and perhaps the threatening character of a world that is also brought into view, may be staging a deeply satisfying stance of the self. So large issues that philosophers have been concerned with for centuries may be at issue even in the matter of literary style, though only if that style is thought of as richly metaphorical in a manner independent of whether metaphors are actually employed within it. There is perhaps something of evolutionary as well as personal significance in the pleasure we take in the emergence of self-sustaining patterns from what appears scattered and meaningless; in our ability to order a lighter world of representations instead of submitting to the heaviness of things; in experiencing the interplay of form and freedom, both the volatile, electric emergence of semantic energy and its ordering and containment; and in finding ourselves in an ultimately enlarging relationship with the nonhuman forces of nature and fate, so that we feel supported on the deep cadences of an activity that has its own rich momentum, apart from what we make it to be. All of these matters of metaphysical and evolutionary interest can have their metaphorical enactments in literature, and especially in literary style.

I grant that the contemporary academic critic may be skeptical here. The claim will be made (by followers of Paul de Man, among others) that metaphor generally, and especially the metaphorical joining of inner and outer, self and world, depends on a magical, identificational thinking that a more reflective stance, grounded perhaps more in metonymy than in metaphor, would have us put aside. Such a critic may believe that the kind of satisfactions of literature just outlined may have had their role in classical Greece and in German idealism and romanticism, in Nietzsche and in modernism, but that they are no longer relevant in the present literary regime. I will have to produce arguments against that objection. (A necessary complication, of course, is that this metaphorical staging of the psyche may, in the movement of the prose, present the postmodern self in its cooler, more fragmented engagements with the objects of a postmodern world.)

A related characteristic of literary space is that it is *aesthetic*. I have been focusing on the way that features internal to the literary work, such as rhythm and style, are not mere ornaments but contribute essentially to constituting a heightened space of significance. It is quite common in recent criticism to play down aesthetic properties. They may be seen either as appealing to regressive psychological interests or as encouraging politically repressive models of organic unity. But if the model of literary space I am defending is correct, then the space of literature can allow for its several functions only if the sequences of language have certain qualities of aesthetic well-formedness. This is not a matter of covering over disagreeable features of the world. A work of literature might be thought of as like a hurricane party in a house on the beach; the stable and well-proportioned architecture of the language allows us to get closer to threatening experiences and insights without fear of being overwhelmed by them, since the architecture of the prose that we identify with seems able to internalize such material without losing its self-sustaining form and momentum. The very tension between the threatening, fragmenting tendencies of the material and the ordering power of form, especially insofar as the latter can let the former appear without repressing it, is one of the great sources of literary power. In one respect, of course, this emphasis on well-formed patterns goes back to the Greek moment of culture. An intensified sense of individuation then, with accompanying anxieties about the risks of dissolution, placed such a premium on beautiful forms that could maintain themselves by seeming to have an internal necessity and rightness. But it is a mistake to suppose that we have simply passed beyond that stage in becoming modern and postmodern. To read some postmodern critics is to assume that with the so-called death of the subject and the triumph of discourse there is no longer any anxiety about individuation and death. That is a serious misreading of our contemporary situation. As is usual, the more radical turn to a postmodern-linguistic space tries to leave behind aspects of living a human life that are still crucial to us, and that indeed are crucial to discourses being meaningful at all. To speak of literary space as aesthetic in this manner is to suppose that it maintains a strong and fertile tension between its world-directed functions, in which it is bringing some truth of the world into view, and the internal functions through which its elements achieve a complex, self-maintaining order and connectedness, an aesthetic rightness.[15]

The space of literature is importantly *prelinguistic* as well as displaying the grammatical, discursive, and rhetorical operations of language. Academic critics, following the linguistic turn, have been more likely to focus on the effects of the linguistic machinery itself, as the material patterns of letters engender meanings unintended by the author, as linguistic items implicitly quote or refer back to other linguistic items, and as the grammars of cultural discourses and social power impress themselves on the text. But that gives an impoverished view of how meaning emerges in our literary practices. We retain the complex brains inherited from millennia of evolution, and earlier forms of cultural experience and organization serve as a scaffolding on which we build our more sophisticated accounts. So semantically relevant patterns may emerge at various levels, in different registers of mental activity: iconic and spatial and kinesthetic shapes; a metaphorical resonance of similar structures in different content areas; primitive representations of the young child's world in terms of form and loss, boundaries and blurring, self and other, anger and desire; moods and emotions that count seemingly unrelated perceptions as linked; musical patterns in the sounds and rhythms of word sequences; bodily feelings of tension and relaxation. Since most of these may be in play in the way that certain novel meanings first assume a scarcely articulate shape for us, literature will be more powerful that also keeps these different registers in play, that finds a nascently emergent pattern that extends, with often a minimal visibility as such, across several levels, including prelinguistic ones. Perhaps those prelinguistic forms of experience are also necessary for a satisfying engagement of the self with the world around it, an engagement that literature might help us realize.

There was a time when philosophers of language and cognitive scientists, influenced by logical and grammatical models of language processing, tended to downplay our handling of images and metaphors and of

other forms of experiencing not fitting the linguistic model. But more recent work with neural-network computer models, and with discoveries
about neural linkages in the brain, have placed an emphasis again on a
holist pattern-recognition that finds analogous patterns across different
experiences and different fields of experience. Steven Pinker suggests, re-
viewing the literature, that our mental activity likely requires both sorts of
processing: the search for fuzzier, shifting patterns across fields of data
(the lion has to be seen as such even when its shape is partly hidden behind
a tree); and the logical, grammatical processing of strings of logically defined symbols.[16] The space of the literary work might be seen as, similarly,
requiring both sorts of processing. (In Shakespeare's comedies the characters often enter a zone where a "grammatical" ordering of social roles is
weakened and more shifting patterns resonate strongly across normal
boundaries, as when a brother and sister who look alike enter a mobile
play of identifications and mirrorings.)

There is a helpful model here: not a radical linguistic turn that puts language in the position of the voluntarist God but rather Daniel Dennett's
model of mind as the processing of *multiple drafts.*[17] Dennett claims that
there is no central location where there is a fact of the matter as to what
we are holding in conscious view. The mind works rather like a legislature
working on a complex bill. Different versions of the bill may be drafted in
different committees and congressional offices, and pressures of outside
lobbyists and constituents will be felt. There are many forces trying to get
their formulations into the final bill, and this will often result in odd com-
promises, in clauses of the bill that may express interests that are virtually
incompatible (as when a proabortion legislator and an antiabortion legislator agree on certain wording for an appropriation). Someone reading the
final bill may see a superficial unity, an apparent logic, but it will take little
effort to realize that quite different texts, and multiple drafts of each text,
have somehow been compressed in the final wording, with the conflicts
often not actually resolved. According to Dennett, the human mind has all
sorts of "homunculi" like those legislators; these have different programs
and aims, and they struggle, in a Darwinian "pandemonium" in which
some aspects of some drafts win out and others are erased, until finally
something is said by the person's voice box and a decision begins to be ex-
ecuted by movements of the body.[18] (That is why you do not know what
you mean until you say it. There is no place where the meaning was determinate already and just needed translation into the words of a natural language.) Of those interior homunculi competing to impress their effects on
the final draft, many may not be embodied in linguistic structures but
rather in prelinguistic ones, of the sort mentioned above. One secret of lit-

erary space may be the writer's ability to keep in play, even in the final text that appears, more of the multiple drafts that in ordinary usage might disappear by the final editing. One has more of a sense of the meaning-forming process and not just of its result.

Literary space can usefully be thought of also as *pedagogic*. Like an athletic trainer or a cook, the author makes the text embody recipes, as it were, for exercises of reading that train us in taking on a more sophisticated stance toward ourselves and the world. As with athletic training, there are some ways in which we come to orient ourselves toward reality that we do not arrive at by applying theoretical knowledge. We must go through certain exercises under the direction of someone who has had more sophisticated and profound experiences. (It should be clear throughout this presentation that I am trying to return more authority to the author, after decades in which that authority was severely discredited. It is true that language is such that a sequence of words produces many semantic effects beyond what the writer may understand them to be producing, but it is easy to exaggerate the significance of this fact.) So literature can provide exercises in establishing a richer psychological and ethical subjectivity. It is not just that we see characters going through kinds of ethical decision-making; we become aware more reflectively of our patterns of identification and investment, of the ways in which we set ourselves in relation to an ethical world, and through reading we develop more complex versions of these patterns. The critic Charles Altieri has insisted on the role of both art and literature in forming and testing models of subjective agency.[19]

Literary space could also be called *selective* rather than proliferative. I intend, with this suggestion, to counteract the notion that a literary text is best understood as endlessly productive of disseminating meanings. On that view each reader, by setting a few puns in motion in the text and by applying personal social codes and interests, can find almost any text desired in the literary work. I believe instead that a literary text is best understood as resulting from the author's intelligent elimination of countless possible combinations that might have gone into that space. Whereas most of us would have made banal combinatory choices, and would have linked our words to obvious images, metaphors, moods, and musical rhythms, the writer, through training, hard work, and intelligence, will have found combinations that let us see things we have not seen before, that let us have more compressed experiences we were not capable of on our own. It is unfortunate that academic literary criticism, in its use of texts for purposes of abstruse theory or of social criticism, has made the reading of those texts almost totally disconnected from the kinds of processes of selection and editing that take place in the writer producing them. (Or rather, if these are mentioned it is likely in a negative manner, as showing how certain cultural issues were marginalized and repressed in that editing.) Whatever dispersive energies the deconstructionist may discover in a text, the space of literature is primarily one of concentration, where normally dispersed meanings converge in an especially intense manner.

Finally, I do not wish to underestimate the fact that the space of literature is a *linguistic* one, where words and sounds as such resonate with one another across an intensely charged linguistic field. Fiction and poetry would mean little if the writer were not a sophisticated inhabitant of such a field. But the radical linguistic turn exaggerates this feature, so that there is a reduction and impoverishment of literary space, a loss of the richer terrain in which it operates. So in readings of literary works I will not spend as much time examining this feature as would be spent if my purposes in writing were different.

This is not, I have granted from the start, an inclusive account of what makes literature matter; there are polemical purposes built into my selection, as I try to pick out precisely those features that a radical linguistic or sociological turn would eliminate. But I should mention one function of literary space whose value I endorse but to which I will give little attention here. One might recall Edmund Husserl's distinction between eidetic phenomenology, in which one examines the experience of different sorts of objects to see what is essential to their form of objectivity as such, and transcendental phenomenology, in which one studies the activities of mind, the mental intendings, that set structures in place necessary for the having of any experience whatever.[20] The latter sort of investigation might be transferred to art and literature. There would be less focus on what is pictured or spoken about and more on the activity of the artist or writer who perceives these or invests in these in a certain way in order to make them significant. One's interest, for example, would be less in the fiction made than reflectively in the act of making the fiction, so that the writer may present those fiction-making moves self-consciously in the text. As this mode of attention develops, both the object presented and the way of seeing it may become less important than the concepts about writing literature or about making art that are being suggested and worked with and tested. The writer's real investment may be not in what is spoken about but rather in a complex conceptual strategy game being played against other conceptual moves and positions regarding literature and language and meaning-making in general. I acknowledge the importance of that sort of literary function, even if my own interests are for the most part elsewhere. My worry regarding it is chiefly that it risks becoming empty play when the more radical linguistic or sociological turns are put into effect. On the model defended here that reflective conceptualizing would still be geared to the work of bringing the world into view and of determining a phenomenology of self-world relations, even if one chose to focus on the conceptualizing itself. With the more radical turns, that conceptualizing enters a realm of frictionless free play in which one engages in an abstract strategy game with other theorists and writers.

That danger applies generally to those forms of attending to texts that emphasize reflective, metalevel stances by the author or reader, that see literature as a space of rhetorical positions and moves able to implicate readers in their machinery, or that expand literary space into a larger cultural space of strategic maneuverings, where cultural grammars may be pointed to or resisted. These attitudes tend to thin out the space of the text in a self-defeating manner; as they are able to produce themselves with less dependence on textual content, they end up generating the same readings of almost any text presented. One may also do such conceptualizing without the constraints of evidence and argument, or of careful distinction-making, that would be required if one were making the same conceptual moves in philosophy. Perhaps one ends up, instead, offering a vague gesture toward epistemic or semantic issues, while taking up the political, moral, and aesthetic attitudes that one was committed to already. Works of art or poetry, rather than being visually or verbally powerful, may end up as mere illustrations of ideas that are neither precisely conceived nor rigorously developed.

The cultural studies model holds that all representations are implicated in regimes of social power that are never innocent. Any text is a site where the culture's forms of representation and its ways of constructing subjectivity are in action, often in destructive ways. So any act of reading must not be neutral or confine itself to the "literary" but rather must see itself as an intervention in these power processes, as an act confirming or contesting or subverting or using for different political purposes those cultural representations. I grant that texts can be usefully read in this manner, but I will argue (especially in chapter 7) that the radical cultural-studies turn will impoverish literary space without offering in return much assistance to those in need of social justice.

While I make no claim to give a general theory of literature here, I believe that a considerable part of the power and value of exceptional works of literature is due to their achievements regarding the aspects of literary space outlined in this chapter. (Sometimes, for the sake of brevity, I will summarize these features by talking of a psycho-metaphysical model of literary space. I will see it as opposing both a linguistic-postmodern model of that space and a sociopolitical or cultural studies model.) Literature matters because these various functions of the space of literature allow for experiences important to the living out of a sophisticated and satisfying human life; because other arenas of culture cannot provide them to the same degree; and because a relatively small number of texts carry out these functions in so exceptional a manner that we owe it to past and future members of the species to keep such texts alive in our cultural traditions.

LITERARY SPACE IN McCARTHY AND PYNCHON, RUSHDIE AND CHAUDHURI

In chapter 3 I will make the case that what may appear naive in the model of literary space defended here, when one looks at philosophical arguments about language and subjectivity, is actually not so. First I will show, in brief and initial fashion, that my description of literary space so far can bring out significant features of literary work, including recent fiction. Here is a description in *All the Pretty Horses* of Cormac McCarthy's character John Grady Cole crossing from Mexico into Texas:

> In four days' riding he crossed the Pecos at Iraan Texas and rode up out of the river breaks where the pumpjacks in the Yates Field ranged against the skyline rose and dipped like mechanical birds. Like great primitive birds welded up out of iron by hearsay in a land perhaps where such birds once had been. At that time there were still indians camped on the western plains and late in the day he passed in his riding a scattered group of their wickiups propped upon that scoured and trembling waste. They were perhaps a quarter mile to the north, just huts made from poles and brush with a few goathides draped across them. The indians stood watching him. He could see that none of them spoke among themselves or commented on his riding there nor did they raise a hand in greeting or call out to him. They had no curiosity about him at all. As if they knew all that they needed to know. They stood and watched him pass and watched him vanish upon that landscape solely because he was passing. Solely because he would vanish.[1]

In a postmodern world of weightless contingency and unmotivated juxtaposition John Grady might meet with the Indians and move off with them to an interesting metafictional landscape. Any combination might easily occur in that thinned-out space where unexpected linkages can happen smoothly, as the postmodern field is limited only by a combinatorial power resembling the arbitrary will of the voluntarist God.[2] But here in McCarthy's text the movements have their own gravity, their own fatal necessity. Either an intersection was going to take place or it was not. The Indians watch John Grady as if watching a storm passing in the distance. Instead of a postmodern space that signs are constantly filling in the gaps of, the emptiness of the terrain here allows a different character of things as real to emerge, so that they continue to have weight on their own, unlike in the theological model. The Indians see him merely as an instance of something that appears for a while and then vanishes, that has an existence temporarily in this vast space and then has it no more. Their wickiups are a minimal adjustment to that metaphysical landscape, not a way of transforming it in the image of the human world as a human construction or projection. Things are left with a kind of deep visibility against a larger background; they are not projections in the shallower space carved out by a radical linguistic turn. There seems to be a broader, nonhuman world that operates by its own rhythms and powers rather than a flat, insubstantial space waiting for a voluntarist productive power to project itself, unconstrained by any gravitational field it has not generated. (McCarthy's prose, it is true, is highly stylized. It is by no means a simple presenting of the world. Yet even in that stylization, and perhaps because of it, it reaches out to bring a hard-to-grasp character of the world into view.)

Note that what is counted here as metaphysical involves more than being given a precise description of some portion of reality. The passage of the rider through the landscape hints at a larger account of the status of individuals; it suggests the sort of reality they have in an ongoing universe for which they are ultimately ephemeral. Similar occurrences can be found in art by painters such as Vermeer, Caravaggio, and Cezanne, in which the space and lighting of the works allow not just an intense and precise taking in of a particular object but also a suggestion of at least one sort of objecthood as such, against a background that is not simply physical but is also an object-determining space, a frame out of which objects crystallize as having the experiential and perhaps spiritual character they do. In McCarthy's case the universe is a vast nonmoral one that does not offer any special significance to the human world, that was not designed to have our purposes fit its operations.

If the space of McCarthy's text is then phenomenological and metaphysical in the senses given to those terms in chapter 1, it is also a ritualized space, with a powerful cadence that presses us as readers to recite the sentences aloud. Through that recital, even if a silent one, we come to assume a more resolute stance toward, and a resigned acceptance of, the inexorable working out of the world's patterns. We are often as humans emerging into a more articulate, isolate, and reflective individuality, while we feel the pull of psychological and cultural forms that once made us feel more dependably sustained, that gave a more archaic support to the frailer movements of individuality. Here, for example, is McCarthy's description of John Grady as he comes upon the faint traces of a trail once used by Comanche war parties:

> At the hour he'd always choose when the shadows were long and the ancient road was shaped before him in the rose and canted light like a dream of the past where the painted ponies and the riders of that lost nation came down out of the north with their faces chalked and their long hair plaited and each armed for war which was their life and the women and children and women with children at their breasts all of them pledged in blood and redeemable in blood only. When the wind was in the north you could hear them, the horses and the breath of the horses and the horses' hooves that were shod in rawhide and the rattle of lances and the constant drag of the travois poles in the sand like the passing of some enormous serpent and the young boys naked on wild horses jaunty as circus riders and hazing wild horses before them and the dogs trotting with their tongues aloll and foot-slaves following half naked and sorely burdened and above all the low chant of their traveling song which the riders sang as they rode, nation and ghost of nation passing in a soft chorale across that mineral waste to darkness bearing lost to all history and all remembrance like a grail the sum of their secular and transitory and violent lives. (McCarthy, *All the Pretty Horses,* 5)

Many critics will likely see this as an image of one text being written over another, with John Grady's route written over the old Comanche one. But this is not a matter of arranging bits of language, of textual palimpsests. It is a vision of an archaic form of life whose energies have not simply been lost but at some level still move us, as in reading Homer. In hinting at forms of ethical life and of metaphysical perception of the world that were once more dominant, the writing points to resources we should not want to lose for thinking about our lives, even if we cannot return to them (nor should we wish to). We are reminded as well that some things worth noticing emerge through deeper and slower rhythms than those that characterize modern and postmodern life. The cadences of the written passage echo the distant music that they recall, the "ghost of nation passing in a soft chorale across that mineral waste to darkness." The length of the two sentences, stretched out with their powerful rhythms over such an expanse, suggests the deeply rolling powers of nature that, according to Nietzsche, Greek tragedy with its chorus could still make real for us. That tragedy stood at the threshold of a new world of more distinct individuation, with the earlier ritual energies (and their less individuating identifications) still vividly evident. Shakespeare was looking forward into the modern world while still feeling the pull of a ritual, theatrical Catholic England. Melville felt the attraction of an earlier world of male bonding and violence, of pre-Oedipal conflicts about individuation, even as liberal Protestant culture was trying to produce a more civilized genteel self.

In all three cases the textual space seems to be working out those oppositions metaphorically in its very style. In each case, as in McCarthy's, there is a virtue to those features of literary space earlier called translational and regressive-disenchanted. The writer remains on a border between what is being left behind and what must be moved into (McCarthy's trilogy of novels is called The Border Trilogy), and represents that space in a way that shows both gains and losses, so that we can ask what resources of the earlier world we might work at retaining, if any. (That is why both the fading cowboy culture of 1950s Texas and the ritual world of Mexico are important spaces for McCarthy's novel. They shape the rhythms and attitudes that remain beneath the present world, in our psyches and in certain cultural patterns. They do this even as their cadences are becoming a distant music we are on the verge of losing, along with the metaphysical and ethical forms that this music carries, relating us as it does so to issues of chance, fate, and destiny and the weaving of individual lives within them.) That sort of space allows a richer staging of the psyche than does the postmodern one. What Hegel described as a structure of self-relating-in-relating-to-otherness can be expressed in a more complex shape, bringing in different levels of engagement with the world and allowing the world itself a more complex way of appearing. We are given, in the accompanying mood of elegy and loss, a sense of the world's thickness and depth as these are both being held on to and lost in the translation into language, even into language as sensitive to these features as McCarthy's.

In the textual space of McCarthy we see a phenomenology of self-formation against a deep metaphysical backdrop. John Grady Cole, the protagonist of *All the Pretty Horses,* seems Greek or Nietzschean in the way his actions occupy an ethical world that gives them gravity, in the way they spring with a seemingly inevitable shape from the style of his character, from a sense of honor and shame that he considers not at all universal but, nonetheless, an unavoidable standard of action for himself. Both nature and ethics come to have a metaphysical weight that the modern turn to free subjectivity, to a self that constructs its conditions of validity for itself, has apparently deprived them of. McCarthy's accomplishment is to have his style not only match, but also endorse, this overall vision. His sentences seem in their rhythms and language to have that weight and inevitability of the ethical and psychological selfhood being described. One's movement through the sentences has the elemental feel of the movements of the characters across the empty plains and deserts of the U.S. Southwest and northern Mexico.

> There were storms to the south and masses of clouds that moved slowly along the horizon with their long dark tendrils trailing in the rain. That night they camped on a ledge of rock above the plains and watched the lightning all along the horizon provoke from the seamless dark the distant mountain ranges again and again. . . . The grasslands lay in a deep violet haze and to the west thin flights of waterfowl were moving north before the sunset in the deep red galleries under the cloudbanks like schoolfish in a burning sea and on the foreland plain they saw vaqueros driving cattle before them through a gauze of golden dust. (McCarthy, *All the Pretty Horses*, 93)

> He rode with the sun coppering his face and the red wind blowing out of the west across the evening land and the small desert birds flew chittering among the dry bracken and horse and rider and horse passed on and their long shadows passed in tandem like the shadow of a single being. Passed and paled into the darkening land, the world to come. (302)

McCarthy's work can stand then as an example of the sort of text one might call to mind in believing that literature matters: that it makes a difference that these particular words have been placed in this particular order to produce experiences not available elsewhere, experiences having to do with fundamental ways in which the self sets itself in relation to the world and to itself; attitudes are enacted that are ultimately more metaphysical than literary toward objects and their way of appearing. Yet it is easy to show that what I have thus picked out as virtues can be very differently read if we are persuaded by recent literary theory. Indeed, it is surprising in how many ways the critic might show McCarthy's text to go wrong. There ought to be something suspect, it will be claimed, in a style of language that aims for that aura of necessity, of stark inevitability, and that encourages a reader to feel his own psyche perhaps strengthened through an identification with the movement of the prose. For we are thus engaging, it will be said, in a form of escapism from the stance of being a self today, from the radical contingency we have discovered to character-ize it. John Grady Cole seems to move across the landscape with a stoic sense of fate, of the necessity of what he does, but in fact we are selves within historical frameworks that might have been other than what they are, and that cannot be justified by any appeal to the strength of our habits of living within them. The qualities of the prose seem to naturalize what is a quite parochial, socially constructed form of selfhood that is rightly dis-appearing. McCarthy's characters avoid not only the modern anxieties of subjectivity but also the postmodern predicament of the self as multiple, mobile, and shifting, as a site where different vocabularies are at play, where diverse ethical notions can simultaneously make a claim on us. They exemplify instead, so it will be claimed, a simplistic and romanti-cized notion of selfhood.

McCarthy's style is regressive (so this criticism will continue) in that it strives for a ritualized, ceremonial feel, a music that absorbs us hypnoti-cally and that, in provoking such an identification with the cadenced power of the prose, produces in us the kind of psychological effects that religious ceremonies once did. But we ought to be seeking not substitutes for religion but a more radical disenchantment from the world of ritual and sacrament, from archaic and magical ways of being a self. We are in need, as modern selves, of a style that is disruptive, that calls attention to itself in a way that makes us see the machinery of language at work, so that we are not caught up inappropriately in its effects. Paul de Man, for one, has insisted that as readers we are always in danger of mistaking lin-guistic effects for worldly or psychological ones; the fundamental (and fal-sifying) nature of metaphor for him is to make identifications across the boundaries of self and other, inside and outside.[3] A stronger, more reflec-tive turn to the linguistic and the grammatical, he supposes, will make us less susceptible to those identifications. So presumably he would recom-mend, as part of that disenchanting process, that we resist getting taken up into a ritualized prose that would make us believe that we have the very qualities, the self-maintaining forward momentum and necessity, the well-ordered form and proportion, that the prose seems to possess. That way of reading must appear, in the end, like the primitive conception of the be-liever in voodoo who supposes that what happens to the representation of something is happening to the thing itself. Quite generally, that sort of identificational thinking may seem an expression of a more primitive style of engagement with things, to be replaced by what a study of language trains us in: an emphasis on differences, on failures of identity, on disrup-tions of any movement toward unity or reconciliation. (Perhaps as nature and history lose that sense of fateful necessity we look to aesthetic objects not only to express that sense but also to project it on what they portray.)

The ritual functions of McCarthy's texts, so the objector will say, hide behind a vague air of necessity the moral and political questions that the text ought to raise. In *Blood Meridian* we read of the terrible and senseless slaughter of innocents, of massacres perpetrated by an American column hired to wipe out Indian marauders. But we get a view from high above the scene, as it were, with the Indians equally vicious and all the action taking place in a landscape (and in a prose) that makes it seem a continuation of the processes of nature. The lighting of the scenes is such that we feel a silence and distance stretching out behind them, so that individual events can seem hardly to matter against the wider frame.

> Glanton turned his horse. The dead lay awash in the shallows like the victims of some disaster at sea and they were strewn along the salt foreshore in a havoc of blood and entrails. Riders were towing bodies out of the bloody waters of the lake and the froth that rode lightly on the beach was a pale pink in the rising light. They moved among the dead harvesting the long black locks with their knives and leaving their victims rawskulled and strange in their bloody cauls. . . . Men were wading about in the red waters hacking aimlessly at the dead and some lay coupled to the bludgeoned bodies of young women dead or dying on the beach. One of the Delawares passed with a collection of heads like some strange vendor bound for market, the hair twisted about his wrist and the heads dangling and turning together.[4]

Even a brief reading in contemporary cultural studies will make one aware that the scenes McCarthy is describing connect richly to a social and political context.[5] There were larger relations, many of them ethically questionable, being worked out at that time between the United States and Mexico and among white Americans, Native Americans, Spanish Mexicans, and mixed-blood Mexicans—all of these shaped by economic and social forces coming to transform the West. But the large configurations of social and economic and political power, and the ways in which these were shaping representations of the world, are mostly absent from McCarthy's texts, even if an academic critic will have little trouble reading them in. Another issue is whether the processes of self-formation that his writing embodies, and also assists, are not universal human ones but rather products of the modern bourgeois (and male) culture that forms us as individuals subject to certain kinds of vulnerabilities, and in need of certain kinds of compensations. Or perhaps some other prose styles are marginalized when we think of his style as praiseworthy. Once these issues are raised, it may appear that to conceive the space of a text as enacting certain psychological and metaphysical functions, as McCarthy's text perhaps encourages, may be not only outdated and naive but also politically dangerous. Then, too, if readers come to believe that the psychological resolutions offered by literature are ritual compensations for frailties of the self that ought to be improved instead through social change, they will be less convinced of the importance of giving an analysis of cadence and literary form in a work of literature.

On almost all the disagreements of assessment just described, the opponents can be seen as disagreeing on whether one ought to make the two radical turns described in chapter 1: to language, on the one hand, or to regimes of social power, on the other. The turn to the linguistic emphasizes how language deconstructs the level of psychology and phenomenology, how it undermines processes based on identification and mirroring, on image and metaphor, on a ritualized absorption in the music and movement of the text, on the intentional and ethical life of the self as involving a stance toward the metaphysical character of the universe. That turn would then lead to a reading of McCarthy's text in a way that goes very much against the grain of its writing. The radical cultural studies turn would advise us to reject the hypnotic power of McCarthy's prose and see all his representations, of Indians and Mexicans for example, as moves in cultural power games that have effects on how those without power are treated. In succeeding chapters I will present an account of literature that would treat McCarthy's text much more positively than my (imagined) literary theorist opponent would allow.

We can investigate similar issues with a look at *Midnight's Children*, by Salman Rushdie.[6] Rushdie's activity of textual production does not ride on a world that remains at a distance or is being lost, as in McCarthy, but instead constructs its items within a thinner space that it produces for itself. So one finds in Rushdie something like a theological conception: the world becomes thinned out over against the self-constructing and self-supporting activity of the fictional space. Normally in literary work the time and space of representation are used to make visible a world of individuals and things that belong to a different time and space, a wider, larger world that comes into view in being represented but whose character is only suggested, and by no means exhausted, by what thus appears. In Rushdie, on the other hand, events and individuals seem broken off from such a larger space; they are already discursive items to be maneuvered smoothly within the discursive world. Rushdie's character Saleem has telepathic skills, his magical power resulting from being one of the children born on the midnight of Indian independence. His too easy access to faraway events, without their having to be approached from a distance and with difficulty, can stand for that theological fictional space in Rushdie that can produce almost any combination from its unchecked activity; or it can stand as well for the too easy availability of items from all over the world in a single marketplace today, or for a postmodern and international discursive space where items circulate easily as signs. So Rushdie's text seems to have accomplished the more radical transition to a linguistic realm where items now move in a relatively frictionless space, so that we are not surprised by the spontaneous generation of marvelous connections that occurs in the text. Even with as many references as he makes to the history of modern India, the characters seem discursive constructs that dissolve easily into the linguistic maneuvers.

The fictional activity in his novel must generate objects and conserve them in their existence or else they fall into a flat nothingness. Rushdie's narrative drive, as theological in this sense, must be self-supporting; it cannot derive its energy from a larger world whose depth it only suggests. If there is anxiety in thus spinning out the conditions of one's own existence (the anxiety is due of course to our inability to occupy that theological slot, as only God could truly be self-supporting), then it will show in a feverish production of new characters and new scenes, of outlandish narrative incidents and coincidences, all intended not so much for themselves but to represent that unflagging narrative energy. He offers a proliferating, expanding universe where any empty spaces that appear as it expands are quickly filled in with new matter and energy. There is an abhorrence of silence, of any space not constructed by the narrative itself, of any emptiness spreading out behind things and extending into the distance.

Rushdie calls attention to the arbitrary and fictional quality of his creation by the astonishing coincidences between Saleem's personal history and the history of modern India and Pakistan. Saleem's attempts to prove himself to a girl cause a bicycle crash into a procession of language demonstrators, and an innocent slogan he then repeats causes war between Gujarati speakers and Marathi speakers and leads to a political partition (Rushdie, *Midnight's Children*, 228–29). There are magicians and magical children and a 512-year-old whore, an army major with ten thousand lovers, and two cobras able to mime, for a political lesson, a rich man refusing to give alms to a beggar—all of which indicate the sovereignty of the fictional space. Rushdie presents a world where linguistic suggestion turns into narrative momentum. The word "Bombay" brings to mind "gin" and then "djinn," and if a rifle has the brand name Daisy it will be used to shoot at flowers in the air. If Saleem's relative has a sign in front of his house, "Aziz and Fly," with the latter expression standing for "family," then there will be several references to the family in terms of the insect (466–69). As with the strong turn to the grammatical, we see here how the linguistic-textual space becomes a realm of spontaneous generation of patterns that are then projected into worldly or intentional form. For Rushdie, it can appear, there are only texts and arrangements of cultural signs. Speaking of Pakistan he says that reality stops existing when leaders have the power to determine what counts as truth (389). But reality does not cease to exist, of course, when leaders lie about what is happening; those whose suffering is unrecognized by the lie continue to suffer. It is only a glorifying of textuality that makes Rushdie's claim seem appealing.

Rushdie's narrative is an allegorical one that links episodes in Saleem's life with events in India from independence to the time of Indira Gandhi's dictatorial rule during a state of emergency. Academic criticism, for its part, also seems to show a strong preference for allegory over metaphor.[7] The characteristic note of allegory is to make linkages between two well-formed, already discursive worlds, such that we can see each side clearly on its own and can then wonder how the writer will link the two of them up. With metaphor, in contrast, at least when it is well done, a relatively familiar pattern is used to bring into view a pattern we have not yet been able to recognize as such. We probably cannot hold the new one in view at all without taking advantage of its resonance with the familiar pattern, and its meaning remains, even with the metaphor, difficult to specify. Rushdie may employ references to earlier Indian religious stories and folktales, but they are already discursive items available for allegorical hookup if necessary. The preference for allegory, then, is consistent with the postmodern view that everything is already textual, a patterned move in a field of cultural strategies. One does not look for moments when meaning emerges into the linguistic field from nonlinguistic worlds, as would characterize metaphorical space, where the beginning shape of a novel pattern is often built on visual or gestural or spatial forms of experiencing. So allegory seems to fit the stronger turn to a linguistic, grammatical, discursive space as metaphor does not.

It might be useful here to contrast Rushdie's writing with the work of another writer often called postmodern, Thomas Pynchon. *Gravity's Rainbow* has many features that make it like *Midnight's Children:* the comedy, the odd characters, the coincidences between historical events and personal ones. But there is another side to *Gravity's Rainbow* without which it would not be a great novel, and that is its powerful sense of elegy and loss. The novel can therefore stand, in contrast to Rushdie's, for the less radical transition into linguistic space, so that one has a keen sense of earlier spaces and of the gains and losses in the passage to the more sophisticated linguistic-grammatical environment. Here is a scene of late-afternoon London:

> Pirate and Osbie Feel are leaning on their roof-ledge, a magnificent sunset across and up the winding river, the imperial serpent, crowds of factories, flats, parks, smoky spires and gables, incandescent sky casting downward across the miles of deep streets and roofs cluttering and sinuous river Thames a drastic stain of burnt orange to remind a visitor of his mortal transience here, to seal or empty all the doors and windows in sight to his eyes that look only for a bit of company, a word or two in the street before he goes up to the soap-heavy smell of the rented room and the squares of coral sunset on the floorboards—an antique light, self-absorbed, fuel consumed in the metered winter holocaust, the more distant shapes among the threads or sheets of smoke now perfect ash ruins of themselves, nearer windows, struck a moment by the sun, not reflecting at all but containing the same destroying light, this intense fading in which there is no promise of return, light that rusts the government cars at the curbsides, varnishes the last faces hurrying past the shops in the cold as if a vast siren had finally sounded, light that makes chilled untraveled canals of many streets, and that fills with the starlings of London, converging by millions to hazy stone pedestals, to emptying squares and a great collective sleep.[8]

Note the chantlike rhythm of the passage, the accumulation of phrases with the sentence ending postponed, as if the style is metaphorical for all those linguistic or psychological architectures that sustain themselves on the edge, through an inertial drive more than through daunting complexity, before dissolving to Absolute Zero. The late-afternoon light is seen as an "intense fading in which there is no promise of return." The Pynchonian world of linguistic dissemination is played off against a gravitational pull toward grief and dissolution, toward the opening out of an emptying terrain against which things appear as inherently fragile. Pynchon even gives an image of the movement of textualization. A Russian character, Tchitcherine, is assigned to Central Asia on a committee trying to provide an alphabet for tribal groups whose language has not yet been written down. He sees how the great expanses of the steppes, the sense of largeness and weight they make possible, will be lost once these perceptions are captured in writing. A female character returns to Moscow and dreams of herself as now a tiny figure who could be easily crushed by her "Central

Asian giantess self" if the latter were to enter Moscow (Pynchon, *Gravity's Rainbow*, 341). Tchitcherine, observing a singing duel between a young man and a young woman of the tribe, knows that the very capturing of this duel in writing is part of the process of losing it forever (356–57). So for Pynchon the move into the space of representation is a compressing and shrinking of an earlier world whose character may be lost, perhaps finally, as it comes more and more to fit itself into the time and space of that representational world instead of into its own. Pynchon's prose alternates between a comic postmodern fertility and the powerful, elegiac cadences of a music it will soon be impossible to hear as the world is transformed, as it becomes fully a realm of circulating, nearly weightless signs (as in the turn to the grammatical and discursive that will come to dominate literary theory). In Rushdie there is no such loss; since things are from the start constructions out of the narrative space, they leave nothing behind in their habitation of that space. Just as Derrida finds in writing itself the characteristic relations that everything else mirrors, so Rushdie's fictional space determines, rather than responding to, the conditions of whatever enters into it. (The Derrida model is one in which nothing can be lost because writing, given theological powers, has in advance projected everything nonlinguistic as an image of itself.) Pynchon shows, even in the tensions and differences within his prose, a world in the act of becoming both modern and postmodern but not quite there yet; Rushdie shows a world that already is and in some sense has always already been postmodern.

One might say that in *Gravity's Rainbow*, Pynchon is portraying and commenting on a process that Rushdie's fiction is merely an expression of. Pynchon's theme is that of modern cultural processes, represented by the system of the Rocket swallowing up all energies on the planet and turning them into aspects of the Rocket's self-sustaining life. (That movement is parallel to the one whereby the representational energies of writing, as with Tchitcherine on the Russian steppes, are transforming the nonwritten, and in so doing are both capturing and losing it.) Pynchon's fictional energies can seem at times, like Rushdie's, to parallel that work of the Rocket in their ability to bring all items into their narrative momentum. But Pynchon is careful to show moments of holding back from these all-enveloping systems, to make us aware of absence and loss. The young lovers Roger and Jessica, on a dark evening during World War II, come upon a small church where Evensong is being celebrated (Pynchon, *Gravity's Rainbow*, 127–36). They recognize that they cannot quite accept these rituals as once they could, yet still they give themselves over to the music and feel temporarily restored as the war continues outside. In another scene two behavioral scientists discuss an issue as they walk along the shore in winter:

> So, the two of them: trudging, hands in and out of pockets, their figures dwindling, fawn and gray and a lick of scarlet, very sharp-edged, their footprints behind them a long, freezing progress of exhausted stars, the overcast reflecting from the glazed beach nearly white. . . . We have lost them. No one listened to those early conversations—not even an idle snapshot survives. They walked till that winter hid them and it seemed the cruel Channel itself would freeze over, and no one, none of us, could ever completely find them again. Their footprints filled with ice, and a little later were taken out to sea. (92)

Children brushing their teeth in the morning are shown to be part of larger processes that link a wide range of activities "home to hedgeless sea," as what were formerly natural processes of individuation and dissolution are being taken over by a technological regime.

> the intricate draftsmanship of outlets feeding, multiplying out to sea, as one by one these old toothpaste tubes are emptied and returned to the War, heaps of dimly fragrant metal, phantoms of peppermint in the winter shacks, each tube wrinkled or embossed by the unconscious hands of London, written over in interference-patterns, hand against hand, waiting now—it is true return—to be melted for solder, for plate, alloyed for castings, bearings, gasketry, hidden smokeshriek linings the children of that other domestication will never see. Yet the continuity, flesh to kindred metals, home to hedgeless sea, has persisted. (Pynchon, *Gravity's Rainbow*, 130)

In the book's very title we can see the pull of death, of gravity, on the system of the Rocket even as that system, within the novel, tries to impress all other energies into its working in order to keep itself suspended against that pull. Sometimes Pynchon's writing can seem suspended over a gravity that will eventually claim it, where it seems to be, as Pynchon says, "a persistence on the hard edge of death" (Pynchon, *Gravity's Rainbow*, 486). So Pynchon's fictional space faces two other geographies that hold out in their different absences: that of earlier cultural or psychological worlds being lost, as the system of the Rocket seeks to transform them into itself; and that of a deeper process whose pull on all individual forms threatens to dissolve them, to return them to the cycling rhythms of nature against which the Rocket and everything belonging to it have been raised up. That fictional space is effective, then, precisely by not making the strong turn to the grammatical, a turn that would have lost the significance of those earlier worlds and of the relations of dependence and compensation between them and the fictional space. Rushdie's fictional world, in contrast, seems to be rather like the system of the Rocket. It is a process of bringing all things into its territory to be used as continual fuel for the narrative energy, so that everything on the outside becomes insubstantial, though there is, from the point of view of the narrative machinery, no sense of loss, no acknowledgment of a pull toward nothingness. (That is why Rushdie can stand for and fit into the space of contemporary literary theory better than can McCarthy.)

Perhaps it could be said that Pynchon's narrative universe in *Gravity's Rainbow* is like a two-star system in which one of the stars has collapsed in on itself, becoming a black hole that is invisible but whose presence can be felt as a strong pull on the other one, leading gradually to its collapse. In Rushdie there is no such threat to the self-articulating energies of the fictional space. (It is interesting that Pynchon's most recent novel, *Mason & Dixon,* comes somewhat closer to Rushdie in this respect.[9]) As the Rocket rises into the sky at the end of *Gravity's Rainbow* it can seem to stand for, among other things, a long cultural history from Plato on, with that history's attempt at a gravity-resistant Cartesian machinery of self-maintenance, a systematic (male) world that achieves autonomy. Pynchon knows, as Rushdie does not, that the Rocket must be eventually betrayed to gravity, that the grammatical, discursive order does not have that autonomy but rises up only on the basis of earlier layers that it tries to deny.

The lighter world of postmodern linguistic fertility, I should be clear, has value for Pynchon. If there is hope to escape the pervasive modern world of the Rocket and its colonizing energies, then it will come from two different sources: the earth and its natural powers as perhaps still greater than that upraised world of the Rocket; and the capacity, expressed in the novel's postmodern dissemination, for all systems, including language, to resist closure and to keep on generating unexpected and self-subverting patterns out of their own materials. In that way the Rocket with its unifying, centripetal powers may seem more modernist than postmodern. But there remains in *Gravity's Rainbow* a sense of earlier gravities pulling on the novel's world, as certain forms of the world's appearing are no longer available. (And so in Pynchon but not in Rushdie there is the complex disenchanted-regressive space that I earlier associated with Greek tragedy, with Melville and McCarthy, where issues of self-formation and individuation over against earlier dissolving powers are joined with the lighter, intertextual movements of language.)

Rushdie's tone is captured well in Richard Rorty's phrase "the world well lost."[10] Rorty continues a philosophical option that we may employ when a serious gap opens between the world of language that we maneuver in comfortably and the world our language is trying to reach to. One trick in this situation is to find a way of conceiving matters that will shrink back the horizon that seems to open up that worrisome empty space. Thus (to take one example of this move in philosophy) if objects are really mental constructs, then there is no problem in explaining how minds can reach out to them. And if a space of absence and loss and emptiness seems to open out behind one's fictional world, then one finds a way of shrinking back those horizons until the fictional world and its constructs exhaust the available space. That is what occurs in Rushdie, and this move can be seen as a further example of the theological model at work. Rushdie would in that case be like Rorty and Hilary Putnam, who in different ways try to shrink back the space of possible meaningfulness so that no profound metaphysical gap can open up, no larger measure of the possible failure of our ordinary ways of speaking and understanding.[11]

Further contrasts with Rushdie, regarding how radical is one's transition to postmodern discursive space, can be seen if we compare *Midnight's Children* with three short novels published together as *Freedom Song* by Amit Chaudhuri, a writer much like Rushdie in background. Chaudhuri's virtues as a writer extend perhaps to a somewhat narrow range of what might be thought of as the possible ways in which literature can be excellent, but a comparison with Rushdie is instructive; unlike Rushdie, Chaudhuri shows some of the aspects of literary space described earlier. In his writing the distant and absent come forward *as* distant and absent in a present field of representation, so that one has access to rhythms that went on before the representational space drew them in. A student at Oxford thinks back to his family's origins in what is now Bangladesh, or Sohanlal, an associate of that student's music teacher, is also associated with such an earlier space: "That world, of gestures and wonder, existing in the wide, silent margins of the land, is gone now. All has been named and brought to consciousness, the colours, the words and their meanings, but Sohanlal is one of those few people who remember the darkness of what was there before, the old language and its life."[12] One might take such a description as nostalgic, but in Chaudhuri this is not the case; he is trying to present a phenomenology of how objects appear against a deeper and earlier background that is weakening but whose effects have not disappeared. Quite generally, one is aware in reading Chaudhuri of objects appearing in the available light, as in Vermeer, a light that raises things up, that lets us see them in their inherent importance simply as real, but also lets us recognize their transience and fragility, their expression of a certain luminosity, one that shines through them only briefly.

> and Oxford, in the evening, resembles what an English town must have looked like in wartime, the small shops open but unfrequented, an endangered, dolorous, but perfectly vivid peace in the lanes, as the eye is both surprised by, and takes pleasure in, a couple linked arm in arm, or a young man conversing with a woman on a polished doorstep, and then the early goodbyes. It is like what I imagine a wartime township to have been, because all the young people, with their whistling, their pavement to pavement chatter, their beer-breathed, elbow-nudging politics, are suddenly gone, leaving the persistent habits of an old way of life, the opening and shutting of shops, intact, a quiet, empty bastion of civilisation and citizenry. It is because of its smallness, repetition, and the evanescence of its populace, that Oxford is dream-like. (*Afternoon Raag,* 129–30)

The space of Chaudhuri's novel is thus a phenomenological and metaphysical one, with moments that are like a sudden step backward to bring into view an overall but usually difficult-to-grasp character of the world. His prose offers a patient attentiveness to spaces and things that emerge slowly and quietly, in the background of ordinary life, according to rhythms often missed in postmodern habits of filling up the semantic field with the mobile circulation of signs. He gives us a clear sense of the space of appearing precisely through focusing on its penumbral effects as it is emptied out. He shows how spaces retain their character, the mood and lighting they place us in, even as the inhabitants disappear and are replaced by others.

> This is the abbreviated, painting-like view that passersby have of the interiors of the colleges. . . . Yet the students do not really matter, because within the college walls there is a world—a geography and a weather—that clings to its own time and definition and is changed by no one. In this world, glimpsed briefly by the passerby through the open doorway, a certain light and space and greyness of tone, and at night, a certain balance of lamplight, stone, and darkness, co-exist almost eternally, and it is the students . . . who, in truth, vanish, are strangely negated, so that, when the passerby later remembers what he saw, the students seem blurred, colourful, accidental, even touching, but constantly skirting the edge of his vision, while it is possible to clearly and unequivocally recall the dignity and silence of the doorway and the world beyond it. (Chaudhuri, *Afternoon Raag,* 190–91)

The space of Chaudhuri's text remains at some level a psychological one where a certain shape of self-to-other relation is being enacted, where a partial regression allows a more intense staging of that relation, so that much seems to be at stake in achieving it. One is being ritually trained, through the very experience of reading the text, in taking up a certain stance of the self toward the world and toward the self, a generous way of letting things appear. The writing self is working for a balance that the psychological self, in its earlier process of self-formation, of separation and individuation, has also worked for: between being overwhelmed by the world and making it a mere projection. The line of prose should be steady enough to stand for the reliably self-maintaining activity of the self, and yet it should have a quiet and openness that allow the world a certain depth and an independent weight.

Chaudhuri's text displays what was spoken of earlier as a doubleness of literary space, its inhabiting of a disenchanted world while reaching back toward a distant music that both grounds that world and is muted by it. Both aspects, the music and the distance, are important, as one looks to a more archaic space where individuation is less rigorously determinate, while raising an articulate everyday world over against that space. It is not difficult to fit Chaudhuri into such talk of distant music because that is explicitly the theme of the middle novel of his trilogy, *Afternoon Raag,* whose title refers to a form of classical Indian music. The narrator, who grew up in Bombay and Calcutta, is now at Oxford studying D. H. Lawrence and other English writers. The occasion of the novel is the death of the narrator's (presumably Chaudhuri's) music teacher in India. That this is distant music is marked by that death and by the narrator's thought of once singing with the teacher in India, and also by the memories of the narrator performing classical Indian *raags* with his mother. In the subtle but absorbing cadences of Chaudhuri's prose, it seems, one is hearing faint rhythms of that music, of an India in whose rituals the narrator cannot quite share as once he could but that remains nonetheless present as shaping his life and writing, and as an aspect of the self's complexity in its form of engagement with the world. The doubleness of the literary space, then, reflects Chaudhuri's position as one separating in some respects from Indian culture while holding on to the earlier world it represents. (He also has chosen English as his writing language while young, rather than Bengali.)

Quite often in the narrative Chaudhuri discusses the nature of Indian music in ways that suggest his own writing: the prolonging and shortening of notes, the wandering movements of the speaker's voice while the instru-

ments maintain the cadence and the signature note that the singer must return to.

> The greater part of the unfolding of a raag consists of a slow, evasive intro-
> duction in which the notes are related to each other by curving glissandos,
> or meends. The straight, angular notes of Western music, composed and
> then rendered, are like print upon a page; in contrast, the curving meends of
> the raag are like longhand writing drawn upon the air. Each singer has his
> own impermanent longhand with its own arching, idiosyncratic beauties, its
> own repetitive, serpentine letters. (Chaudhuri, *Afternoon Raag,* 151)

It is literary style as well that is at stake in such descriptions. I especially
want to call attention (for the sake of making a contrast with Rushdie) to
the way that the line of prose may be said, by analogy with the music, to
ride on other formations.

> On some mornings we would sing raag Bhairav together, our two voices and
> styles mingling closely and floating over the other sounds of the house . . .
> his voice sometimes carrying my hesitant voice, and negotiating the path-
> ways of the raag, as a boat carries a bewildered passenger. (151)

> The four strings provide only two notes as a background to the song; *sa*, or
> *shadja,* the first, the mother-note, from which all other notes come, with
> which one's relationship is permanent and unambiguous, and the second
> note, depending on the raag, the father-note, circumstantial but construc-
> tive. (152)

> While the pretence is kept up, and the singer's rhythm appears to have lost
> itself, the tabla-player, with emotionless sobriety, maintains the stern tempo
> and cycle, until the singer, like an irresponsible but prodigious child, decides
> to dance in perfect steps back into it. . . . The tabla- and harmonium-players
> behave like palaquin-bearers carrying a precious burden, or like solemn but
> indulgent guardians who walk a little distance behind a precocious child as
> it does astonishing things. (167–68)

These passages suggest that the space of the music, as portrayed by
Chaudhuri, is simultaneously the scene of writing, with the prose line
working itself over a deeper rhythm that supports it, "as a boat carries a
bewildered passenger"—the "distant music" that Joyce mentions in "The
Dead"—and also the space of early childhood, with the child's movements
of individuation supported by the unobtrusive presence of a parent who

can be returned to, whose rhythms have not fully disappeared, the *sa,* or "mother-note." In Chaudhuri the textual field seems constructed on that earlier, less evident scaffolding, both a psychological landscape and a spatial and musical order that is not itself discursive but helps to shape the discourses that appear. The textual articulation comes forward out of a background world that is half-forgotten.

> Maand was a raag which, when sung by my guru or Sohanlal, revealed its airy, skeletal frame, with holes and gaps in it, its unnameable, magical beginnings, and its spirit-like mobility in covering distances, in traversing scorched mountainsides, deserts, horizons, water, following back on the route of migrations that had led away from that country. The raags, woven together, are a history, a map, a calendar, of northern India. (219)

With Rushdie, in contrast, there is no distant music, no denser and less evident scaffolding, no disappearing world held there elegiacally as we become disenchanted modern selves. In the way one finds that certain forms of modern and postmodern morality thin out the ethical space of the self, and thus impoverish its multilevel engagement with the world and with itself, so too one can find literary space impoverished. The implicit self-to-other relation that one is being trained in, through a postmodern literary space, allows one's investments in the world's meaningfulness to become shallower. Neither world nor self can appear with a depth and integrity of its own as discourses break free and circulate autonomously, generating their objects. Chaudhuri, more than Rushdie, tries to guide us in resisting that process.

I drew a contrast between Pynchon's literary space and Rushdie's in that the latter involved a reduction and thinning out, in spite of its energies of production. That contrast between richer and more impoverished spaces of literature is important to this book throughout but also echoes larger issues in the history of thought. Hegel criticizes Kantian ethical space, for example, precisely because of its reductive thinning out. More generally, Hegel wishes to defend modernity by letting emerge in its field a richer array of materials than Kant or the empiricists could appeal to or account for. One finds in his picture a fertile set of tensions and oppositions that he tries to keep in play as he articulates an overall activity of resolution that should not win out by denying or weakening the underlying stresses. There is the tension, for example, between the internal working of the grammar of Hegel's conceptual machinery and the phenomenological stance of self-other relations, the ways that the subject sets itself in relation to the world within a culture and within history. This tension may appear as that between antihumanist and humanist tendencies. There is the related tension between the moment of bringing the world as it is into view and the moment of moving laterally within the layout of language or culture. One may feel in Hegel both the sweeping pull of modernity and the appeal of earlier cultural layers already worked through, though Hegel is never nostalgic.

There is a sense in which modernism is more Hegelian in this respect and postmodernism is more like Kantian ethical space. More clearly, modernism in literature tries to work within the rich set of Hegelian tensions, even as it puts pressure on them and revalues them and rejects Hegel's resolutions of them and his defense of modernity.[13] If we look, for example, not at what Eliot said but at what he did in *The Waste Land,* we see that as much as one experiences there the cultural circulation of linguistic fragments and the decentering of self, one also sees that the stance of the experiencing individual consciousness still matters deeply, as the poet tries to master deep layers of personally and culturally unconscious material. So Eliot retains in that poem, as modernism in literature often does, the Hegelian tensions between grammar and phenomenology, between sideways linguistic or conceptual relations and the stance of the self toward the world and toward itself, between an ironic attitude toward vocabularies and a deep investment in letting reality appear, between metalevel reflection on one's literary activity and a commitment to that activity in its ordinary form. (This is a claim about richer versus more impoverished spaces of literary engagement. It is by no means a claim that one should write poetry in the manner of Eliot or Stevens or anyone else, nor does it have much to do with modernism, say, in architecture or music.) The postmodern strategy tends, like the Kantian one in ethics, to be more radically reductive. In order to focus on the operation of the sign machineries as such, one drastically thins out world and consciousness in order to see them as projections of language or of cultural grammars. Or if one wants to focus on the feel of the postmodern self, in its being a receptacle for so many rapidly circulating cultural signs, one performs a reduction whereby that sort of social space is all that is real. These two reductions are, of course, very different from the ones that Kant undertook in ethics, but they are like his in their efforts to form a more reduced space that leaves a wider and richer context behind and tries then to generate the features of that context out of itself. Such reductions, and then the attempt to construct the rest of the field out of that reduced space, will often fail because what one has left behind in making the reduction must actually remain in view for the reduced space to have any content.

Even if contemporary culture would contribute to the process of postmodern reduction and thinning out, that is no reason to endorse that process but rather to bring into view experiences that resist it, that refuse the glib shallowness that the turn to theory and to cultural studies may encourage in the reading of literature. Suppose it is true that we are now in a late capitalist information culture in which bits of information are more pervasive and mobile than ever before; they move through us at such an increased rate that a new kind of self is being shaped, one that is less substantial and more a shifting, resonating product of the flows of words and images. There is no reason why it should follow that it is the goal of art and literature to give themselves over to that sort of cultural formation; to repeat its moves in a manner whose irony and self-consciousness are supposed to make up for the thinness of that world; to train us as readers and viewers in having more sophisticated, ambiguous attitudes toward the consumption of cultural signs. Why not ask how literature can contribute to a more satisfying kind of self-formation? We can then see literary space as training us in richer rather than thinner shapes of self-relating-in-relating-to-otherness (to use Hegel's expression).

Consider a poem written rather late during James Merrill's fatal illness, "Press Release."[14] I have been defending the sort of space that keeps a richer set of tensions in play, rather than a reductive postmodern one. Two possible tensions within that richer space are, first, that between humanist and antihumanist tendencies and, second, that between the formal ordering powers of art and, over against them, threatening psychological energies or difficult material from the world. With a reduction to a postmodern discursive space these two tensions will dissolve. The antihumanist tendencies will win out over the humanist ones through a deconstruction of the modern self. And since language or culture for the postmodernist is productive of the very energies it is ordering, there is no longer the tension between the ordering power of form and the psychic or worldly material and energies that resist it. Therefore much less value will be given to the aesthetically well-made artifact; it is no longer seen as doing a kind of work that has valuable and analogous psychic and cultural forms. Instead one ignores the self-unifying character of a text and sees it as formed by external social energies and as disseminating meanings beyond itself. Merrill, then, will seem extremely old-fashioned as he offers in "Press Release," while facing his own death, a poem that follows the strictest of formal rules. In the poem there are nine stanzas of nine lines each. In each stanza lines 1, 3, and 7 must end with the same word or a close variant of it, and so must lines 2, 4, 5, and 9. The word at the end of line 6 in one stanza becomes the end word for lines 1, 3, and 7 of the next stanza; the word at the end of line 8 becomes the end word for lines 2, 4, 5, and 9 of the next stanza. Nines or addends of nine are everywhere. There are eighteen end words for the eighty-one lines, nine of them used four times and nine of them used five times, and so forth. Is this just another well-wrought urn that the theorists were right to warn us against?

Yet the poem has a natural, even colloquial flow to it, and the literary form is doing important work. There are a number of concepts in the poem, such as *concentrate, crystallize, substance,* and *solution,* that have to do with how substances form in nature and with activities of the poetic and psychological self. The poet, reading about a substance crystallized for the first time in a laboratory, wonders whether a reconfiguring of self is awaiting him with his death, a new crystallizing of his essence, or whether the only form of such a transformation, the only concentrate of his substance, will be the poetry. So instead of appearing artificial the poem's nine-sided crystal form has a complex continuity with the architecture of natural forms, and new crystallizations of nature are probably forming inside the poet right then and helping to bring about his death. The analogies between art and nature, at the level of crystalline forms, are deeply real and are no longer mere New Critical triggerings with symbolic charge. The poem as a nine-sided prism is compared to an insect's eye, as in dreams the poet sees multiple forms of possible suicide that are available to him. There is a play in the poem's words between nature and mind (as *concentrate* may refer to the form of a substance and to the act of paying attention), between active intervention into nature and letting natural processes happen. There is, then, a kind of small heroism, a linkage with the processes of the universe that are bringing death, in enacting this beautiful crystallizing of patterns in the poem, using, as nature does, rather simple building blocks (the eighteen end words) over and over in a complex structure. The result is hardly a mere aesthetic triumph; the existential and metaphysical weight of the poem could only have been carried by such a well-made artifact.

Or take the modernist tension between humanist and nonhumanist tendencies. The postmodernist would dissolve the former into the latter. But a distinction should be made here. It is proper to criticize Renaissance humanism for its conviction that humans have a special position in the universe, endorsed by the universe itself. But even if the universe was not designed for us and offers no larger picture that makes us significant, and even if we are formed by impersonal processes, still the character of an individual life matters, at least on the scale where literary work itself matters. The way the individual sets himself in relation to the universe and to death, the way he sees his life as taking on an overall shape, and the role that art plays in these projects, all have importance even after we understand the antihumanist claims of the academic critic. Merrill's poem acknowledges fully the larger natural processes that dominate us and that have no concern for us; at the same time he shows how, continuous with that recognition and consistent with it, the concentrate of self that an individual life produces, and that a poem expresses, can matter greatly. In both of the cases just considered (the tension between aesthetic values and dispersive energies, and the tension between humanist values and antihumanist ones) the postmodernist reduction of those tensions, through the dissolving or absorbing of one side of them, sacrifices too much of the resources needed to make sense of our projects. The supposedly naive continuer of the richer fields of play that Hegel and literary modernism, in their different ways, left us with is in much better shape.

THE PHILOSOPHICAL BACKGROUND

A likely criticism of this account is that it employs conceptual patterns that are naive, regressive, outdated, and nostalgic. In this chapter I want to show that work in semantic theory and metaphysics does not support that criticism. I will begin by examining two philosophers whose works might serve as models for this undertaking in that both may appear to support positions that are historically regressive. The first example is Bernard Williams, who considers and rejects a certain progressivist account of human ethical notions.[1] On such an account the ancient Greeks come off as immature and undeveloped. Their notions of shame, necessity, chance, and fate, and of the project of giving shape to one's life as a whole, do not seem to allow for the rational autonomy, the intensified inner life, and the nonegoistic moral ideas that characterize the modern system of morality. In some respects, though not in Williams's way of presenting it, his account repeats a structure central to this investigation. The older ethical stage emphasizes a phenomenology of self-concern and of self-formation, expressed for example in the notion of shame, as one is engaged with a universe not designed to fit one's ethical life. The modern stage has to do with one's fitting into positions that are defined by a moral grammar and regarding which moral agents are interchangeable units, as in a formal language or as in the turn to the grammatical. It is true that traditional ethical systems will also determine somewhat formal spaces that are defined positionally in terms of who can do what to whom. But the modern systems intensify that sort of space and underplay the way honor and shame express the relationship between the demands of ethics and an overall project of self-formation, so that one loses track of how the shape of the life makes sense as a whole to the one living it.

Williams argues that as we make advances today in the philosophy of mind, we come to see that such a modern sphere of pure autonomy, free inner acts, and determinate responsibility is an illusion. The modern morality system collapses when it tries to stand on its own. It fails to see how a much larger ethical context that it would dismiss as premodern or immature actually is still in place in the modern world and makes the morality system to some degree workable. So the turn to the morality system shares much with the turn to the grammatical. It tries to isolate out a particular sphere from the larger metaphysical and phenomenological context that gives it life, and then to make that sphere autonomously productive of certain formal patterns that world and self must match.

John McDowell works within a different area, that of metaphysics and epistemology, but a certain analogy can be drawn between his project and that of Williams.[2] McDowell is also considering a case in which we seem to have made a transition to a more sophisticated account. The Kantian and empiricist notion of the *given* in experience has been rather thoroughly demolished (one even speaks of the *myth* of the given), and instead one considers representations and beliefs as maneuvering within a holistic epistemic space where no position within that space has any privilege as truth-revealing. But McDowell argues that such a space becomes blind and frictionless; it is hard to see how what occurs within it has any meaning whatever, has any purchase on the world. It turns out that even if the traditional notion of the given in experience was in error, Kant was nevertheless correct that our accounts of belief need both the moment of spontaneous conceptual activity and a moment in which we are perceptually engaged with the world, in which we bring it into view.

As we might put it (these are not McDowell's terms), the grammatical moment of a semi-autonomous conceptual intertextuality, of patterned movements within a discursive space, is not enough. It requires as well a moment (supposedly more philosophically naive) of the phenomenological, of the stance of the self in relation to the world, of its taking the world to be a certain way and of its taking itself to have such an engagement with the world. As with the case of Williams in ethics, the stance we have supposedly given up, in becoming more sophisticated about a grammatical sphere of laterally related items of language, is actually required if the latter is to make sense. Only in the richer context of the phenomenological, whether expressed ethically as structures of self-concern linked to shame and character and to the overall shape of an individual life, or expressed epistemically as a moment of bringing the world into view for a subject, can the more laterally productive grammatical realm function. With literature as well it is certainly not that impersonal linguistic machineries and regimes of social power are unimportant. It is rather that the larger context that makes them important must include an understanding of how an individual life matters to the one living it, of how it takes on weight, or does not, in relation to the overall character of the world in which it finds itself. Literary space is then like ethical space in Williams and like epistemic space in McDowell.

Literary criticism, as I argued in chapter 1, tended to favor first a radical linguistic turn and later a radical sociological turn. The effect of both of these was to empty out the world and the space of subjectivity so that they became thin projections of the structuring machineries of language or of social regimes of discourse/power. These more radical turns are not justified, and a convincing account both of epistemic space and of literary space requires that richer notions of the world and of subjectivity remain in play. I want to support this claim now by looking at further work in philosophy. My principal target will be the radical linguistic turn, but similar arguments might be made against the radical cultural studies turn as well. One issue to be examined is how vulnerable our notions of truth, reality, representation, and subjectivity are to the destabilizing effects of the grammatical and deconstructing mechanisms of language. In literary theory such an examination tends to lead to quite radical conclusions about semantic and referential indeterminacy and about the decentering of subjectivity.[3] These conclusions undermine notions of textual objectivity and authorship and of aesthetic space and aesthetic value. Then the emptied-out field is taken over by those who use a social constructionist notion of meaning and value, of form and canonicity, to place literary texts in the context of systems of social and economic power.

In philosophy, on the other hand, it often happens that the arguments about linguistic indeterminacy, when pushed to their conclusion, actually favor considerable referential and semantic *stability,* perhaps weakened but still significant notions of truth and representation, and considerable place for the role of the experiencing and intending self. Such notions become more complicated but are not undermined or rejected. Indeed one could say that the linguistic turn in philosophy, once pressed with such vigor, has been given up as such. Even if it continues to be a demand that one be well trained in the philosophy of language and be good at conceptual analysis, there are relatively few now who believe that the core questions of philosophy are simply disguised questions about language. There is less support, then, for the view of language as a semi-autonomous activity that projects its grammatical patterns on the world. Perhaps the philosopher and the cultural studies theorist can agree on giving up that view, but they will do so for very different purposes and with different results. The latter may see the failure of the linguistic turn precisely as a reason to widen the field and see social configurations of power and discourse as what constitute truth and selfhood. The philosopher supposes that this sociological turn would just repeat the errors of the linguistic turn at a different level. A better response to the failure of the linguistic turn is to note its underlying cause: its misunderstanding of the rich notions of world and subjectivity that must remain in play for experience and meaning to emerge. A defense of that response follows.

The arguments of Wittgenstein and others force us to reject notions of a meaning-giving inner activity that is unmediated by language and by the lateral connections that entry into language imposes. But it is wrong to suppose that we thereby make language into a power that is projecting its forms on everything else. Wittgenstein has given us the tools to bring about a disenchantment of subjectivity, a recognition that it has no mysterious "spiritual" power to generate semantically determinate speech and action. But those same tools allow us to see that there must be a disenchantment of language itself.[4] Language, no more than the inner activity of mind, can confer an intrinsic meaning on its own items; it cannot play a theological role. So we have to ask about the conditions under which strings of linguistic shapes can be meaningful, can actually count *as* linguistic shapes.

Donald Davidson's work is especially useful in this regard. Consider an interpreter trying to make sense of a string of marks or utterances.[5] As they are not intrinsically meaningful it is only when they are set in a worldly context, such that they vary in regular ways in accord with variations in the world, that meaning can be ascribed to them. The layout of the world, in its given articulations, casts its shadow across these marks or utterances and in so doing makes it possible for them to be meaningful. Someone interpreting a speaker would not even be able to divide up his supposedly linguistic strings into meaningful segments unless they could be read, at least as a starting point, as registering the way the world is laid out. So in fact the theological model, at least as applied to language, turns out to be incoherent. As one metaphysically thins out the world, in order to see language as projecting its structures on it, one gradually reaches a point at which the world is no longer rich enough to provide the context needed to make linguistic utterances meaningful. This does not mean that language simply mirrors patterns already determinate in the world. Nor need we suppose that there is a way, through an epistemic examination of the apparatus of individual experience, to describe what the world is like apart from any particular way of viewing it and talking about it. Rather our decisions about degrees of objectivity are made through our attempts to share our perceptions and beliefs with others who are differently situated and perhaps differently endowed. (That is why a meeting with intelligent extraterrestrials would be so epistemically significant.) But a global antirealism such as what is called here the radical turn to language must, on the preceding argument, be rejected. It is true also, in this context of radical interpretation, that selfhood cannot be a pure construct of language, however it may be shaped by it. For, again, even to begin to count a string of marks or brain states as expressions of a meaningful language requires, in the Davidsonian account, a context of interpretation in which creatures can be seen as possessing mental states many of which, at least, have a richer provenance than their representations in language. So both world and self must be aspects of a richer context than the more radical linguistic turn can allow; the reduction it seeks would end up destroying the linguistic level itself.

Now I want to use that argument to ask about the degree to which our metaphysical and semantic notions become destabilized by the powers of language. One should note how the account of the basic conditions for mental or linguistic items to be meaningful already introduces a considerable measure of stability. In the model of modernity all the burden of stabilizing meaning was placed on the intending activities of selves. But there was no reason why those intending activities could not differ massively and arbitrarily from one person to another, one occasion to another, one culture to another. (Kant attempted to answer one version of this problem.) In the account just given, however, much of the meaning-conferring burden has been removed from language or thought. The world itself, in its relative stability as the site of our actions, plays a role in fixing meaning and so brings a considerable stability to our semantic activities. On the earlier paradigm, when meaning and determinacy were conferred almost fully from the side of subjectivity, then it might be supposed that sharply different conceptual schemes were being employed by different speakers. But once the conditions of meaningfulness are understood, says Davidson, then radical differences in what different subjects take the world to be must disappear.[6] Those intelligent enough to take the world to be one way or another, to have a meaningful scheme in the first place, must count as mostly agreeing about a largely shared world, given the conditions for counting beliefs as interpretable. Davidson advises us to give up the very notion of a conceptual scheme that projects its structure on an inarticulate world. And as we consider these conditions for meaningfulness, which are intrinsically linked to the possibility of interpretation by others, we see that those who count as speaking meaningfully must share, to at least a rough degree, a basic conception of rationality.[7] Again, it is precisely because language and subjectivity do not have an intrinsic metaphysical determinacy that we can eventually justify a considerable measure of stability and sameness, rather than concluding that we are in a realm that is radically unstable and undecidable.

A similar argument might be made in the area of science. Those in literary theory who favor notions of difference and historical discontinuity may be tempted to suppose that Thomas Kuhn's notion of paradigms is still the last word in discussions of scientific rationality. Supposedly we move out of one way of talking and into another and the two are not sufficiently commensurable to allow epistemic judgments as to which is superior. But in fact Kuhn's work has been superseded. Once again the key is to understand the stabilizing effect of the role that the world plays in determining reference. We do not have to assume that two speakers with different beliefs regarding a phenomenon are actually speaking about different objects. As long as ancient thinkers had some notion of natural kinds and certain causal connections to the world, then we and they can be speaking about the same natural kind *gold* even if our scientific paradigms are not the same.[8] So the claim that in transitions to new scientific accounts we are simply changing the subject, rather than talking about the same world in a better way, is, at least as a general claim, false. Again, oddly enough, a certain indeterminacy in our mental or linguistic items results in semantic stability. To disenchant only the world and not thought or language is to open the door to sharply different linguistic schemes that project their structures on the world. To be more radical in one's disenchantment so as to include language as well is to understand that at least a rough fitting of beliefs to world and of speaker to speaker must be present.

Some may point to Wittgenstein as a supporter of a more radical linguistic turn, for he did argue that many traditional questions in philosophy are really questions about how we use language, are questions of grammar rather than factual or causal ones. But Wittgenstein did not wildly inflate the power of language or attribute to it a radical undecidability, as many in literary criticism did at least during the heyday of deconstruction. It is true that our moves within the various language games are not, for Wittgenstein, a mirroring of metaphysical articulations built into the universe. But these moves hardly exist in a free-floating space unconstrained by the gravities of the world. Our conceptual patternings are like twisting cityscapes on uneven and complicated terrain; they must be constantly accommodating themselves to that terrain even if they are not precisely mirroring it, and that terrain must be rich enough to give our conceptual moves across it weight and consequence. A strong antimetaphysical tendency in Wittgenstein makes his arguments defeat any attempt to find fixed anchoring points that can absolutely secure meaning, reference, intention, and extralinguistic determinacy. But this situation does not lead to massive indeterminacy and undecidability. It is rather that we see how it is both wrong and unnecessary to look for such fixed points. Our practices of speaking and intending are multiply pegged to a range of other features that they cannot determine from inside the language game. David Pears puts the matter well:

> His point is only that the authority is not supplied by any single item, but by the whole language-game with all its complicated attachments to the world. . . . The answer opposed by Wittgenstein is that there are special points inside the system at which all the required support is concentrated. Not only is that not so, but really it could not be so, and here his usual reductive arguments are brought to bear. The support is spread throughout the structure, eventually reaching the ground at many different points each of which makes its contribution to the stability of the whole.[9]

That conclusion echoes the finding above. The problem with models of the modern sort, and of the theological sort generally, is that they try to concentrate the meaning-conferring power at one point or one level; then wild difference and arbitrariness may seem to result. To distribute metaphysical and semantic support across the system, as when we let the world play a role in fixing meaning, is to reduce that arbitrariness substantially. Pears's overall account here shows how Wittgenstein uses that form of argument in his critique of empiricism. Once one asks in a radical way how meaning is formed and stabilized, then one sees that the inner world of the empiricist would be blank, would be meaningless, except that it occurs within a larger taken-for-granted space, one that importantly includes three features devalued by the empiricist: patterns of regular happenings in the surrounding world, a context of possible repeatability by others, and lower-level desires and tendencies in the bodily life of the self. The empiricist move inward toward a supposedly richer inner foundation would bring about only emptiness if it succeeded. The necessity for this wider distribution of support shows why reducing a complex semantic (or ethical or literary) field to a thinner aspect of it, and then attempting to construct the former out of the resources of the latter, will usually fail.

Davidson gives another example of finding convergence and stability where others fear that seemingly related entities might come uncontrollably apart, in ways that threaten our sense of the stability of ordinary practice. Suppose we ask whether we might be seriously mistaken about what our own words mean.[10] There seem to be two different moments in play, what the words mean and what we take them to mean, and nothing keeps those two moments from coming radically apart, so that we can have no confidence at all that we end up meaning what we take ourselves to mean. But Davidson claims that this cannot happen because neither one of the two moments has an intrinsic semantic determinacy; they are determinate only in the context of an interpretation that makes overall sense of a speaker's full range of linguistic and nonlinguistic behaviors. A constraint on that interpretive activity is that the interpreter assigns meaning on the basis of a certain overall picture, one that takes what a speaker says and believes as at least roughly grasping what the world is like. In addition that assignment will take what the speaker *understands* his words to mean as, roughly, what they do mean according to the holistic interpretation being developed. The settling of a certain description on one phenomenon is part of an overall process that automatically settles a certain parallel meaning on a different phenomenon, so that the close fitting of the two is not *discovered* (on the basis of causal relations between independently described entities), but is built into the very way they are picked out as what they are. This argument would press the linguistic turn in a way that makes us see that wild indeterminacy cannot result from it.

Crucial here is the Wittgensteinian notion of there being multiple pegs through which the linguistic is linked to the nonlinguistic such that semantic and referential stability is possible even when none of the points of attachment has a rigorous determinacy on its own. That notion helps us understand how philosophy of language and literary criticism went in generally different directions. Consider the contrast, for example, between Wittgenstein and Paul de Man. For the latter, linguistic indeterminacy is so inflated that meaning takes on for him a radical undecidability and even impossibility. Language, de Man believes, is a material, grammatical, and rhetorical machinery that is inherently destabilizing to whatever enters it. Any attempt to match inner and outer realms, whether through one's referring to the world in order to capture its features or through having one's intentions shape the meaning one's actions take on in the world, is hopeless. The linguistic machinery takes over and keeps engendering meanings that have nothing to do with the referential world being aimed at, or with the intentions that supposedly did the aiming. (De Man likes to push indeterminacy over the line into impossibility. It is not so much that reference and communication are less stable than we might have thought. If we take him seriously then it seems that nothing is ever referred to, nothing is ever communicated, no actions are performed; yet the pathos of being caught up in language is that we inevitably go on acting as if these phenomena actually occurred, as we cannot help our built-in error of mistaking linguistic patterns for worldly or psychological ones.)[11] One way of reading de Man is to see him as performing a radical disenchantment that is parallel with the earlier disenchantment of nature. Once people believed that nature was full of signs and resemblances put there by the design of God as a guide for humans. But with modern science we recognize that there are no such analogies, that nature is a blind, impersonal machinery that may have generated humans out of its material processes but that gives no special recognition or relevance to human activity. In a similar way, de Man seems to believe, we are now discovering language to be also a blind machinery whose pattern-generating processes are in a fundamental sense inhuman and are not there to serve human interests or goals. We are the effects of these processes but the processes do their work in a way that undercuts, because they have nothing fundamentally to do with, human enterprises.

But that account, while a dramatic one perhaps, ignores the central ways that language, even as disenchanted, is not like nature. We might usefully refer again here to Wittgenstein and Davidson. Language is not an autonomous, all-enveloping system but rather emerges in the context of complex, nonlinguistic phenomena. There must already be a stably articulated world as its setting or else the mental or vocal shapes that develop could not count even as language. Language arises as well in a context where there are sophisticated animals with wants and needs and living situations in which certain kinds of communication will aid survival. Davidson's holistic account of interpretation assumes that such a context is in place; language's emergence in that context, its being multiply pegged to those surrounding features, enables a semantic stability that language by itself, from the inside, could not generate. The instructions sent through space from NASA to astronauts in a badly damaged capsule are quickly interpreted to produce the exact adjustments needed to return safely; a radical semantic impossibility does not threaten, even if a particular sequence of linguistic shapes, taken on its own, might be interpreted in wildly different ways. (It is not that the nonlinguistic context provides a final determinacy; someone clever enough might still come up with alternative readings. It is rather that as a practical matter we come readily to agreement.)

The Davidsonian answer seems more sophisticated here. The failure to find an anchoring metaphysical determinacy at a single point in the system is actually good news, a way of reducing overall indeterminacy. One can see a large part of Davidson's work as showing how the *reifying* of such phenomena as reference, meaning, intention, empirical content, language, and so forth, actually works against the possibility of communication. The mediating entities between speaker and world that philosophers typically put forward in order to explain meaning and truth actually make matters worse; once we put them in place with a certain determinacy of their own then they can be barriers rather than links (for example, when we suppose that our experience is of such mediating entities rather than of the world itself). We must see rather, says Davidson, how all of these phenomena are the fallout of our overall practices of interpretation; some degree of metaphysical "give" in our language-to-world linkages, with correspondingly less reifying of semantic entities, is helpful in making the interpretation go through. The resulting overall stability is the reverse side of all those local indeterminacies.

The conclusion is that giving language its full, supposedly destabilizing play actually works to give us relatively stable semantic notions of truth, meaning, and aboutness. It is just that these notions end up much more complicated than when we started out. Consider, for example, the notion of reference. Perhaps it is true that for Quinean reasons the attempt to find a simple word-to-world linkage keeps failing, as one finds oneself shuttled in a lateral movement toward other words, other instances of language use. But one should not then draw the conclusion that the notion of language as referential is somehow illusory. When Quine speaks of the "inscrutability of reference" and Davidson talks of "reality without reference," they are by no means denying language's fundamental relation of *aboutness* to the world.[12] Rather they are challenging the idea that there is a particular sort of relationship of reference between words and things that could serve as a fundamental causal notion in our overall scientific account of the world.[13] Our words, says Davidson, are tested against the world as whole *sentences,* as units that can turn out to be true or false, that can be justified. In making sense of the language of a radically alien group an interpreter would have to take as fundamental evidence their reactions of assent or dissent to sentences. On the basis of that evidence and evidence about what the world is like, a theorist of the language might then draw up an account that assigned referential value to individual parts of the whole sentences. Reference would thereby be a fallout of the overall theory, as one attempted to match the theory to evidence regarding sentences. But even if reference cannot play a certain *theoretical* role in science, we will still end up perfectly justified in saying that *bacteria* refers to bacteria or that *Mississippi River* refers to the Mississippi River. The completely wrong conclusion to draw is that we must somehow give up the notion of language as referential and see it as free-floating conceptual space.

We have to guard against a pernicious form of argument here. A philosophical argument will be successful against a certain metaphysically strong notion (of reference, intention, subjectivity, freedom, and so forth), and then other thinkers assume that the notion itself, in any version at all, is in jeopardy. But that conclusion does not follow. When we speak we are bringing the world into view and successfully referring to it with at least a rough degree of reliability. A similar argument might be made for the notion of representation. It is true that certain notions of linguistic or mental items as mirroring the world must be given up; there is for the most part no such mirroring relationship. But after one understands how we are engaged with the world as perceivers and believers one understands that a bit of language might represent the world as ordered in such a way that a right-hand turn is necessary to get to a desired location; fortunately these items often enough represent the world accurately.

It is true that philosophers disagree as to just how rich a content can be assigned to the world itself as the site of our intendings and believings. This is a topic regarding which debates may seem endless. The point here is to show how little justification there is for the picture that language or regimes of social power project their schemes on a thinned-out world. Even if there is controversy regarding what degree of realism we are entitled to, that controversy offers little support for a radical linguistic turn or a radical sociological turn. As it turns out there is considerable support in philosophy of science for modestly realist claims. When we try to come up with the best explanation, all things considered, for why our beliefs about viruses and DNA molecules and tectonic plates have been successful, the most persuasive answer seems to be that there really are viruses and DNA molecules and tectonic plates. The answer that social power enabled some group to project its favored answers on a neutral world is ludicrous in comparison. It is significant that many present theories are effective in guiding novel discoveries, and not just in managing to account for an already given set of data, and that these theories often explain new data they were not constructed to explain. The assumption that there really are DNA molecules, and that they are pretty much as our theories take them to be, guides new experiments, new therapies, and the construction of new investigatory machines that enable further discoveries. The best explanation for the success of these novel moves is that the original assumption, that there really are DNA molecules, is justified. By assuming that this DNA theory picks out real causal processes, rather than just pictures helpful at making predictions or thought patterns favored by those in power, one is led to engage in activities aimed at changing the world in certain ways, and the success of these activities strengthens this belief in the reality of such causal processes. (I should grant that the relation between inference to the best explanation and truth is more complicated than I am making it out to be, or than I can possibly consider in a few sentences in a book on philosophy and literature.)[14]

Nothing in science is certain, and it is not impossible that intelligent aliens might describe the world adequately without mentioning DNA molecules. Or perhaps a more exact future science will find, at its level of precision, that it is no longer helpful to talk about viruses or DNA molecules and the like. Even if that were so, even if we had to take our talk of such molecules as more weakly realist than we formerly did, still we would be getting a purchase on worldly phenomena in that talk and would be, at least roughly, getting matters right in doing so. We might have to speak of theories as tending toward truth, as truth-tropic, rather than as simply true. Of course some of our more speculative theories of astrophysics and subatomic particles may not be close to how matters truly are; and some of those theories, so we may decide in the long run, were successful, if they were, only in an instrumentalist manner.

Some philosophers of science, it is true, will favor more pragmatist accounts, rather than straightforwardly realist ones, regarding our scientific languages. But they do not do this in any way that gives solace to the relativist.[15] This remains the case even if there is much greater skepticism today about the possibility of discovering a unified science that gives a complete explanation of a fully law-governed universe.[16] So a literary theorist has no justification for resting secure in a global antirealism or social constructionism. Contemporary philosophy of science offers virtually no support for relativist notions that our scientific theories are little constrained by how matters stand in the world; that they are merely linguistic or social projections; that they so strongly determine what will count as evidence for them that they cannot be objectively tested by evidence; that ways of thinking bring their own standards of rationality and so cannot be measured against one another; or that scientific beliefs are just expressions of social power.

The notion, as in Rorty, that truth is just a matter of social agreement, a language-to-language match rather than a language-to-world match, has little to support it. Otherwise a scientist should spend less time on experimentation and more on a social-studies investigation of what would make other scientists agree with her. The backers of social agreement as a criterion usually add "in the long run." If intelligent life should disappear from the universe, then it is supposedly a matter of what agreement *would* have taken place if those intelligent beings had stayed around for an infinitely long period. But why grant such a role to "the long run"? We do so because we assume that at any stage of social interaction, the world may not have yet had its fully adequate say in shaping our beliefs. The language-to-language relationships have no significance unless they participate in a larger process of language-to-world accommodation. Again we need a stronger conception of humans as getting things right in speaking about the world.

According to the schema being developed here we not only need and can justify richer notions of the world, but we also have to show that subjectivity, and the phenomenological space of self-to-world relations, do not collapse into being a mere projection of language or social power. In order to make sense of experience we need a richer version of our intentional relations to the world than either the radical linguistic turn or the radical cultural studies turn can allow for. (The word *intentional* as used here does not mean "purposeful" but refers rather to mental states that have the character of being directed toward an object that they are about.) We can look at crucial features of that space of intentionality if we examine, in considerably more detail than above, the work of John McDowell.[17] I consider that work because those who favor the more radical turns in question do not consider the complexity of the story that needs to be told about what it means to have perceptions or beliefs about the world.

The issue McDowell is examining, in developing his version of that story, is what happens when we give up the "Myth of the Given," the idea that between the world and our beliefs about it there is a stage of experience that is the sensory input to our thinking, a stage that we do not contribute to conceptually and that we must simply take for granted as the basis for theory. If we accept that notion of givenness, then thought's activity does not reach all the way to the world itself, but only to some intermediary stage whose offerings cannot be further questioned. If that seems an undesirable outcome, the temptation is that in rejecting it we adopt what seems the only alternative: emphasizing the freedom of thought to move in its own space, to determine itself through its lateral relations to other linguistic items, rather than by a frictional or confrontational relationship with how things are happening in the world.[18] Even in Davidson, who in other respects wants to call on the world as the justifying measure of our thinking, McDowell locates some features of that model of a free-floating activity operating without friction from the way things actually stand.[19] Davidson claims, for example, that beliefs can only be measured against other beliefs and not against some portion of the world. In some respects this is more a matter of Davidson misspeaking than a position essential to his philosophy. What he ought to say is simply that we must give up the notion of a belief-world confrontation insofar as it is supposed to play a foundational epistemic role, as if there were a feature in some experiential encounters that could make certain statements self-grounding. But if there are no language-world confrontations of that privileged epistemic sort, it remains the case, in spite of Davidson's claim, that we compare our beliefs all the time with the way matters stand in the world. It is not that one occupies an inner space and suddenly a perceptual belief pops into that space. One is engaged with the world itself and has it directly in view.

But what capacities, McDowell asks, must be in place if we are to have perceptual beliefs that are genuinely about the world in that fashion? (Davidson fails to answer this question adequately because he does not have a rich enough notion of the self-to-world relationship, of subjectivity itself.) At a basic level our thought needs to "track" the world, varying as it varies, in the way that even an insect's mechanisms might track the world. But for genuine belief there must be a richer structure than that in place. McDowell asks about the conditions for counting something as experiential content, for example, having a belief that something is colored. To experience colors as such, he says, is to take certain features of the world *as colored* and to bring them into a larger framework of beliefs, including the belief that colors are the surfaces of objects that could remain the same even if their colors should change. To have genuine empirical content means to have a rich implicit conception of objectivity as well as an implicit self-understanding, a sense of oneself as engaged in a project of comprehending reality. The world is not just given to me; I must *take* it to be such and such.

But my taking it to be so has complex structures. To be a sophisticated belief-former is to act under what McDowell calls the idea of rational freedom: our capacity to form our beliefs about the world based only on considerations of what is rational to believe. But then it is not enough that the world causally affects our mental states in reliable ways. Suppose the world causally influenced certain inner experiences, but as far as the experiencer was concerned, these just happened, inward along the chain leading to belief, and his conceptual activity then went to work on these experiences. That way of accounting for belief-acceptance, based on what is given, would only be exculpatory; one could not be blamed for the beliefs built on it. But our project of doing well as believers aims at justification, not exculpation.[20] That means that the range of our rational freedom, of what we can bring up for review in our overall project of forming well-supported beliefs, must extend all the way to the world. Everything along the chain leading to belief, including the nature of our sensory apparatus, must be a candidate for this sort of review. We show this, for example, even in so simple a matter as getting eyeglasses when our vision deteriorates. It is not as if we simply accept the deliverances of the senses and then form our beliefs on them. We show our self-understanding of the project of being a believer when we are willing to make any change, even surgery, along the route between belief and world, provided that the world will thus come more reliably into view.[21] But that fact shows how complex must be the structure of our intentional relations to the world, our structures of self-relating-in-relating-to-otherness, as Hegel called them. In our ways of having and evaluating experience we must bring to bear a sophisticated conception of ourselves as believers, and of what it means to experience the world.

McDowell shows, then, how empirical content requires rich structures of intentionality, of one's taking the world to be a certain way. Without that complex self-understanding and world-directedness, our mental or verbal items would not succeed in being genuine beliefs about the world. A frictionless space of circulating concepts or linguistic items or cultural representations would be meaningless without that complex phenomenology of self-to-world relations. Again the stronger linguistic and sociological turns are wrong in their demotion of that phenomenology. They seem to take it for granted that simply appealing to the circulation of cultural signs through the mouths and brains of individuals is sufficient to explain the structure of believing.

We may now ask, more generally, how rich a notion we need of subjectivity, beyond what we have just seen by examining those arguments of McDowell. One notes surprisingly widespread agreement across many areas of literary theory that the subject is dead, that the stance of the self-conscious experiencer is no longer relevant.[22] It is true as well that some positions in philosophy, especially in cognitive science, can be similar. Having a mind may be thought of as a processing of strings of a formal language. But then it seems that subjectivity is nothing more than the running of certain grammatical patterns. Anything else running the same formal program ought to count as having mental states. So we are given thought experiments in which the Chinese nation, for example, is presented as running such a program, with individuals holding flags up or down to represent the ones and zeros of the program.[23] Would the Chinese nation, thus configured, count then as having intentions and beliefs? It seems mysterious to many in cognitive science why it would not.

But there never was a chance that the nation as a whole could have mental states. Whatever formal grammar it may be exemplifying, it does not begin to have the sophisticated structures of subjectivity that are essential to the having of empirical content.[24] There is no self-articulating, self-maintaining individuality that is at least a minimal condition for subjectivity; no self-other differentiation, no implicit self-understanding of a stance toward objectivity. To leave these out is to lose hold of the conditions for how any meaningful intending of the world can emerge. The cognitive scientist who believes that having an intentional relation to the world is simply a matter of running the right grammatical patterns, then, is very much like those in literary theory who would reduce subjectivity to other versions of what I have called the grammatical level. If there is to be semantic content to language, then there must be selves whose subjectivity involves complex self-relational activities, including those described by McDowell but others as well. There must be selves that experience the world through a sophisticated way of taking themselves to be engaged with it; whose self-unifying activity is complex and sophisticated and the result of a process of individuation and differentiation; and whose apparatus of knowing is an aspect of the world-directed character of their self-concern, their caring that things are one way rather than another. These aspects of subjectivity are not linguistic constructions, even if language and culture help to shape them. We cannot account for social constructionism itself unless there is a much richer self than the social constructionist can allow for.

An opponent here might continue to claim that the subject has now been deconstructed into a collecting point for fragments of cultural languages. But even if we must give up any strong metaphysical notion of the source of unity for a subject, still it is important that there is an ongoing work of synthesis that selves engage in. The dangerous form of argument here is that once we see the weakness of arguments for something as strong as Cartesian self-identity, we may suppose that we are driven to an extreme opposite view: that self-identity is illusory except as a marker of what cultural vocabularies and social power temporarily construct us to be. It is true that typical accounts of self-identity today emphasize a more dispersed quality, as if each of us should be seen as a collection of homunculi without any central "I" where experiences are gathered and decisions made, or as a legislature with different drafts of possible statements or actions competing to impress themselves on the mechanisms of speech and movement.[25] The "I" seems to emerge from all this activity the way a university emerges from all the activities and buildings and persons that make it up. And since many of the inner drafts or homunculi will have been implanted by cultural training, there is some truth to the notion that we are played through by larger vocabularies rather than having language at the service of our wants and intentions.

Yet it remains true that we hold ourselves together as selves, connecting events across the frame of a life and saturating our activities with an implicit self-concern. It is not just the continuity of a single body. Evolution has surely designed our brain engineering so that the self's concern for itself, its implicit awareness of itself in whatever it does, its connectedness to a past that still matters and to a future in which it will die, its anxiety about living its life well, its intense interest in protecting this particular self from dissolution, and its being at home in a certain feeling of being itself are all strongly supported by biology. Perhaps a few mystics rise to a level where the difference between one self and another seems illusory. Perhaps we might develop in the future, with technological change, so that our sense of what counts as a whole life, worthy of concern in its passage from birth to death, becomes weaker. But the basis for this entire phenomenology of the self goes deep and is not simply a matter of linguistic or social construction. (Poets, of course, depend on that fact if they want future readers.)

In addition it is not the case that our increasing scientific knowledge shows that we are just the surface playthings of forces that work through us from behind and that we cannot be aware of or master or control, so that the notion of a self that forms itself, is responsible for itself, and is self-determining must be given up. Daniel Dennett shows how even if we adopt a quite mechanical view of mind and consciousness, we can still show how sophisticated creatures could gradually emerge that are self-unifying and self-controlling.[26] They do not get to be this way through any special metaphysical ability but through a long biological and cultural evolution that gradually makes them more self-reflexive and more capable of forming themselves through a responsiveness to good reasons. This is not absolute freedom, of course. We are controlled by mechanical and historical forces that gradually determine us to be more self-determining, to believe and act for good reasons and to be capable of a self-making that makes us more responsible for what we are. If that is a limited way of being a self, still it is strong enough such that it will remain the task of fiction and poetry to reveal the lives of selves of that sort, as they appear to themselves in the living out of a life. There should be little support for the assumption that once we have deconstructed traditional metaphysical notions of self-identity and subjectivity, we have no alternative but to accept radical claims about the death of the subject. Dennett's response is much more interesting: after our philosophical arguments have left us with apparently more impoverished materials for building self-consciousness and subjectivity, let us see how far we can get with those materials. He shows that we can get quite far, even if he does not arrive at a fully satisfying account of consciousness.

To say this is not to deny the often multiple, shifting, and poorly integrated character of psychic life. We may discover in our strong desire for something how much we also want to fail in our attaining it, or in our acts of genuine kindness a foundation with elements of rage and fear. There is not just a doubleness in us but a tripleness and quadrupleness. One of the powers of literature is to give ourselves over to those aspects in us that are marginalized by the unifying habits of consciousness, perhaps to a certain freeplay of signifiers, so that the sounds and shapes of language instead of already determinate meanings generate possible linkages. But for the most part the material we have a hard time dealing with, and that the language of literature helps us to manage, has to do with the quite common experiences of human selves rather than with a transgressive shifting of signifiers. Such common experiences include grief and loss, guilt and aloneness, shame and emptiness, the sense that one's life has been wasted, that it has missed what is essential to living a human life well. The interest of literature is less in the unleashing of such feelings than in the ways, enacted through the literary work, through its patterns that model those of subjectivity, that selves find ways of managing them. It is right to point to the creative potential of the fragmenting, mobile self lost in a torrent of signifiers, with their various substitutions and displacements. Just as interesting are the ways that selves who acknowledge these aspects are still able to be reflective, self-managing, and, to a relative but still satisfying extent, self-unifying. Literature can model this possibility through its own doubleness of repeating the deep rhythms of forces beyond the self and enacting, in its prose, the movements of a more reflective, disenchanted individuality.

There is something odd, anyway, about the notion that there has been a paradigm shift and now we should talk about cultural discourses instead of talking about subjectivity, or should talk about the latter only as a construction of the former. It is not as if, prior to that shift, we had succeeded in understanding what human subjectivity consists in. It remains a largely mysterious phenomenon to us, so much so that there are philosophers, such as Colin McGinn, who hold that we may not be able to give an account of it within our present scientific ways of understanding, if ever.[27] Work in artificial intelligence has not disenchanted the realm of subjectivity but has shown rather how difficult it is to imagine what it would be for a machine to have subjective states. Even the implicit feeling of being a self that seems to saturate my awareness as I walk through a city is profoundly difficult to explain philosophically. Nor do we have satisfying accounts of why the conscious experience of tasting pepper or smelling chocolate seems so different from merely having accurate information about stimuli, as computerized robots could possess. Subjectivity is perhaps at the present time especially suitable for study in literature and poetry. At the very least it is a crazy notion that literary criticism should focus only on the play of discursive vocabularies and forget how poems and fiction can reveal the life of selfhood in an especially intense manner. When we speak of the death of the subject all we can properly mean is that it can no longer play certain metaphysical and epistemic roles as self-supporting ground and center. But we are rather early on in understanding the rich field of subjectivity, in making sense of how experience feels to us and of how we feel to ourselves.

I hope I have shown, in my turn to philosophy, that it is not naive to hold out for richer notions of reality and subjectivity, and stabler notions of truth and meaning and representation, than either of the two radical turns in literary theory would grant us. Those movements are themselves philosophically naive. My reading of literature as we go on will not be intimidated by their claims that earlier ways of reading are somehow regressive.

JAMES MERRILL AND THE MAKING
OF LITERATURE

Two poems by James Merrill, "Lost in Translation" and "Santorini: Stopping the Leak," are especially useful in setting out important features of the model of literary space I am defending. I have chosen Merrill because he is a good example of the weaker or less radical turn to the linguistic or grammatical: earlier ways of being engaged with the world remain in play in his work even as a somewhat autonomous realm of linguistic arrangement and pattern generation becomes important. Merrill's poems often consider one's passage into that realm, with an awareness of what that passage both captures and leaves behind. In chapter 1, I claimed it was important to see literary space as *translational*. The title of the first of these two Merrill poems shows how that feature of literary space is his preoccupation as well.

"Lost in Translation" is about several ways in which there is a transition from one space to another: from childhood to adulthood, from French to German, from unconscious turmoil to linguistic resolution.[1] One contrast especially stands out, that between what might be called the "iconic" and the "compositional." In the principal scene of the poem a boy whose parents are getting divorced, presumably the poet at that age, is working on a jigsaw puzzle whose picture is that of an orientalist painting about Egypt. There are two levels of focus: the images that appear on the puzzle and the compositional arrangements based on the shapes of the puzzle pieces. Those compositional arrangements are compared throughout by Merrill to the arrangement of word-shapes in the poem. The suggestion is that in making the puzzle the boy is moving from anxiety-producing images whose meaning is often unconscious to a cooler linguistic arrangement that in some ways handles this difficult material; the fitting together of the puzzle pieces (the fitting together of bits of language as such) allows the emerging into view, and the successful handling, of the larger picture implied by the puzzle's scene. (In the primal scene portrayed by the puzzle the orientalist sheik, lady, and pageboy suggest another threesome.)

There is a suggestion as well that this move is repeating the move of a young child into language, into an understanding that he can gain power in that way over certain unconscious conflicts and worries about individuation and identity. He can move into a space where grammatical rules and positions mark out a field allowing a stable selfhood to be more securely established. So there is in the very occasion and theme of the poem a reflection on the move to the grammatical. As Merrill says about a puzzle piece: "What it seems to show is superficial / Next to that long-term lamination / Of hazard and craft, the karma that has / Made it matter in the first place" ("Lost in Translation," 280); or: "Each with its scrap of highly colored / Evidence the Law must piece together" (279). The karma or law, as in a formal language, gives a set of items and also rules determining which arrangements of them are acceptable or unacceptable. Also, as in Derrida, the puzzle shapes, which stand for the shapes of linguistic items as such, keep suggesting new meanings beyond the representational content they portray. Thus the "Witch on broomstick, ostrich, hourglass. . . . These can be put aside, made stories of." These puzzle shapes suggest the woman who is replacing the boy's mother as his parents are divorcing; his own lack of awareness, as an ostrich with its head in the sand; and the hourglass that represents the passage of time between these events and his later memory of them. So we see how in this case at least, if not elsewhere, something of the deconstructionist account is correct: features of the language as such (here the puzzle pieces) begin to generate patterns on their own, apart from their representational character (here the vivid picture on the puzzle), and suggest a referential reading that is then projected on the world. Merrill nicely captures the sense of poetry as compositional, as the putting together of the sound-shapes of language, when in his very description of the puzzle pieces he talks of "a thousand hand-sawn, sandal-scented pieces." The repetition and varying of syllable sounds in that line are able to suggest, on the side of language, the compositional nature of the puzzle and the existence of language as a realm of material shapes that can generate novel semantic connections on their own.

A passage from anxiety-producing image to the cooler arrangement of words can be seen when the poem talks of how a certain puzzle piece was produced. This is not part of the puzzle the boy is making but belongs to a scene, years later, when a medium is asked to guess what object has been placed in a "plain tole casket" while he was out of the room. The poem describes the scene that comes to his mind:

> A dry saw-shriek drowns them out,
> Some loud machinery—a lumber mill?
> Far uphill in the fir forest
> Trees tower, tense with shock,
> Groaning and cracking as they crash groundward.
> But hidden here is a freak fragment
>
> . . . .
> Plywood, Piece of a puzzle.
> ("Lost in Translation," 280)

The castration scene with its tense, jolting language becomes, as the language cools down, a puzzle piece, a bit of linguistic material separated from that unconscious message and ready to be arranged according to the grammar and laws of the language, like the pieces of the boy's jigsaw puzzle with their matching shapes. The puzzle piece, "an object at once unique and common" (and so both a proper name and a syntactic slot), finds its proper place not only in the overall grammar of symbolic arrangement but also as an iconic shape (as in another primal scene); it appears in a box in which it has been hidden, as one watches the "Panel slid back, recess explored," so that the shape is discovered "by an opening of lids / Upon the thing itself." The overall translational activity here reminds one of the process of thinking for Spinoza: when we understand matters imperfectly, he says, we see them as external and arbitrary, as forced on us from without; we come to understand their real nature, and to accept them, when we see them as aspects of internally necessary arrangements of which we are also a part. The poem as an internal arrangement of linguistic items uses such features as rhyme, cadence, and the internal resonance of one word with another to suggest that cooler necessity of an ordering scheme capable of internalizing and containing the difficult material.

A parallel claim about writing is contained in another scene from the poem. The boy is now grown and, while living in Athens, is trying to find a translation that he remembers Rilke having made from a Valéry poem about a palm tree. The transition from French to German has changed the feel of the poem, he recalls. He thinks of "How much of the sun-ripe original / Felicity Rilke made himself forego / . . .

In order to render its underlying sense." The translation is compared to a physical landscape, a "Rhyme-rutted pavement," where "the warm Romance / Stone by stone faded, cooled" ("Lost in Translation," 283). That landscape is itself a scene of writing where Rilke gives up the warm sounds of the French words for a "sublime and barren" ground plan whose "fluted nouns" are "Made taller, lonelier than life / By leaf-carved capitals in the afterglow. / The owlet umlaut peeps and hoots / Above the open vowel" (284). As with the poet's move from childhood to adulthood, the warm, livelier sounds and images give way to a cooler, linguistic understanding that captures the "underlying sense." The barren shapes of the written German, with the umlauts and the capitals and the fluted nouns, as described so well by Merrill, bring a greater peacefulness but also a sense of loss; the landscape of the writing, of language itself as an arrangement of shapes, is presented almost as a ruined city in the twilight. Wisdom comes but does so rather late in the game, and even that wisdom is ironically deflated by having Hegel's owl turn into a mere owlet, a diacritical mark over a material shape rather than a principle of spiritual understanding. The transition from passion to the written word repeats a process of gain and loss that has gone on since childhood, since a time when the child's entrance into the structural, rule-guided field of language (the "Law" that holds the puzzle together for Merrill) helped him overcome his own fragmentation, like the fragments of the puzzle. But that way of holding the pieces together through one's accession to language has lost some of the energy, some of the desire and pleasure, that was present in the child's prelinguistic, image-laden relation to his mother and to his surroundings, in just the way that Rilke has both captured and lost something in his translation from the French. (Merrill's portrayal of the ambiguity of that accomplishment is one of the strengths of his poetry.)

Unlike in a more radical turn to the space of the grammatical, by which the phenomenology of the self in relation to the world is left behind, Merrill shows the psychological context in which the move to the grammatical has its function. (Recall here the treatment of Williams and McDowell in chapter 3, where such a larger context had to be kept in play if a narrower, supposedly more autonomous realm was to function.) He makes it clear how the space of the poem is a psychological one and is not simply linguistic. First there is the point that in putting the puzzle together the boy and his French nanny do the boundaries first: the outline of the puzzle as "Straight-edge pieces / Align themselves with earth or sky / In twos or threes, naive cosmogonists / Whose views clash" ("Lost in Translation," 280). Only with that arrangement of pieces do we get a clear demarcation of the inside of the puzzle from what is external to it; setting up those boundaries by first doing the puzzle outline represents the child's marking out of self from other; and the question of whether pieces should be aligned with earth or sky suggests an issue of gender identity as well. That reading is affirmed when we look at the scene in the orientalist painting on the puzzle's face: a "Sheik with beard / And flashing sword hilt" is facing "a dark-eyed woman" who is being helped by "a small backward-looking slave or page-boy." That this triangle concerns the poet himself is seen when Mademoiselle, the nanny, writes to a cleric friend and worries about what will happen to the poor child and his innocent mother. The boy mistakenly thinks she is talking about the puzzle scene, though she is talking about the divorce. The triangular scene of the painting is emphasized when the poet mentions the Great Pyramid that can be seen at a distance in the painting, calling its apex the "Eternal Triangle," and claims that the boy in the scene "wonders whom to serve, / And what his duties are, and where his feet." The boy is unclear about gender identification in that triadic scene, and there is an image of castration in the fact that the puzzle piece representing the page-boy's feet seems to be missing even after almost all the rest of the puzzle is done. The space of the poem is a privileged scene of ritual and also the transitional space of early childhood, both of which require the feel of being set off from the space of ordinary life, as the puzzle is defining its separate scene clearly. Merrill is able as he writes to stage a partial return to that childhood transitional space where intense anxieties of self-formation and gender formation, and of securing an overall style of relation to objects, were still in play. The poem does not reduce itself to an autonomous linguistic machinery engendering meaning on the basis of its sounds and shapes. It is built on an earlier scaffolding of spaces that are psychological and prelinguistic, so that the accomplishments and losses of the move into language can still be felt.

If the poem is about such a transitional scene in which both individuation and gender identity are at stake, there is no sense here of a successful resolution that leaves the earlier weakness of identity behind. One might suppose that the triadic structure will settle matters by its grammatical rules (Who is allowed to combine with whom? How is A's relation to B determined as well by A's relation to C and C's relation to B?), which are set against an earlier dyadic scene characterized by a blurring of boundaries and an oscillation between opposing poles. But even after the puzzle is finished, the regressive blurring keeps happening. It turns out that Mademoiselle has taught the boy French with a German accent because she was only French by marriage but had a Prussian father; so the transition the poem represents as a linguistic translation, from French to German, is more ambiguous than it first appeared to be. The child's transition to the grammatical field of adulthood may also, it seems, be incomplete and ambiguous. Additionally, the cleric Mademoiselle writes to is in Alsace, again a blurred historical boundary. Her nephew is now "a UN interpreter," both a successful translator from one set of items to another and (the blurring again) an *un*-interpreter, for whom such translation will not occur as matters remain uninterpreted. The next project after the puzzle will be a puppet show, for which the boy will play the part of the "goosegirl," so gender identity is still at issue. The question of identification with the power of the father remains unclear. While the father-image in the painting is one with a "flashing sword hilt" as the Sheik steps forward "on a tiger skin" whose "fangs gnash out at us," there is a double meaning to the claim that "he is all but finished" beyond the obvious meaning of completing that part of the puzzle. After the puzzle is allowed to come apart, after its Law no longer operates, that fierce tiger skin is repeated, in a deflationary way, in the "mangy" tiger skin rug in the room where the puzzle was worked on.

The boy's "missing feet" are at last found, but of course they are the missing feet of a poetic line, so that the wholeness achieved is a literary rather than a personal one, though the self may temporarily borrow from the literary language that sense of being made whole. We do not get here, then, a full transition to a new psychological structure, one defined by culture's grammatical rules prescribing how one's boundaries and gender position are to be articulated. Instead we seem to have the language of literature as a necessarily repeated, even obsessive, reworking of that transitional space. There is a continuing exposure to the world one has supposedly been translated from, with its oscillations and intensities, and there are rituals that relive, and reassure us about, the movement into an arrangement of words that both brings the earlier material under control and makes us accept a compensatory resolution. And "missing pieces" remain:

> Before the puzzle was boxed and readdressed
> To the puzzle shop in the mid-Sixties
> Something tells me that one piece contrived
> To stay in the boy's pocket. How do I know?
> I know because so many later puzzles
> Had missing pieces—Maggie Teyte's high notes
> Gone at war's end, end of the vogue for collies,
> A house torn down.
>
>   ("Lost in Translation," 283)

That mobile signifier, the puzzle piece seen earlier in the poem as what was made, symbolically, from a tree's crashing down in the forest (so that it could find its place in a concealing box), has managed to attach itself to the boy, but only as part of a world of loss and missing pieces. The puzzle was "readdressed," on the one hand, to the shop "in the mid-Sixties," an area of Manhattan, and, on the other hand, as the author in the mid-1960s is reflecting as a man thirty-five or forty years old on the puzzle of his boyhood. It is only in being sent thus to a different place, later on, that it can be understood.

Merrill seems again to be reflecting in "Santorini: Stopping the Leak" on the relation between the writing of literature and certain rituals that secure processes of self-formation.[2] The island is one that suffered a massive volcano in the ancient world and then gradually reformed itself: "The curtain on a universal hiss / Would fall; steam cover all; millennia pass. / An island surface. Two. three. Vineyards wax. / The plume of smoke with airier emphasis / Slant from the inky crater" ("Santorini: Stopping the Leak," 334). The poet is traveling there after breaking up with his lover in Greece and after having a plantar wart destroyed by "God willing lethal x / Rays." As with the island, dissolution of the self will be followed by a reforming of what seemed to have disappeared: "We felt / A stone heart quicken, a deep fault made whole. / Far and wide around us infant waters laughed" (339). Even the wart will come back: "From some remotest galaxy in the veins / A faint, familiar pulse begins. The wart, / Alive and ticking, that I'd thought destroyed" (337).

This process of risking dissolution and having the self restored is shown to apply especially to the writing of poetry. A description of the island's volcanic catastrophe ends with the lines: "A molten afterbirth transmuting these / Till Oedipus became Empedocles" ("Santorini," 333). Besides the rearrangement of sounds in the two names, so that there is a literal transformation as well as a conceptual one, the move from Oedipus to Empedocles suggests a certain mathematics. Oedipus stands for a triadic structure, while Empedocles pictured a world with two principles, Love and Strife, that caused an endless cycle of pulling apart and coming together. The legend is also that Empedocles killed himself by leaping into a volcano; as Merrill has it: "Leaper headlong into that primal scene / And deafening tirade. The mother tongue / At which his blood boiled, his brain kindled." So Empedocles stands for a dissolving of one's boundaries, a regression to a pre-Oedipal stage of psychic formation where boundaries have not been well-secured, where there is an oscillation between poles, between identity and differentiation, as in the Empedoclean philosophy.

But that regression is also into a form of experiencing for which language becomes the "mother tongue," in which it dissolves and comes together in new ways, so that a soul clinging "to its own fusing senses" might eventually crawl away from that volcanic linguistic activity, perhaps with a poem. The "fusing senses" are the different registers of meaning that are compressed into a single word or phrase, as in that phrase itself, where the senses are both the organs of sensation and the meanings of words.

The poet goes through a dangerous weakening of individuation and returns to earlier psychic stages of experiencing, so that language itself comes apart and reforms. Through that ritual the self relives its own move from pre-Oedipal oscillation and mirroring to the well-ordered arrangements of language, which give it a securer sense of its own self-maintaining articulation. Merrill insistently links poetry with that risk of loss of self. After speaking earlier of vampires on the island the poet forms a petition to his Muse, "Those revels' Queen, in easy ownership, / Sated, my vigor coloring her lip: . . . even as I fall / Back out of mind, yours, anyone's to this / Upsteaming human thaw, bubble and brawl / Of now no thought" ("Santorini," 337). Elsewhere in the poem he feels that "random, ravenous images" from someone else's life are taking over his psyche, though he knows "whence / My trouble springs. Psychic incontinence." ("Santorini," 336). To give oneself over to the poetic space is to surrender to a vampiric muse using one parasitically for her own life, as one slips into an "upsteaming . . . bubble and brawl," or it is to let oneself be invaded by a mental life that is not one's own. With a more rigorous establishing of boundaries, a more strategic sense of selfhood, one may not be open to those linguistic workings, the fusing of senses that occurs with the Empedoclean leap into the volcano of images and half-formed words. (One way of reading Merrill here is in terms of the notion, introduced earlier, of Dennett's multiple drafts. As hordes of psychic homunculi try to impress themselves on the various drafts that will eventually express themselves in speech and action, most lose out in the Darwinian struggle as the self puts forward a relatively coherent draft. A poet wants to enter a less coherent stage of the self where many different drafts are still in play, where some of them may come off as foreign voices speaking through one. But that means a risk to one's sense of oneself as unified.)

Merrill eventually makes the island into a three-level image of the space of writing poetry. The middle level in Merrill's island-picture is perhaps that of the everyday self making its way in a self-interested manner through the terrain of the world. The lower level is represented by a visit to a monastery with an underground classroom where, during Turkish rule of the island, the Greek language was clandestinely taught. It seems that there is now a primitive memorial to that time in "this nocturnal / Limbo of straw children, scarecrow sleeves / Lifting their Book of Life mute with neglect, / While overhead a flickering in fetters / Descended on the office of dead letters" ("Santorini," 338). The children had learned only "the Alphabet / Pruned of meaning to dry glottal kernel." This underground room is, then, what a follower of Derrida or Lacan might call the "graphemic" unconscious, the arrangements of "dead letters" apart from their semantic content, as the children had memorized and combined the Greek letters without quite knowing what they meant. And if the "flickering in fetters" is at one level a torch strapped in place in some manner, it is also the flickering self trying, perhaps through poetry, to shed light on that underground chamber whose language is a repressed one (the Turks forbade the Greek language to be taught). Yet there remains as well the level of the iconic, the nonlinguistic, the phenomenology of self-other relations, in that image of scarecrow children in flickering light; one sees in them the poet's anxieties about the fragility of individuation.

On the same excursion the poet goes to a high point on the island, to the "precinct of Apollo of the Herds / . . . Its highbrow wholly given to the Sun" ("Santorini," 338) / . . . Apollo stands for the ideal patterns and forms (for "highbrow" culture perhaps) that the poetry is seeking to embody and for a "radiance" that will shine through the poems. Service to the god is also dangerous, however, since as the poet takes a picture of the sun at that spot on the island, it burns a hole in his film. The radiance the poet is seeking from that higher world echoes, elsewhere in the poem, the "radiologist's / Black box (335)"; the X ray "Threatening forever to unmake / The living form it sees through in a trice (333)"; and the "eerie radiation" that as the gods decline "eats their armor (334)." As the sun may either make vision possible (recall Plato's myth of the cave) or cause cancer, so there is danger in the poet's reach upward to a higher vision. "As for our meal tonight," says Merrill, "which far-out lab / Prepares and serves it: Gemini? the Crab? (335)" One hopes for a double vision, a twinning of higher and lower. The underground classroom and the hilltop devoted to Apollo are called in the poem the "double site" of our excursion, a double sight as well. (The poem elsewhere mentions "double vision," and the elderly woman who accompanies the poet to the island lost her twin brother many years earlier in a lightning strike.) But the ruling sign may also be Cancer instead of Gemini, a destruction of the self instead of a radiance that, from a higher world, shines through the lines of one's poems and gives them double meaning. The higher world of ideas that radiates through our lives and our literary work is given a Christian form as well as a Greek one in the poem. As the poet ascends to the "precinct of Apollo" he passes a "toy chapel to Saint Michael," and that reference to the archangel, along with the poem's earlier one to the Byzantine "avian-angelic iridescence," gives a hint of the angelic realm that will, in Merrill's long poetic trilogy *The Changing Light at Sandover,* communicate larger truths through the poet.

So poetry involves both a surrendering of the self to higher patterns and a regression to a pre-Oedipal, volcanic loss of self and to a graphemic unconscious. (That model is, of course, opposed to one that a more radical linguistic turn would favor. Such a radical turn would devalue or deconstruct the phenomenology of self-other relations, of stages of self-formation, that is so crucial to Merrill's conception.) Through a ritualized linguistic activity that works through both those forms of surrender the self hopes to be restored, with a reaffirmation of its own articulate self-movement, as in the lines of poetry themselves. As so often in Merrill, there is at the poem's end a sense of calm peacefulness from having come through the ritual loss successfully: "Our 'worst' in part lived through, / part imminent, / We made on sore feet, and by then *were* made, / For a black beach, a tavern in the shade" ("Santorini," 339). (Note with the reference to "sore feet" that Oedipus has returned after the Empedoclean leap into the volcano.) Merrill's linguistic resolutions here are always temporary, however, as the description of the island indicates: "Here was Santorini / Once more, blue deeps, white domes, in imbecile / Symbiosis with the molten genie" (337). We may recall, reading this, how the puzzle in "Lost in Translation" came apart: "All too soon the swift / Dismantling. Lifted by two corners, / The puzzle hung together—and did not. / Irresistibly a populace / Unstitched of its attachments, rattled down" ("Lost in Translation," 282–83). The poet's work, in that surrender of self, is in imbecile symbiosis with the ongoing life of Poetry and Language. They live off the poet's blood, vampirelike, in order to keep themselves developing in ways that may have little to do with the individual good of the poet but that leave him exposed, again and again, to the threat of dissolution, of being consumed by that molten genie. Merrill is sensitive to, on the one hand, that symbiotic (or is it parasitic?) relationship between the needs of these symbol systems to develop and reproduce themselves and, on the other hand, the configurations of the human psyche that are useful for satisfying those needs, given how the turn to language plays a decisive role in them. (The energies that drive the need for poetry might express themselves in other ways: "Here, finally, music that would take Satie / Twenty-five hundred years to reinvent / Put naked immaturity through paces / Of a grave dance—as if catastrophe / Could long be lulled by slim waists and shy faces" ["Santorini," 339]. Satie's "Gymnopédie," a kind of training done in the nude, as it were, recalls Minoan rituals performed by the young, rituals that had been unable to prevent the volcanic destruction of Santorini. For Merrill, of course, the "slim waists and shy faces" belong to the young as those one is erotically attracted to, and that attraction, we are told, is unlikely to be successful against forces threatening to dissolve the self.) The obsessive return to a more anxiety-ridden space, and then the resolution of those anxieties through an accession to the grammatical level, make a productive engine for poetry, necessarily repeated, but not perhaps a successful way of life.

I want to develop this treatment of Merrill by linking it more clearly with the distinction, in chapter 1, between weaker and stronger versions of the turn to a grammatical space. Merrill shows how we might focus that issue more clearly on matters of individual self-formation and how we might make use of certain work in psychology, especially in object-relations theory, along with work in literary criticism having to do with expanded senses of metaphor and metonymy.[3] Let us begin with an extremely simplified and somewhat speculative account of child development but one that will be useful in thinking about the space of literature. In early stages of that development one is concerned especially with dyadic, self-to-other relations, first of all to one's mother though eventually to different individuals as well. There is often a blurring of boundaries, and one works at being a self through activities of identification and separation, of projecting and taking in. The other may serve as a kind of mirror in which one is reflected, so that the baby finds in the mother, for example, a mirroring response that seems determined by its own movements. Through that identification with the other's securely articulated form one may find assurance of wholeness and identity against painful feelings of fragmentation and dissolution.[4] Much work at this stage is toward securing that firmer sense of individuation, of clear and stable boundaries, within a world dominated by shifting images and by patterns of holistic similarity. (Such a world is often visible in the magical thinking of early myth and religion.) Since the child must succeed in setting itself in relation to a stable world of objects a constant testing of what is self and what is other occurs; eventually the child can take pleasure in having before it a world of independent objects that are not a mere reflection of its supposedly omnipotent psyche. A relatively firm style of engagement with objects, of an implicitly metaphysical stance of the self over against otherness, emerges.

A stabilizing of that earlier level is helped by a new level of organization, one that is triadic more than dyadic. The child must learn to take up a position in an already formed language and culture, with its rules de-

fined positionally. The I-you structure now is complicated by a third grammatical person (he, she, it, they), and each of these positions can be taken
up by others in ever-shifting relationships, so that the self is sometimes an
I, a you, a he or she in relation to different others. There is also the triangular relationship of self, mother, and father, again with its culturally defined rules that, as with the grammar and semantics of the language, open
up some modes of relationship and close off others. One will feel a sense
of loss at giving up the earlier dyadic relationship, with its promises of
grandiose power, of a possible merger with the other, or at least of identifications that might secure identity in the wholeness of the other's image.
But at the same time there are clear gains in the more developed stage one
has moved to. One's identity no longer depends on a mirroring by others,
on a narcissistic finding of wholeness in the other, but rather is positional
or grammatical; that is, it is defined by its place within a repeatable structure the occupants of whose various positions are changeable. I no longer
need to merge with my mother or father in order to have an identity like
theirs. Instead I recognize that if I play by the rules of the culture I can one
day take up my father's position, for example, in the triangular pattern in
which I now take up a different position. So repetition of structure and positional mobility within it, rather than self-other identification, becomes
the principle of identity (as in a formal grammar or language), and I can
thereby gain a richer, more stable sense of objectivity. The object I am directed toward is not just involved in a boundary-blurring, oscillating relationship with me; that object is also seen by and desired by an other, by
the third person in this triangular grammar, and from other viewing positions that I might come to stand in myself. So I must arrive at a sense of
the objective as what remains the same both for me and for others who are
different from me and differently situated, who may compete with me as I
try to establish relations with a world of objects. In moving within this
grammatical space of moves and positions one is more self-consciously involved in something like game-theory strategies against others seeking the
same goals.

Even as we engage in far more developed intellectual enterprises there
may still be reminders of the distinction we are exploring here. If the earlier structure may have a certain affinity with metaphysics and aesthetics,
because these disciplines often appeal to that pattern of subject-object
identifications and to an interest in well-formed individuation, the affinity
of the later structure is more with sociology and economics and linguistics,
with their rules for the circulation and transformation of abstract units.[5] I
would claim that the interest of recent literary criticism in sociological,
economic, and linguistic models, and its turning away from the vocabular-

ies of metaphysics and aesthetics, is related to those different affinities. (It is true, of course, that deconstructive criticism works at destabilizing and disrupting the operation of cultural grammars, but that is still to do one's work at this grammatical level rather than at an earlier level emphasizing a phenomenology of self-formation.) I would also suggest, as before, that the two levels being treated here have parallels (in some respects while not in others) in the distinction Steven Pinker makes between modes of information processing best modeled by neural networks and those best modeled by the sequences and moves of formal, logical languages.[6] (While the grammatical may be a stage we arrive at in our understanding of being a self, that kind of maneuvering within a positional grammar has, of course, gone on from birth, as Pinker suggests, in some of our ways of processing information about the world.)

To some degree I am trying to read this structural contrast out of Merrill's poetry. He plays on it throughout "Lost in Translation"—in his contrast between the compositional aspects and the iconic, mimetic aspects of both the jigsaw puzzle and the poem; in the emphasis on boundary-blurring; and in the transition from a "warm romance" to a cooler linguistic ordering that both resolves earlier anxieties and does not. In "Santorini" there is a contrast between the dyadic system of Empedocles, with its oscillating energy and its threat of a dissolution that will not be followed by restoration, and the cooler triadic system of Oedipal resolution, which returns with the poet's "sore feet" at the poem's end. (In speaking of Oedipal resolution here I am not supporting the Freudian notion of sexual desire for the parent of the other gender but referring rather to the resolution that occurs when one sees identity positionally and grammatically: one can take over one's father's or mother's position in a repeatable structure whose occupants are not fixed.)[7] Throughout "Santorini" there are references to mirroring, as in the "looking-glass rim" of the crater and as in a dream "I hobble to the mirror" and see reflected there a vampiric muse, "my vigor coloring her lip." There are several references to twins, to double vision, to an image that "would clone in depth a double." But ultimately it is the lateral, structural ordering of words in the poem that resolves the Empedoclean anxieties about dissolution, that sets things in a more secure position.

We might line up the metaphor-metonymy contrast at least roughly with the two forms of experience investigated here. Metaphor can be seen as having to do with imaginary identifications; these may occur between different fields of experience, through resonance among similar patterns, or between what is self and what is other, through the ways one sees oneself mirrored in the latter. Metaphor for many critics today encompasses what we might ordinarily think of as wider, more properly epistemic and referential relations.[8] Insofar as certain notions of representation and reference seem to imply a mirroring or identifying of structures across the boundary of self and other, of language and reality, some critics speak of those notions as, in this much enlarged sense, metaphorical. For many there is something suspect about metaphor when one understands it in this fashion. Its tendency, so the objection goes, is to find unities, similarities, and mirrorings where there are none, and especially to project what are properly linguistic qualities onto the world or onto the psyche. We might, for example, take the rhythmic advance of literary language, its rightness of arrangement, to be capturing either the status of our own psyches or a metaphysical structure of the world. (One might then see German idealism as favoring metaphor, in this general sense, in its desire to resolve oppositions.)

There is, correspondingly, an expansive notion of metonymy in contemporary criticism. It typically refers to those linkages occurring because of associations along the chain of linguistic signifiers, due to the movement that language generates from some items of language to other ones. Given that sideways motion internal to language, metonymy (used here as a term of art rather than in its precise traditional sense) seems to resolve dyadic self-other relations as in metaphor into triadic ones: the self-to-other direction of reference is shown to be dependent on a lateral movement toward other linguistic sayings or repetitions. (The philosopher Charles S. Peirce held that reality could be explained in terms of three sorts of categories based on monadic, dyadic, and triadic relations.[9] Dyadic relations are those that involve the experience of being "up against" what is other, as in that aspect of experience where the brute resistance of the world as something opposed to him emerges for an experiencer. The most typical triadic relation for Peirce, on the other hand, is that of the sign, for no sign is able to mean what it does simply by being placed over against something. The sign must be interpreted; it must mean something for someone or in relation to further signs. So the move that tries to direct the sign toward a meaning-giving confrontation with what is other keeps getting shunted sideways, as it were, toward interpreters or other signs.) Perhaps the basis for that specialized and broader notion of metonymy lies in its association with contiguity. For instance an athlete says that he wants his ring when he means that he wants to win a championship; while the ring does not resemble the championship, it is in well-known contiguous association with it. That contiguity-based metonymy can then be expanded so that the rhetorical figure comes to include reinforced associations along the chain of signifiers.

The mathematics of two and three is evident as well in Davidson's arguments against empiricism. Empiricist models employed a dyadic confrontation, whereas today the model is more likely to be Davidsonian triangulation, where speaker, world, and interpreter must all come into play for anything like meaning to occur.[10] In Davidson we see coming together the following notions: that meaning can be understood in terms of the arrangement of shapes in a logical language; that there is no direct relationship of reference between units of language and the world; that metaphor is unimportant in a study of meaning; and that we need a triadic relationship to account for our sense of objectivity. These four themes can be seen as exemplifying the turn to the grammatical-positional and away from the mimetic and metaphoric. (McDowell, we have seen, thinks that Davidson's account remains too dependent on lateral, coherence relations and does not allow a rich enough sense of what it is to have the world itself in view, as what ultimately justifies belief. Davidson makes the third position in the triadic field, that of the interpreter, so dominant that he says it is not the speaker who makes his beliefs match up with the world but the interpreter, by interpreting them to be about what, generally, in the world is causing them.[11] But that impoverishes too much, and gives too little status to, the character of the dyadic, self-other engagement with the world. It replaces the confrontational moment too thoroughly and radically with the metonymic, grammatical moment.)

The contrast articulated here has other sorts of cultural manifestations. In Foucault's account of European intellectual history in *The Order of Things* he claims that a medieval and Renaissance worldview based on symbolic resemblances was replaced by the ordering of information through systematic grammars of construction; living things fit on a table based on how their parts are combined instead of having iconic resemblances to features of the heavens.[12] So an iconic, metaphorical thinking was replaced by a positional, grammatical one. Or Catholicism will be seen by some as holding back in a culture of images and magical identities instead of accepting, for example, a modern ethics based on substitutions within a formal grammar of decision-making. Modernism in literature was often attracted to such earlier forms of experiencing.

One of my themes throughout will be the debate between a less radical and a more radical turn to the linguistic, the grammatical, the metonymic, the discursive. To find a model for the virtues of the weaker turn refer to the last lines of Merrill's "Lost in Translation":

> But nothing's lost. Or else: all is translation
> And every bit of us is lost in it . . .

And in that loss a self-effacing tree,
Color of context, imperceptibly
Rustling with its angel, turns the waste
To shade and fiber, milk and memory.

(284)

The palm tree in the desert recalls the quote from Valéry's poem about the palm that Merrill has set at the beginning of his text, in its German translation by Rilke: it has roots that "drink deeply." For Merrill this means that the structures of language in his poem are built on the scaffolding of much earlier forms of experiencing, childhood scenes that were not understood at the time and may still be understood poorly. Proust is of course in the background here. The desert waste around the palm tree that is being transformed slowly into shade, fiber, and milk is also the apparently wasted time of earlier life that is now actualized in a satisfying way in the poetry of adulthood. In terms of the two developmental patterns considered here we can take Merrill's solution to be that the positional-grammatical form of ordering experience (arranging the puzzle pieces or arranging basic linguistic shapes as such into poetry) does not replace earlier forms of engagement with the world but builds on them. The palm tree standing solidly in the desert at the poem's end is understood on the level of image and metaphor (it recalls and reverses the earlier castration scene where the tree in the forest crashes down before being sent to a lumber mill) and at the level of linguistic metonymy (it makes a lateral reference to the Valéry poem and to Rilke's translation of it, and its "rustling" with its angel linguistically recalls Jacob's earlier "wrestling" with an angel). Even the shape of the tree is the linguistic signifier "I" and also iconic, a reaching upward of the self (not only as phallic) toward transcendence while remaining deeply rooted.

The attention to intralinguistic patterns does not give arbitrary rewards but has a definite payoff; the linguistic transformation of "wrestling" to "rustling" is a wonderful way of suggesting the transformation of one kind of passionate energy into a quieter way of coming to have a certain power, which has indeed been one of the themes of the poem. That translation has its effect only if the psychological tensions it resolves remain real and not just mirrors of linguistic tensions. Instead of a forced contention, like the Sheik in the puzzle with his flashing sword hilt, there is a quieter growth of a tree in the desert. The poet's quiet waiting, his seemingly passive taking in of useless material all through his childhood, has produced a readiness so that even a slight happening (in Valéry's poem the alighting of a bird on the tree's branches) can come to have great value.

That slight happening will be for the poet a linguistic one, the coming together of pleasing linguistic shapes, but it generates powerful meanings
precisely because it is not simply linguistic but, like the tree's rustling,
takes advantage of years of experience, much of it nonlinguistic, in which
the roots of the meaning-making process were established. In being "self-
effacing," sinking invisibly into the background, becoming the "color of
context," the poet is, like the palm tree, turning "the waste / To shade and
fiber, milk and memory." There is a sense, so Merrill says in the poem, in
which nothing is lost in the translation from one space to another, and
there is a sense in which we ourselves are lost in it.

What matters for Merrill is a translational space in which is enacted the
passage of experience into representational form, with what this process
both grants us and takes away. Consider a scene in Venice (from "The
Book of Ephraim") as tourists head into a museum to sit out a storm in
front of Georgione's *Tempesta*:

> Air and water blown glass-hard . . .
> Glaze soaking inward as it came to mind
> How anybody's monster breathing flames
> Vitrified in metamorphosis
>
> To monstrance clouded then like a blown fuse
> If not a reliquary for St. James'
> Vision of life: how Venice, her least stone
> Pure menace at the start, at length became
>
> A window fiery-mild, whose walked-through frame
> Everything else, at sunset, hinged upon—[13]

There is a certain semantic register suggested by references to "glass-
hard," "glaze," "vitrified," "monstrance," "fuse," "window," "frame,"
and "hinged." Earlier in this section of the poem there is a reference to
looking at Giorgione's painting behind its "shatterproof glass," (120) and
the poet mentions being glad he lost his camera so that he will not any-
more "overlook a subject for its image." (120) So we are dealing with
frames of glass that might be more or less cloudy or transparent, that
might capture or reflect images more or less well. (It is important that the
similarities that engender this field are built on iconic rather than linguistic patterns.) There is also the semantic field contrasting "monster breathing flames" with the "window fiery-mild" and the suggestion (Venice as a
city of glassblowers) that one has vitrified into the other (though the win-

dow retains the "fiery" character out of which it was produced). That theme continues earlier themes in this section of the poem: people are coming into the museum from a storm; as they walk over a bridge two by two they suggest to the poet Noah and the flood (they are "entering the dark / Ark of the moment" [119]); the name of the painting is *Storm,* and later the storm outside is described. Representation is seen as turning powerful unconscious material (Venice's "least stone pure menace at the start") into something cooler and more transparent. The storm is described as "the old man of the Sea / . . . Bellying shirt, sheer windbag wrung to high / Relief" (120–21) (where "relief" has the double art-historical and psychological meanings), and just a few pages later in the poem we learn that according to one art-history account the Giorgione painting being considered paints over an earlier scene in which Saint Theodore rescues his mother from a dragon, the same Saint Theodore, who "Grown up . . . will / Destroy a temple to the Magna Mater" (127). (In a few lines the poet's mother will be transformed, because of her cigarette smoking, into that dragon.) That family image of "Man, woman, child" is said by the poet to be the scene of *Tempesta,* "earthly life in all its mystery" (120).

Yet in transforming all that tempestuous material into a cooler representational space, one that gradually allows transparency, we also lose something; a photograph is said to be a "Receipt (gloom coupleted with artifice) / For holding still, for being held still" ("Book of Ephraim," 120). That the transformation has a ritual nature is suggested by the terms "monstrance," and "reliquary," each of these having a small glass window, the former for viewing the host. If Venice becomes a "walked-through frame" that everything else hinges on, are we entering such a representational space with its various gains and losses? And what of the monstrance, which typically is a small circular compartment with a window one can open to get at the host, surrounded by rays of gold metal? Is that a sexual image representing the "menace" of a feminized Venice— "*her* least stone"? How does that represent "St. James' [Merrill's] vision of life"? The power of the poem depends on its finding patterns that cut across several registers of the psyche, including a prelinguistic realm of images and mirrorings, instead of turning more radically to a linguistic, grammatical ordering. As the images of Venice suggest, the poem is about nonlinguistic psychological states and anxiety-ridden visual images *becoming* language. A more thorough linguistic turn would make that space of poetic power impossible.

Perhaps some might claim that Merrill in his poetry remains too occupied with pre-Oedipal concerns. One might even give a narrative in the style of Rorty in which cultural vocabularies and the tasks they encourage should be replaced as they seem to lose their energy and interest. It might be said that we have now been through a long period, from the ancient Greeks onward, in which the large undertakings of high culture had to do with the kind of anxieties that arise in a pre-Oedipal stage. The Greeks were concerned with issues of individuation, of form and dissolution, while modern thinkers were concerned with a phenomenology of self-other differentiation, as in empiricism. Now we are past those vocabularies and interests, the Rortyan might say, as we can note in our giving up both the interests of modern empiricism and the interests the Greeks had in an aesthetics of the well-formed. Now we will see ourselves instead as postmodern selves maneuvering on a hang glider, as it were, on the currents of multiple vocabularies and codes. Then Merrill's poetic interests will seem regressive.

But that analysis is wrong. It just is not true that we leave our earlier tasks and interests behind as we move into a postmodern world of cultural grammars and signs. We remain selves for whom the concerns linked to pre-Oedipal anxieties are real: loss and grief; fears of death and dissolution; the upwelling of childhood anxieties about the fragility of the self; the maintaining of a style of selfhood over against external forces. There remain for us those times, as in an earlier staging of the self, when the entire feel of the world seems to be at stake, when the style of our engagement with things seems to be in jeopardy, when the space in which things appear seems to have an overall bleakness or emptiness. One may perhaps imagine strange science-fiction futures in which these are no longer our concerns, and sometimes literary theorists seem to read literature as if concerns about death and the overall meaning of an individual life should no longer be asked about. But the beings in such a future will certainly not be living lives that we can recognize as our own.

THE RADICAL LINGUISTIC TURN IN
DE MAN AND PERLOFF

My treatment of Paul de Man's account of literary language will look especially at his *Allegories of Reading*.[1] In making a radical linguistic turn he ultimately gives a picture of language as an inhuman, impersonal machinery that generates formal patterns, whether phonetic, grammatical, or rhetorical in character. These then project themselves to produce referential and psychological effects that are both illusory and unavoidable. The literary space of my own model will surely appear, from this point of view, a result of error; one takes merely linguistic effects as if they were expressions of nonlinguistic or prelinguistic worlds that come before, and are themselves the conditions for, the meaningfulness of language. I choose de Man because he is an almost perfect case of the view I am opposing; for him not only the world but also the level of phenomenology and psychology collapse back into the workings of language, which itself assumes a theological position. One might suppose that this is now a historical matter as de Man represents an earlier generation of literary theorists. But in fact the very terrain in which literary theory still works, including that of cultural studies, was carved out and made possible by work of which de Man's is representative. One find ideas that spread widely in the field taking clear (and sometimes extreme) shape in his work, so that it is useful to look at those ideas as he developed them.

It is typical of de Man's readings that what may seem a rich psychological phenomenon that language is trying to grasp is treated as the production of a linguistic mechanism. Thus he considers the passage in the *Confessions* in which Rousseau speaks of betraying the servant girl Marian, by accusing her of stealing a ribbon that he is accused of stealing.[2] Because he had been thinking about Marian her name comes to mind without any forethought on his part. De Man insists that this should be seen as a case of the automatic, nonsemantic functioning of the linguistic machinery, which on its own is generating arbitrary sequences of sounds and shapes and then positing a world as what will seem to have produced these shapes. (Hume, a good analogy here for de Man, says that the functioning of the associative mechanisms of the mind, in their mechanical impetus from one impression to another, generates a psychological feeling of forceful connectedness that is then projected on the world as a causal impulse between things. That projected effect is then considered the cause of the mental movement. For de Man it is linguistic rather than psychological features that are thus projected.) De Man says that we have here, in Rousseau's case, a "form detached from meaning and capable of taking on any structure whatever, yet entirely ruthless in its inability to modify its structural design for nonstructural reasons" (*Allegories of Reading*, 294). Rousseau's excuse, says de Man, is produced by an almost mechanical and arbitrary generation of signifiers that are in themselves meaningless, and then the psychological state of guilt is projected as what that language pattern is supposedly responding to.

> Far from seeing language as an instrument in the service of a psychic energy, the possibility now arises that the entire construction of drives, substitutions, repressions, and representations is the aberrant, metaphorical correlative of the absolute randomness of language, prior to any figuration or meaning. It is no longer certain that language, as excuse, exists because of a prior guilt but just as possible that since language, as a machine, performs anyway, we have to produce guilt (and all its train of psychic consequences) in order to make the excuse meaningful. Excuses generate the very guilt they exonerate. (299)

This analysis appears simply wrong. It is true that our capacity for having the rich psychological states we have depends on language, but those psychological states are grounded in states of the organism that are not linguistic, that are continuous with states that might be experienced more simply, say, by chimpanzees or by early humans. Guilt and shame and desire are aspects of a complex psychological realm that language helps us to articulate and to make more sophisticated. The term "Marian" on Rousseau's lips was surely "in the service of a psychic energy," though de Man denies this, and the guilt and shame he feels are not just a function of language having worked mechanically, even nonsemantically, to produce an excuse that then needed to manufacture a psychic counterpart. Such emotions run deeper in the psyche, and in our biology, than that. But once a radical linguistic turn assigns a theological role to language, as de Man does, these are the kinds of consequences one is left with.

De Man makes a similar move in treating Rilke's poetry.[3] He is against readings that suppose Rilke's own psychological states to stand causally behind his frequent consideration of such negative experiences as "the insatiability of desire, the powerlessness of love, death of the unfulfilled or the innocent, the fragility of the earth, the alienation of consciousness" (*Allegories,* 50). In fact, says de Man, these are not reflections of Rilke's own lived psychological experience; rather they are generated by linguistic, rhetorical, textual mechanisms, and the psychological form of presentation is a secondary effect. Chiasmus is one of the chief figures of speech used by Rilke. As a formal pattern (and de Man's notion here goes much beyond the traditional meaning of the figure, in which it refers to a reversal of grammatical order), this is a movement of exchange and reversal, of an X-like crossing of categories. So chiasmus, in de Man's generous reading of the figure, comes down to a structure of oscillation or rotation of qualities between the different poles of an opposition. One might oppose language to eros, for example, and then have certain erotic categories cross over and describe linguistic facts and vice versa. That formal pattern is, for Rilke, present in linguistic functioning as a mechanical operation, in the manner in which a Chomskyan grammar can blindly generate a different kind of structure; the resulting pattern is at any time ready to impose itself on available content.

But that rotational movement of exchange and reversal can go to work only if there is a lack, says de Man: "Chiasmus . . . can only come into being as the result of a void, or a lack that allows for the rotating motion of the polarities" (*Allegories,* 49). So Rilke finds himself, in one poem, describing the declining motion of a ball. The declining motion, repeated in the line of poetry, is not expressing a psychological feeling of loss, says de Man, but is demanded as a reflection of the figural motion of chiasmus, which needs both the rising and falling motions of the ball to express its rotations and reversals. Perhaps the most important example of this figure, for de Man, occurs when the rotating polarities are the inside and outside peculiar to the structure of subjectivity. Here chiasmus sets in motion the exchange that takes internal features to be external or referential ones, and external features to cross the line and become inner experiences. To indicate that sort of motion Rilke must choose psychological experiences, and he must choose negative ones because, as with the declining ball, it is only a lack or void that can set the figural energies into motion.

So it turns out that all those negative experiences mentioned as central to Rilke's poetry are not there because of their psychological relevance to Rilke's life, "but because their structure allows for the unfolding of his patterns of figuration" (50). He speaks about sadness not because he was sad but because his rhetorical figure needed a downward motion to express its structure, and sad emotions are the psychological equivalent of the downward motion of the ball. In turn that lack or void demands, by chiasmus, a positive assertion as its polar counterpart, and so Rilke's poems tend to take on as well a messianic fervor and exaltation.

This argument appears odd. Take, for example, the idea that the structure of chiasmus requires a lack in order for the exchange and reversal between the polar opposites to occur. The required lack would be such only in the vaguest, most banal sense: that some further description was still possible. Thus a reversed application of erotic and linguistic terms requires that human sexuality has not been so fully described that some new description, from a different semantic realm, cannot helpfully be added. But that is a lack in the most trivial sense possible. To say, on this basis, that the figural structure requires negative psychological experiences of pain and loss is a leap without justification; any rotating of qualities from one side of an opposition to another would have done as well. It may be that the falling movement of the poetic line is in some sense for the poet prior to any content and that he looks around to find a motion in the world, that of the ball, that can match what is already a linguistic motion. But when one asks about the appeal to the poet of that falling poetic line, it is not at all persuasive that what generates the line is a reversal-rotational movement of chiasmus that, independently of any meaning or psychological state, waits around to impose its structure mechanically. It seems instead that if there is a music to literary language that is prior to having that music filled in with content, then it is psychological mood and need that are imposing themselves on the line. The movement of Hemingway's sentences, for example, can seem an occasionally desperate effort to retain the self-maintaining rhythm of the self in the face of the gravitational pull of more regressive states, so that the falling motion of certain lines would have a psychological rather than fundamentally linguistic or figural origin. The interest would be in the movements of language as playing a compensating role in a psychological space that is already complex.

I have mentioned the detail of these arguments in order to show features that keep repeating themselves throughout de Man's work, which tends to make more explicit, than do the works of other theorists, the model of language as having a divinelike capacity to be self-generating and to posit reflections of itself. But unlike the self-determining activity of the medieval God, the grammatical and figural machineries of language for de Man keep also undermining themselves, both producing certain linguistic effects and then undercutting them by showing them to be *merely* linguistic. Language for him is like the arithmetic system for Godel: since it is capable of self-referential statements it must produce paradoxes and undecidability, as it demands one sort of reading and then shows how that sort of reading is impossible.[4] De Man makes this point by considerably enlarging our notions of metaphor and metonymy. What happens, over and again, is that the metaphorical energies take linguistic effects and project them across the inner-outer boundary, so that they seem to belong referentially to the world, to be features of the world that are actually imposing themselves on language. Then the metonymic activity of language deconstructs these apparent language-to-world linkages and identities, showing them to be constructed out of, or posited by, operations that are merely linguistic. So language is in a continual process of positing and deposing, projecting its movements referentially and then showing that referential status to be an illusion.

In a case taken from Proust, de Man sees what he takes to be the interaction of metaphor and metonymy.[5] He is commenting on the passage in *Swann's Way* in which the boy Marcel is reading in his room at Combray. The narrator speaks of the sounds outside that remind him of summer. He compares the "chamber music" of the insects, which seems linked to the summer days in a necessary manner and contains "some of their essence," with a human tune that is connected with the summer only by the chance that one happened to hear it then, when it might have been heard at any time of the year. De Man believes that any text is implicitly self-reflective; language or rhetoric is at some level commenting on its own activity. Here, says de Man, the text is saying that metaphor, represented by the music of the insects, is superior to metonymy, represented by the human tune heard perchance. Metaphor, says de Man, is concerned with identifications that have a sense of rightness and necessity to them, that join together different semantic fields in what seems a satisfying wholeness, a proper fitting together. Metonymy, in contrast, has to do with accidental, contingent connections along a chain of signifiers, with words that are linked more by the associational habit of past usage than by any necessity or rightness of connection, or by any natural fitting together into a whole. So in valuing the chamber music of the flies over the human tune heard perchance, the text is supposedly valuing metaphor over metonymy.

But how does the text actually achieve that goal? De Man sees the general activity of metaphor as showing itself especially in linkages of inner and outer, as when mind and nature are seen to fit one another. The

Proustian passage in question here presents that inside space as the room in which Marcel is reading and the outside world of nature as seemingly more powerful and active. But the passage then takes the passive activity of reading and describes it in terms of the power and activity belonging to the external world (thus accomplishing the metaphorical leap joining inside and outside): "The dark coolness of my room . . . matched my repose which (thanks to the adventures narrated in my book, which stirred my tranquillity) supported, like the quiet of a hand held momentarily in the middle of a running brook, the shock and animation of a flood of activity." But that metaphorical success is accomplished, says de Man, by the use of a phrase, "flood of activity" or "torrent d'activité," which is in French a kind of cliché, a phrase whose words are held together by habitual usage (*Allegories,* 66). So the phrase is an instance of metonymy at work. Therefore the text both states the superiority of metaphor and then undermines that statement by having its metaphorical movement necessarily rely on metonymic connections within the language. "A rhetorical reading of the passage reveals that the figural praxis and the metafigural theory do not converge and that the assertion of the mastery of metaphor over metonymy owes its persuasive power to the use of metonymic structures" (15). The reading of the Proust passage "shows that precisely when the highest claims are being made for the unifying power of metaphor, these very images rely in fact on the deceptive use of semi-automatic grammatical patterns" (16). Thus we can draw the conclusion that a literary text "simultaneously asserts and denies the authority of its own rhetorical mode" (17). It posits identities and a referential world that mirrors the linguistic effects, but the very operating of the linguistic machinery, necessarily metonymic and mechanical, keeps undercutting the status of all that has been posited.

It seems evident that the rules of the game that de Man is playing here are extraordinarily indulgent. He wants to prove that in any text he can find the self-reflexive structures of rhetorical tropes reproducing themselves and generating worldly counterparts. But he defines metaphor so as to be able to find it everywhere. Anywhere you have identity, necessity, totality, or any fitting of mind or language to the world, any finding of similitude across an inner-outer boundary, there will be an example of metaphor. So it will be extremely difficult to find any text that does not appear to be assigning value to metaphorical activity. But it is also the case that wherever one finds what was referred to earlier as the lateral or sideways linkages of language, the deflection of word-to-world connections onto word-to-word connections, there will be an example of metonymy. But that lateral deflection, even in the simplest attempt at reference, is ubiquitous. Then metonymy is everywhere, in any usage of language. There is no way one can say anything without relying on the mechanical operation of grammatical and other linguistic patterns. So again, it will be extremely difficult to find any text where there is not both the valuing of metaphorical linkages and the mechanical operation of metonymic chains. The rules of the game are so generous that it is impossible for de Man to lose. But that very generosity means as well that his conclusions are only weakly significant; they were bound to come out true just by the setting up of the investigation. De Man supposes that his argument shows a radical and paradoxical undecidability about language; but it is, instead, inflating facts of the most ordinary and unsurprising sort.

A similar indulgence is shown as de Man tries to make rhetorical theory take the privileged place of epistemology and metaphysics. Reading from Rousseau, he claims that all conceptualization is metaphorical. "And conceptualization, conceived as an exchange or substitution of properties on the basis of resemblance, corresponds exactly to the classical definition of metaphor as it appears in theories of rhetoric from Aristotle to Roman Jakobson" (*Allegories,* 146). It is not only that we count things as the same in order to universalize; there is also typically an exchange of inner and outer features, which is always for de Man the sign of metaphor. Thus, according to Rousseau, primitive man first called other men by the name "giant" because he projected his inner fear and made the other seem larger than he was. Of course if early conceptualization had a metaphorical quality to it, it is still easily possible that subsequent refinements, scientific testing, the habitual use of a rigorous, replicable vocabulary, and so forth, can produce concepts whose principles of application are now clear, whatever may have been the origins of the term, metaphorical or not. But de Man cannot look at that possibility because he wants to show that "conceptual language, the foundation of civil society, is also, it appears, a lie superimposed upon an error" (155). He thinks he has discovered in the rhetorical, deconstructing machineries of language a radical undermining of every single human epistemic and political undertaking. But our language is a lie superimposed on an error only if we look to the supposed origins of usage, rather than to our ways of clarifying language, and also continue to use *metaphor* extremely indulgently, as applying almost anywhere we wish it to, wherever we find any categorizing or any epistemic directedness. Early conceptualization was necessarily figural, he says, because one takes qualities associated with a familiar set of objects and supposes them to apply to a new but similar object. But that is simply to redescribe an obvious and noncontroversial truth in a manner that wildly inflates the role of rhetorical figuration. It will hardly follow that our entire conceptual system is based on an error, or that all attempts at truth and reason dissolve into a rhetorical play. The only conclusion we must accept from his argument is that sometimes we need to apply our concepts to situations and objects we have not encountered before. What could be surprising about that? (What is surprising, against de Man, is how successful we are over time at doing this.)

De Man is intent on showing that what is really at stake in texts does not have to do with what the world is like, or with the complexity of human psychological states, but rather with the operation of the self-reflexive machinery of language. Since conceptuality is already involved in our experience of individuals (since picking out that individual requires some sense of what *sort* of individual is being picked out) and since concepts gather together individuals, then it follows that "to the extent that all language is conceptual, it always already speaks about language and not about things" (*Allegories,* 152). That is a bad argument, as can be seen by returning to McDowell's work as described in chapter 3. The fact that conceptuality is operative even in one's having of intuitions, says McDowell, does not mean that it is working on something inward, something itself linguistic or conceptual. Rather it is a necessary part of one's general openness to things, his having them in view. Even if one's linguistic machinery is already at work in his perception of individuals, it does not follow that he is really perceiving *language* rather than those individuals, as de Man claims. (That is another error deriving from the model of the radical linguistic turn, where the way language is about the world dissolves into the sideways linkages of language.)

De Man then continues: "If all language is about language, then the paradigmatic linguistic model is that of an entity that confronts itself. It follows that the exemplary situation described in the *Essay* (man confronting man) is the correct linguistic paradigm" (*Allegories,* 153). The psychological and political interactions of humans are thus seen as the (illusory) granting of referential status to what are primarily linguistic effects, resulting from the play of language with itself, its always ending up talking about itself; so a reflecting of that linguistic activity in the real world will appear as the reflexive situation of man facing man. But it is nonsense to suppose that human interactions and confrontations are an illusory effect of language's self-reflexive activity, of a structural necessity that it is always talking about itself. First of all, language is not always talking about itself; and secondly, the situation of man facing man is not a mirroring effect of what is primarily a linguistic paradigm but goes deep in our biology.

De Man also insists that "the political destiny of man is structured like and derived from a linguistic model that exists independently of nature and independently of the subject," so that society and government are about a tension between man and his language and are not about ethical relationships among human beings (*Allegories,* 156). "In this sense, ethics has nothing to do with the will (thwarted or free) of a subject, nor a fortiori, with a relationship between subjects. The ethical category is imperative . . . to the extent that it is linguistic and not subjective" (206). But that is an impoverished and inaccurate view of ethics. We are not, as ethical, misapplying a linguistic model to the human sphere, by getting caught up in language's self-reflexive activity, its concern only with language-to-language relationships, and then setting human-to-human relationships in place as an invalid reflection of the linguistic ones. Rather we are coming to recognize the intrinsic worth of others as self-determining selves, as subjects. If the selfhood of the other does not emerge as in itself worthy of our consideration, then we are not being ethical. (Put simply: we could not be good "grammatical" Kantians if we did not have earlier emotional identifications and investments with regard to others; that is what the psychopath is lacking, not some structure of language or reason.) De Man's strong need to reduce subjectivity and psychology to the mechanical functioning of language makes him misread, in dangerous ways, the nature and depth of ethical relationships.

Even human needs turn out, for de Man, to be the product of language. He is not making the obvious point here that cultural vocabularies and advertising can make us feel needs we did not have before. His point is far more radical. "The reintroduction of the intentional language of needs into the allegory is not itself intentional but the result of a linguistic structure. The entire assumption of a nonverbal realm governed by needs may well be a speculative hypothesis that exists only, to put it in all too intentional terms, for the sake of language" (*Allegories,* 210). Thus millions of years of biology get dismissed in a sentence. There is another, equally odd argument: Rousseau has claimed that the language of love is rhetorical and love is often a passion whose object may be nonexistent or arbitrary. But de Man translates those claims into a very different one: that the passions themselves are projections of rhetorical, linguistic effects, a referential illusion posited by language, as if the emotional selves we are, including our passionate attractions, did not emerge from a long animal history in which even much of our own development was prelinguistic (198–200).

Some of de Man's overplaying of the productive power of language, and undervaluing of the realm of subjectivity and self-consciousness and psychology (as well as that of biochemistry), can be considered just good, clean nonsense. But his moves are more dangerous when he talks of ethics and politics. He conceives of the difficulties of politics as linguistic, not in the ordinary sense that communication is difficult and misunderstanding prevalent, but in the sense that the political structure itself reflects the deconstructive, self-undermining, incompatibility-producing machinery of language. "The circular, self-destructive pattern of all civil institutions mirrors the self-destructive epistemology of conceptual language when it demonstrates its inability to keep literal reference and figural connotation apart" (*Allegories*, 158). He is operating here as before: if an *extreme* latitude to the application of the notion of metaphor is allowed, then our understanding of our relation to the political sphere may involve metaphorical operations on our part, as when we take attitudes familiar in ourselves and suppose they exist in others like us. It turns out for him that there is something fundamentally undecidable about our basic engagement with political institutions because we do not know whether to read that engagement literally or metaphorically. But all he can mean by this is that if, for instance, I see you as relating to the government as a citizen in the same way that I do, then I am being "metaphorical", since I am finding similarity across differences. But that sort of claim will not produce even the slightest undermining effect on our relation to the government; it merely gives, again, an extremely expansionist application of rhetorical terms to a commonplace fact. The difficulties of politics are for de Man, then, not political and psychological ones that could be worked out through negotiation. Rather the blindly productive, arbitrary, rhetorical machinery of language, apart from anything we understand, produces political institutions as a mirror of its own profoundly self-undermining, delegitimating rhetorical powers, which in themselves have nothing to do with human needs and hopes. If we know this, we have little motivation to commit ourselves to political institutions.

Even more, de Man says that politics mirrors the "incompatibility" of constative and performative meaning. Language as an activity producing effects may always be doing something more than expressing the meaning it seems to express. De Man takes this obvious truth and makes it seem to threaten the deepest structures of politics (again, not in a way that politics and negotiation might alleviate, but as expressing a structurally necessary movement of self-undermining that is always at the base of human institutions). What happens here is that de Man takes the ordinary tensions of human psychological and political negotiation, as expressed in the complexity of language, and raises them up as instances of fundamental paradox and undecidability. It is true that the American Declaration of Independence is both constative and performative; it states certain things as true as a way of making them true. But that does not mean that we are caught up blindly in a linguistic machinery that makes our very political existence paradoxical. Usage will always make language say more and less than what the syntactic and semantic rules of the language might determine; and the application of the law will help decide what actually has been stated in the original stating of the law. But these facts do not make either language or politics undecidable and contradictory and impossible, as de Man claims. They are just complex human phenomena; they show why we have to work at communication, clarity, and so forth. Politics will involve, says de Man, projects whose ultimate legitimacy may depend on the transformation of the populace into a certain kind of individuals, namely, those who flourish under the sort of regime thus instituted. Liberal democracies, for example, help form people into selves who will find liberal democracies legitimate. But again, that is a feature that belongs to the difficulty of politics. It is not that politics, as a projection of linguistic and figural structures, must share their specifically linguistic and self-deconstructing character.

Over and over de Man presses his analyses until he can draw some conclusion about undecidability, incompatibility, paradox, the "impossibility" of reading, the self-contradictoriness of textuality. He can make ordinary reading seem like one of the most daring things a person can do on the planet. We can develop further here a contrast I drew between de Man and Wittgenstein in Chapter 3. One could easily see Wittgenstein's rule-following arguments as leading to the conclusion that meaning is impossible. The philosophers G. P. Baker and P. M. S. Hacker present Saul Kripke's account of Wittgenstein as claiming that such impossibility is indeed where the arguments, philosophically speaking, end up. "Initial scepticism, according to Kripke, leads us to doubt whether we are applying words in accord with how we have in the past meant them. This led, by a quick route, to conceptual nihilism which denies that there is any such thing as meaning, and faces us with a paradox: language is impossible."[6] We are forced then, says Kripke, to adopt a Humean solution to the paradox: we just go on doing what our intellectual arguments have shown we have no ground for doing.

But that is not Wittgenstein's position. He argues instead that there is something wrong precisely with those who think that conclusions about skepticism and impossibility follow from these investigations. We are shown that where we go astray, rather, is in our expectation that what holds our practices together is some highly intellectualized operation, one that determines a relatively deep metaphysical fact against which the ordinary practice can be measured. There are no such facts, says Wittgenstein, but we do not need them; the error was in the philosophical expectation rather than in some worrisome ungroundedness of our practices. Wittgenstein's solution is quietist: to disarm the habits of thought that create the appearance of difficulty. De Man's solution is anti-Wittgensteinian: to inflate as much as possible whatever gives the slightest hint that we are left as speakers in a situation of rhetorical difficulty. For him the fact that language is material and mechanical and that its pattern-forming processes work apart from any conscious intentionality means that there is almost no predictable connection between what one means to say and what one says, between what one intends and what one does, between the external world and how one takes it to be. But that is to exaggerate wildly the degree of instability that enters with the various sorts of referential and semantic indeterminacy we have discovered language to possess.

In conclusion, de Man's arguments in favor of the linguistic-postmodern model of literary space, characterized by a radical turn to the linguistic or grammatical, are of unusually poor quality, even though he is often referred to in literary theory as an especially rigorous thinker. It is true that the formal or phonological or figural patterns of language often break free of their subservience to meaning, or to comprehension of the world, and operate on their own as somewhat mechanically productive. But that play will be satisfying and effective only within a larger context in which the world and the mental life of the self are much richer than de Man takes them to be, and as much the shapers of language as its mere projections.

A second version of the linguistic-postmodern model of literary space is Marjorie Perloff's.[7] Her narrative of twentieth-century literature begins with Rimbaud and Gertrude Stein and, so she claims, shows the possible direction of a radical modernism, one that was marginalized by the less radical modernism of Eliot, Yeats, and Wallace Stevens. Rimbaud and Stein, by Perloff's telling, offer projects that are closer to the linguistic or grammatical turn that would eventually dominate philosophy and literature, in that they are more intent on examining the potential of the machinery of language. They would free that potential from language's subordination to the need to capture the layout of the referential world, to present the texture of perceptual experience, or to portray the character of human psychological states. Rimbaud shows an intoxication with linguistic sounds in their own right; unlike in Eliot's *Waste Land,* with its clear location in London, says Perloff, Rimbaud's spaces are impossible imagined ones created by the linguistic connections that his poetry generates, with its high level of semantic indeterminacy.[8]

That direction for poetry is intensified in Gertrude Stein; she investigates English as if it were a second language whose purely linguistic features, its syntax and sounds, could be examined to a considerable degree independently of the meaning they are conveying.[9] (I am repeating Perloff's story rather than endorsing every aspect of it. Sometimes Stein presents herself not as a poet of referentially indeterminate language but as describing carefully the manner of appearing of objects, without using their names, or as working on a level of imagery with a vague sexual content.) In Stein, says Perloff, the normal linguistic rules for ordering words and, even more, the strong cultural habits of using language are resisted so that a reader is forced to look at language in a new way, to be more aware of it as such and to see more liberating possibilities of how bits of it might be put together. What meaning emerges seems to be conferred less by what the poem is supposedly about than by the repetitions and transformation of words as one follows the linguistic line across and down the page, just as meaning in painting may be conferred less by what is represented than by the repetition of bits of color and their vibrations with related colors. If Eliot takes a perceptual image or scene and builds up a symbolic meaning around it, Stein makes a more radical linguistic turn and presents objects as items taken up into a free-floating linguistic web.

What Perloff favors is a kind of poetry in which the projecting of referential spaces from the patterns of words becomes a much more open process. Stein's "Susie Asado" can be looked at as a cubist distribution of semantic items across different planes, and when a reader tries to link these to ask what the poem is about, she finds that several of them might work together to make the poem about a Spanish dancer and the rhythms of her dance, while different ways of bringing words together might make the poem about a Japanese woman serving tea on a tray.[10] A third reading might link up some of the available words in a way that takes them to hint at sexual activity. None of these is the right way to project a referential world from the words; the reader is free to find different word patterns that project still other worlds. Just as competing perspectives may appear simultaneously in a cubist work, so competing and even incompatible referential perspectives may be read out of a Stein poem. We have to acknowledge, much more honestly, that we do indeed project referential worlds from language with a certain freedom and arbitrariness, rather than just reporting on what is out there.

Perloff's story of twentieth-century poetry is continued by Charles Bernstein with his "Language School" of poetry.[11] For Bernstein poetry is political in its very nature, for he sees cultural authorities as often doing their work through a control of language: specifying a standard diction, a grammar of combination, that one must employ in order to be taken seriously, while marginalizing the discourse of those not in power, such as women and blacks and Hispanics. So a principal work of poetry is to undermine the power of that standard diction by bringing words together in unexpected ways so that one's typical ways of reading them do not work, and by favoring the language of marginalized groups whose usage subverts our notions of how language ought to be put together.[12] For Bernstein these strategies force the poet to focus on language as such, as a composition of sounds and shapes, in the way that Stein did.

General objections that I have put forward in criticizing, or in suggesting the limits of, a radical turn to a linguistic, grammatical, and postmodern space could be repeated here as applicable to Perloff's narrative. Instead of repeating those objections it may be more interesting to confront her narrative of twentieth-century literature. Two of the key players in her account are John Ashbery and Samuel Beckett. She believes they are excellent examples of the turn that Rimbaud and Stein initiated and that she herself favors. I believe, in contrast, that to read Ashbery and Beckett is actually to find support not for Perloff's account but for the conception of literary space articulated in chapter 1. Those two writers are the focus of the debate with her in chapter 6.

JOHN ASHBERY AND
SAMUEL BECKETT

For Marjorie Perloff the writers John Ashbery and Samuel Beckett represent what I have called the stronger turn to the linguistic and the grammatical. One finds in their work, she says, the predominance of a more purely linguistic space whose compositional, pattern-generating powers, apart from any links to truth or reference or to the subjective life of experiencing selves, begin to produce connections and possibilities on their own. Perloff's favored writers, she says, take language in a manner that is "compositional rather than referential," where the focus "shifts from signification to the play of signifiers."[1] Since Ashbery and Beckett are powerful writers, if Perloff's account of them is correct then perhaps my overall defense of a weaker linguistic turn, in both philosophy and literature, is problematic. But neither writer offers a good case for her narrative; neither one, therefore, will be useful in demoting the psycho-metaphysical model of literary space I am defending, and in replacing it with a more radically linguistic one.

One feature of the poetry she praises is its resistance to our habit of seeing the linguistic items of a poem as tending toward a (possibly never arrived at) coherence and unity. She quotes James McFarlane as arguing that modernism generally, for all its focus on a threatening disintegration and dissolution, was actually in the service of more centripetal energies, so that objects and topics normally kept separate would collapse in on one another, would overlap and blur.[2] Perloff's more radical modernism, in contrast, would resist just those centripetal energies. In Ashbery, on her reading, readers are defeated when they look for any larger symbolic network because the linguistic fragments are not meant to cohere in that fashion; they are more arbitrarily juxtaposed and are not a teasing out of unifying energies already articulating themselves in the poem. These fragments cannot quite be attached to definite referents in the world; nor can they be attached to each other through the mediation of such a common referential world or through the ties of a more abstract symbolic world.

But is Perloff correct in her reading? It is useful, first of all, to describe a certain kind of poetry that might be called "postmodern." Such poetry would see the items of language as ready to follow, as if along the tracks of a roller coaster, the linguistic grooves by which our utterances typically arrive at meaning, and it would use the disseminating energies of language to frustrate those tendencies, would make the arrival less likely or forever delayed. Its energies would be more lateral and metonymic, with meaning deferred along a chain of words that present themselves as admittedly cultural fragments already part of the discursive field of signs, so that they have the status almost of clichés or near-quotations. Novelty would be generated not by the metaphorical compression of different semantic fields but by an unexpected, unnatural juxtaposition of already articulate cultural units. Instead of feeling that the poet is losing himself in a pre-Oedipal regression we would have a stronger sense of him as expressing attitudes, often ironic or coolly noncommittal, toward his use of words. As with conceptual art, poetry would be there to trigger reflection about concepts of meaning-making. We would be forced to acknowledge, at a certain level of abstraction, the usually hidden machineries by which we invest ourselves in objects and in what we say about them, and we would take a skeptical attitude toward those very machineries. The poet's work would admit that his consciousness is not a generator of meaning but a place where the random discursive elements of culture, including its detritus, happen to be gathering.

There is surely something right in taking this as a description of Ashbery's work. We easily find there a sense that one's poetic phrases are self-consciously bits of cultural discourse, that the move of using certain "beautiful" poetic words has already been played out: "About what to put in your poem-painting: / Flowers are always nice, particularly delphinium. / Names of boys you once knew and their sleds, / Sky rockets are good."[3] There is the disenchanted attitude toward experiences that seem to arrive secondhand: "The light sinks today with an enthusiasm / I have known elsewhere, and known why / It seemed meaningful, that others felt this way / Years ago."[4] There is the cooler, ironic postmodern attitude: "The buildings, piled so casually / Behind each other, are 'suggestions / Which, while only suggestions, / We hope you will take seriously.' . . . / . . . And, is this a silver age? / Yeah, I suppose so" ("Spring Light," in *Houseboat Days,* 68). There are, as Perloff says, often juxtaposings of linguistic items that seem to sit on the page as bits of language and do not contribute to an overall coherent meaning.

Yet what makes Ashbery an important poet goes well beyond this, goes well beyond the role he is assigned in Perloff's story. Actually most of the poems in *Houseboat Days* and *Self-Portrait in a Convex Mirror* do not serve well as models of a linguistic turn, as compositional works arranging linguistic tokens at a considerable remove from their meaning and reference. I will argue that both Ashbery and Beckett are exemplars of, rather than counterexamples to, the account of literary space presented in chapter 1. (This is not an account of Ashbery's work as a whole. Two especially good collections will be examined because they present well a vision of Ashbery that is opposed to Perloff's.)

Here are samples of Ashbery's work.

> How are we to inhabit
> This space from which the fourth wall is invariably missing,
> As in a stage-set or dollhouse, except by staying as we are,
> In lost profile, facing the stars, with dozens of as yet
> Unrealized projects, and a strict sense
> Of time running out, of evening presenting
> The tactfully folded-over bill? And we fit
> Rather too easily into it, become transparent,
> Almost ghosts. One day
> The birds and animals in the pasture have absorbed
> The color, the density of the surroundings
> . . . .
>   if we were going to
> To be able to write the history of our time, starting with today,
> It would be necessary to model all these unimportant details
> So as to be able to include them; otherwise the narrative
> Would have that flat, sandpapered look the sky gets
> Out in the middle west toward the end of summer,
> The look of wanting to back out before the argument
> Has been resolved.
>   ("Pyrography," in *Houseboat Days,* 9–10)

> Don't be shocked that the old walls
> Hang in rags now, that the rainbow has hardened
> Into a permanent late afternoon that elicits too-long

Shadows and indiscretions from the bottom
Of the soul.
   ("Business Personals," in *Houseboat Days,* 19–20)

One finds in these lines a treatment that might properly be called phenomenological, a study not just of objects but of the background space of appearing that gives them a subtle and hard-to-grasp character as real. There is a suggestion of the advent of a new way that objects are coming to be present for us, of complex moods that characterize our engagement with things, our forms of investment in them. Ashbery makes us focus on that object-determining space by frustrating the process through which we quickly bring the world toward ourselves in ways we already understand it. Or there are places that previously were saturated with meaning but now are emptied out, so that we are aware of that emptying process, of the shape of possible meaningfulness still remaining but unlikely to be filled in. He notes how things, and how we ourselves, become less substantial as individuals and seem to be more transparent to the surrounding space, to absorb its coloring. What makes his work valuable is that the background spaces of appearing that he investigates determine not a familiar form of objectivity, and not the linguistic feel of bits of cultural discourse, but the penumbral, barely evident textures of how things are real for us now. He also gives us a cool-elegiac rather than sentimental-elegiac awareness of endings and loss, when the panning movement of an invisible camera seems to show one from a distance, as the space of one's life seems to be missing a fourth wall, to be exposed to an unexpected distance and emptiness, and the appearance of evening suggests a settling of accounts, the presentation of a "tactfully folded-over bill," as the life comes into view as what it is.

   Even if Ashbery is extremely sophisticated regarding the various linguistic moves that compose his poetry, the stance of the experiencing consciousness, with its forms of openness to the world's ways of appearing, never dissolves here into being a site for the playing through of cultural grammars. It is true that the perceptual spaces he brings into view may not be fully grounded in a detailed geography, may dissolve quickly into other spaces, and often are used metaphorically to talk about conceptual moves or to refer self-reflexively to the writing of poetry. But even with these uses the perceptual spaces usually retain their integrity, a thickness of their own irreducible to the conceptual or poetic functions to which they are put. Note a difference here with what Charles Altieri has said regarding Stein. He claims that it is the *syntactic* resources within the linguistic space of her poetry, such as reversals and repetitions, that embody metaphorically what the poem is trying to say.[5] But in Ashbery it is often the *perceptual* space that serves as a scaffolding or template for ordering and suggesting a more abstract space, one that suggests a conceptualizing about seeing as such, or about poetry. When in the poem just quoted he says that one's narrative, if it does not pay attention to the details that determine the background feel of a scene, will have "that flat, sandpapered look the sky gets out in the middle west toward the end of summer," that phrase is not just a piece of language that is being maneuvered in discursive space. It is bringing into view a scene that has a lasting visual effect. If he goes on to say that such a sky has a "look of wanting to back out before the argument has been resolved," we are forced to examine both the perceptual image we have in mind and the less visible matter that the poem is about. Perhaps a sky can appear in its end-of-summer state to be dissolving into a universal flatness that ignores details and oppositions we ought to have paid attention to. Perhaps a narrative can have a smoothed over, sandpapered feel when we miss the sort of details that affect our subject matter not centrally but in the way that painting the furniture makes a room feel different (as Ashbery mentions in "Pyrography," 9–10). But the perceptual scene does not dissolve into the conceptual one, as it often does in recent art. When the passage talks of a sense of time running out, of evening presenting "the tactfully folded-over bill," we can imagine an evening scene as one having just that quality of an ending that demands a more reflective accounting.

That is why I want to support the somewhat odd pairing of Ashbery with the philosopher John McDowell. The latter, as treated in chapter 3, criticized accounts of belief (he saw such accounts in Rorty and to some extent in Davidson) that portrayed the believer as maneuvering within a conceptual space where bits of language could be measured only against other bits of language, and not against the world. He claimed that a proper account of our mental operations must include both concepts and intuitions; that is, there must be moments in which we have the world itself in evidence, in which we bring it into view as that toward which our processes of belief-formation are directed. Otherwise the conceptual space becomes empty and meaningless or, at least, whatever goes on in there does not have to do with belief and justification. Ashbery remains likewise someone for whom the moment of bringing the world into view is important; the perceptual level does not fold itself neatly back into the conceptual, as it does for those making the turn to language more radically. Ashbery is not simply asking readers to step back and look at his phrases as fragments of cultural discourse, items that should be experienced as having invisible quotation marks around them. He is putting together words in unexpected ways in order to make us see, to experience a subtle perceptual and emotional pattern we have not, ourselves, been able to stabilize linguistically. Yes, there are metapoetic suggestions here about what relation to the world poetry can have now that we are so self-conscious about poetic moves as such. But this awareness is not for Ashbery (as for de Man) a reason to reduce our field to a linguistic (and metalinguistic) one but rather makes more important our attempts at seeing and describing what experience now offers us. What is thus brought into view has a depth to it, a metaphysical character, and is not a mere projection of our linguistic schemes.

Ashbery, then, remains a poet for whom the death of the experiencing subject, as one speaks of in literary theory, is greatly exaggerated. But the consciousness he uncovers is considerably more complex than that of Descartes or Husserl. In Ashbery there is a multiple, mobile, shifting consciousness whose investments in what it is doing poetically, and in its ways of having a meaningful world of objects, express various ironies and refusals and commitments, especially in its attitudes toward the language it uses.[6] He shows an awareness of how language arrives in juxtaposed segments that do not quite cohere; how our moves of investing ourselves in what we say may fail when they try for too much, so that they have to settle for being flatter, less capacious, and yet precise and attentive, even generous; and of how ordinary clichés can suddenly open out into a fresh vision of how matters stand, in the way "the rainbow has hardened into a permanent late afternoon that elicits too-long shadows."

I am arguing, then, that at least in *Houseboat Days* and *Self-Portrait in a Convex Mirror*, the literary space of Ashbery's work is close to what I described in chapter 1. It is phenomenological and metaphysical in the senses articulated there. The space of his work is also translational in that he is concerned with the passing of vague perceptions and moods, of the subtle patterns of our engagement with the world as such, into language, with the gains and losses entailed by that process, the sense of what slips away even as we grasp it. A play with cultural signs that already inhabit a discursive realm would come too late in this process. Ashbery's poetry also reoccupies a transitional space: one repeats aspects of the profound metaphysical work of the child, in the way that the child must come to an overall sense of its relation to an objective world, must satisfy its hunger to grasp what is not the self, and must come through that process to a less grandiose sense of self-identity. (The pity, Ashbery says in another poem, is that the soul is small and "fits its hollow perfectly.") Reoccupying that space as an adult makes one more aware of the initiating moves by which things first emerge into meaningfulness but that we usually miss in our habits of cultural engagement. The poetic space here is also aesthetic in that however much the linguistic baggage of culture circulates through the poems, one still has a sense of crossing over a threshold into a privileged space where a special kind of linguistic arrangement is occurring. (Many forget this fact and suppose that Ashbery's style will be easy to imitate successfully, but it is not so at all.) The poems are often profoundly beautiful. Ashbery gives us a disenchanted, sophisticated attitude toward both language and world, but if one reads his poems aloud there is often a subtle music, a kind of ritual enactment of a stance toward the world that we might come to participate in. So the space of these poems compresses several aspects of literary space as described in chapter 1.

More generally, I wish to set Ashbery in the context of the schema presented in that chapter, which described four levels (world, subjectivity, language, practices of social power) that allowed for three radical reductions of certain levels to other ones, as in the radical linguistic or sociological turns. I claimed that these supposedly radical reductions were not radical enough, in that they did not allow modern disenchantment to extend all the way. Instead they assigned a theological status to one of the levels, so that it would project its patterns on the now-thinned-out space occupied by the other levels. When one performs the more thorough disenchantment then no theological stance is possible. But then the radical thinning out of these other levels does not occur and they can retain a richness of content, a metaphysical integrity and depth, even if not a full autonomy, of their own. Ashbery fits better into that schema as one who has made the more thorough disenchantment, rather than as one making the radical linguistic turn that Perloff credits him with. With all his sophistication as someone maneuvering within language, he sees how language is disenchanted just as much as the world and subjectivity are. So he will not assign it a theological role but is free to let the world's ways of appearing and the phenomenological stance of subjectivity retain a depth and richness of their own, as Perloff does not allow for.

Ashbery can be compared on this issue with Davidson. Davidson recognizes that the disenchantment of language, so that it has no magical powers to determine reference and meaning on its own, is not bad news for our hopes of finding ourselves in touch with the world as it is. Ashbery too recognizes that language cannot, and does not have to, carry the weight of a heroic romantic projecting of the self on the world. The poet can be as easily at home in banal, hackneyed language or in slang. But such a use of language is not a celebration of postmodern juxtaposition or collage, or a Rortyan satisfaction in a world well lost. To understand the disenchantment of language is, instead, to understand how one resides within a quiet openness to the world, so long as one patiently attends to the ways in which it brings itself forward. With the radical turn to language one sees only how language destabilizes and deconstructs whatever it touches. But a more thorough disenchantment makes us ironic and skeptical about those linguistic moves as well, so that they lose some of their erosive powers, and world and subjectivity can appear again with a certain depth (even if not the depth that a strong realist would attribute to the former or the Cartesian would attribute to the latter). To understand language as Ashbery does is to see how the synthesizing activity of the individual consciousness in relation to the world is not simply deconstructed, even if we are more aware of energies of fragmentation. The space of poetry remains a space where the experiencing consciousness is bringing materials into a pattern that matters. With the more radical linguistic turn we would emphasize only the centrifugal, dispersive energies of language. With the less radical turn that is demanded by a full disenchantment all the way up, we remain in a richer space (a space the poet takes advantage of) where the synthesizing forces of conscious experiencing are still in play; literary power can often be found in the interplay of those two sorts of opposing forces.

Ashbery asks what kinds of openness to a larger world are still possible if we refuse to settle for what our language gives us now, if we do not try to cover up loss, if we do not try to reduce the space that lets distance and emptiness appear in the first place. It is not that he is nostalgic for what we can no longer have; he acknowledges that the romantic poet's kinds of investment in the world, and especially in the activities of the poetic self, are illusory. But he looks then for more sophisticated kinds of investments in things and in our patterns of engagement with them; and he trains us in coming to embody that more complex subjectivity. In letting go of the world as we once believed it to be, he wonders what we may still retain of it from within our disenchanted framework, what kinds of openness to the real it would be wrong to give up. That stance is not a regressive one but merely a statement of confidence that the postmodern realm does not exhaust either the world or our worthwhile forms of attention to it.

I will look at Ashbery's poetry now to see if this description of his work is supported by the poems.

> More chairs
> Were brought, and lamps were lit, but it tells
> Nothing of how all this proceeded to materialize
> Before you and the people waiting outside and in the next

Street, repeating its name over and over, until silence
Moved halfway up the darkened trunks.
        ("The Other Tradition," in *Houseboat Days,* 2)

In asking what it is about the time and weather that causes people to note it painstakingly in their diaries, Ashbery says: "Surely it is because the ray of light / Or gloom striking you this moment is hope / In all its mature, matronly form, taking all things into account / So that if one can't say that this is the natural way / It should have happened, at least one can have no cause for complaint" ("Grand Galop," in *Self-Portrait in a Convex Mirror,* 17).

These poetic landscapes have a strangeness about them, and yet there is a mood that holds them together. Ashbery captures as well as anyone our sense of those late-afternoon or evening moments when our focus suddenly widens and we are more aware of the background frame of our present experiences, so that we are conscious of how they "materialize before" us as silence spreads gradually "up the darkened trunks." In the first of the two passages the scene is perhaps a summer cottage where chairs have been brought and lamps lit for guests, but the awareness is of the surrounding space, with its silence or emptiness that is nevertheless insistent and pervasive ("repeating its name"), so that the scene is held there in the light against penumbral forces that both heighten it and would one day dissolve it, that we may sense with a certain late-afternoon dread and yet also find satisfaction in identifying with. Ashbery's flatness of tone is important; there is no call here for existentialist trauma but a cool description of the overall texture of things.

These are moments when we are less taken up into a strategic way of seeing but instead step back and let the shapes of things, including the shapes of our own lives, declare themselves: a "mature, matronly" point of view that is "taking all things into account," that accepts without complaint the way things are, even if they could have been otherwise. We tend to note the light and weather in diaries, Ashbery says, because in certain moods we identify with these phenomena in the way we let objects and events come into view as, if not quite inevitable, still aspects of a natural unfolding, not to be regretted.

All of our lives is a rebus
Of little wooden animals painted shy,
Terrific colors, magnificent and horrible,
Close together. The message is learned
the way light at the edge of a beach in autumn is learned.
        ("The Wrong Kind of Insurance,"
        in *Houseboat Days,* 49)

Yes, friends, these clouds pulled along on invisible ropes
Are, as you have guessed, merely stage machinery,
and the funny thing is it knows we know
About it and still wants us to go on believing
In what it so unskillfully imitates, and wants
To be loved not for that but for itself:
The murky atmosphere of a park, tattered
Foliage, wise old treetrunks, rainbow tissue-paper wadded
Clouds down near where the perspective
Intersects the sunset, so we may know
We too are somehow impossible, formed of so many different
    things,
Too many to make sense to anybody.
We straggle on as quotients, hard-to-combine
Ingredients, and what continues
Does so with our participation and consent.
                    ("The Wrong Kind of Insurance," 50)

Here again Ashbery is excellent at giving the phenomenology of a certain kind of mood with several components to it: our need to have nature respond to us but our awareness that it now has a flatness, an artificiality to it, as a construct of our seeing, as something already described too often so that it seems a poor imitation of those descriptions; our sense of ourselves as fragmented and unable to give an overall meaningfulness to what is around us; the pressure of a certain aloneness as we recognize these things; a sense of a calm, resolved letting-go as we stare at "light at the edge of a beach in autumn." These passages are not primarily generated by their intralinguistic connections, as Perloff would suggest, but rather by the great difficulty of a perception that Ashbery is trying to put into words. It is true that light at the edge of a beach in autumn is something learned differently from the way other things are learned; the phrase picking that out is making us *look,* instead of being just an already processed item in the culture's economy of representations. We cannot inhabit the perceptual world in the same way as earlier. A cloudy sky at sunset is by now such a cliché that we have to see it as something already meant too often, so that it seems to appear as a stage setting that stagehands, familiar with the task, can wheel into place quite easily. Nature is repeating scenes that we have already made artificial through our repeated acts of knowing, so that it seems a poor, tattered theatrical.

But then the tone of the poem changes and somehow the scene in the park still matters; that sense of a space already colonized by language weakens, and the park is still a place where the form of our engagement with the world is becoming visible, where the nebulous but insistent character of our selfhood is felt. Our tendency to resist the scene, because its features seem pulled along on invisible ropes in an evidently unskilled fashion, becomes instead a more complex form of identification with the scene that deepens us, as we see that "we too are somehow impossible, formed of so many different things." Nature even when it is processed in what at first is too obvious a manner, even when we can no longer be Wordsworth, can still teach us something that is profound and worth knowing. The elements in the park do not leap to life so as to give the scene a unified, organic, and satisfying way of presenting itself, but neither do we, and that is not a bad thing. Perhaps the psychological movements within us are also like an unskillful stage machinery dragged along on invisible ropes, rather than deeply original. But the tone of the passage shows that these still have an important integrity about them. The self in these passages is a poorly understood scattering of moments like those of the afternoon in the park as portrayed in the poem, moments that have a vague feel or mood that seems to join them but that are flat and without any logic that would link them more reliably. Yet the world before one is still being held together by the viewing consciousness (and not just by the lateral frictions of language), so that what continues "does so with our participation and consent." The reason the "murky atmosphere of a park" and the "tattered foliage" seem meaningful is that they are experienced by a self for whom having an ethically and metaphysically substantial world is still important. For Perloff, on the other hand, it is a severe criticism of Wallace Stevens that he still works within the structure of subject and object, self and world.[7] Presumably her favored poets are beyond that.

There is also the notion here of one's life as "a rebus of little wooden animals," so that we think of a kind of picture puzzle whose solution, requiring a turning of images into words, eludes us but is comprehended, if at all, only in the way we seem to grasp the background mood of a scene. Such a notion places the difficulty not as one emerging within language but as having to do with the border between image and language, with what we grasp in a preunderstanding that is in various respects nonlinguistic, as are the images of a rebus. (And the nature of those images is suggested in the description of the wooden animals as "painted shy, terrific colors, magnificent and horrible.") The perceptual information is already on the way to becoming linguistic, sentential, but it seems mysterious how that process is to complete itself; we have not yet entered a discursive space that breaks off and becomes autonomous. Admittedly the perceptual information of a rebus is used to stand for syllables of a language. An image of someone pouring a pitcher of water joined to an image

of a tent may stand for the word *portent,* thus leaving the visual information as such behind. But an Ashbery poem does not become a rebus in that
sense. The "light at the edge of a beach in autumn" retains a perceptual
thickness that does not translate fully into being a metaphor for language.

Perloff's claim that poetry is more advanced when it is beyond a
subject-object structure, as in her criticism of Stevens, fits the narrative
being shaped here, for that subject-object structure seems to belong on the
less developed side of the distinction I have been examining between
different stages of psychological investment. There is on the one hand a
stage where one is dealing with individuation, boundaries of self and
other, and the overall metaphysical feel of the world over against the self.
On the other hand is a stage where the self maneuvers positionally and
strategically within cultural grammars, within a circulating movement of
linguistic representations, where truth is a matter of (lateral) social agreement or of successful moves in the conceptual game, rather than of reaching forward to grasp reality as it is. Ashbery remains interested in the
metaphysical and phenomenological stance of the first stage even as he inhabits the second one, rather than moving more completely into the latter
in a way that leaves the former issues behind. Death and the threat of dissolution still matter to the individual's experience of itself in its way of
taking in the world. Riding the roller coaster of linguistic and cultural circulation is never enough.

Ashbery as a phenomenologist wants to make us aware of the space of
possible meaningfulness, rather than of what appears within it, by presenting it as it has emptied out: "In school / All the thought got combed
out: / What was left was like a field. / Shut your eyes, and you can feel it
for miles around. / Now open them on a thin vertical path. It might give
us—what?—some flowers soon?" ("What Is Poetry," in *Houseboat Days,*
47). There can be an exhilaration in that sudden opening out, in the horizons that can be visible when the mind's normal furniture is no longer in
the way, when the mind's general openness to the world, prior to any particular engagement with it, is briefly in view. The danger for the postmodernist stance is that this kind of seeing will be lost. There is in that stance
the strong temptation that all available spaces will be filled in by the endlessly productive and disseminating machinery of cultural signs, as in films
that cannot allow the quieter opening up of a background space that has
its own kind of insistence. Perhaps it will be said that in this postmodern
world of rapidly moving signs, where everything becomes information
that is easily transmitted and quickly changes its configurations, where
things seem less substantial and more readily consumable as they respond
to changing styles, the task of the poet is simply to give the feel of being

within that world. But a different task is more important. As the character of experience changes in the ways described, there is the danger that we will lose our capacity for a wide range of experiences: those that emerge in accord with slower, deeper rhythms, in the background perhaps, that require silence and a patient attentiveness before the significant pattern in question is able to appear. Poets are one resource for holding out against the loss of those possible modes of experiencing; they should not be expected to feed us back the styles of processing that the information revolution is training us for. The mark of the importance of Ashbery's poetry is the way it refuses to be simply postmodern, the way it lets the space of possible experience open out in depth without filling it in, the way it chooses scenes that allow that background to come into view.

In another poem ("Houseboat Days," in *Houseboat Days*, 38) Ashbery refers to the "trouvailles" of the senses. The use of that word suggests that our sensory perceptions have a "found" quality that is in some ways artificial, a matter more of our willingness to count things as significant than of what they are in themselves, as when some count ordinary objects as antiques. Unlike with the romantics we are ready to see those sensory findings as giving us rather little, as objects with little staying power. But the empty terrain against which they appear remains something worth attending to, as a matter of understanding ourselves and our forms of knowing.

> Here is nothing, not even
> Lazy slipping away, feeling of being abandoned, a
> Distant curl of smoke above a car
> Graveyard. Instead the shadows stand
> Straight out. Uninvited, light grabs its due;
> What is eaten away becomes etched impression
> Of mutability, but nothing backs it up.
>   ("Fantasia on 'The Nut-Brown Maid,' "
>   in *Houseboat Days*, 74)

That "etched impression of mutability" is what remains as the things appearing within that lighting disappear. Light "grabs its due" so that things must present themselves as they are; we thus see with clarity their metaphysical fragility. As things disappear they leave behind that sense of fragility as a quality of the landscape. The metaphysical lighting does not even allow us the satisfaction of a human sense of loss, a "feeling of being abandoned," a mark of human absence such as the curl of smoke above a junkyard. As Ashbery says in "Valentine" (in *Houseboat Days*, 62), things in withdrawing leave an emptiness that is perhaps "bathed in freshness" but may be instead "just a new kind of emptiness."

Ashbery is also a phenomenologist of time-consciousness:

> The insipid chiming of the seconds
> Has given way to an arc of silence
> So old it had never ceased to exist
> On the roofs of buildings, in the sky.
> ("On the Towpath,"
> in *Houseboat Days,* 22)

> Yet in the end each of us
> Is seen to have traveled the same distance—it's time
> That counts, and how deeply you have invested in it,
> Crossing the street of an event, as though coming out of it were
> The same as making it happen.
> ("Saying It To Keep It from Happening,"
> in *Houseboat Days,* 29)

> Better the months—
> They are almost persons—than these abstractions
> That sift like marble dust across the unfinished works of the studio
> Aging everything into a characterization of itself.
> ("Grand Galop," in *Self-Portrait in a Convex Mirror,* 15)

Again, however fine the language is in these passages, what gives them their power is their sense of the self in time, so that the viewpoint of the experiencing subject remains crucial. We are made to notice the difference between attending to measurable calendar time and attending to what seems to sift quietly over things, like dust, in a hardly noticeable, yet perhaps anxiety-producing process that everything around us comes to exemplify. We note the ways we invest ourselves in events or else come through them to the other side, as if crossing a street inattentively, and the way time can seem almost spatial, a silence out of which things are crystallizing. Ashbery talks of his working in an "other tradition," one that would let us attend to the small moments, the indistinct textures of consciousness, the penumbral moods that invest the world, the hard-to-grasp overall feel of the most ordinary scenes, everything that is ordinarily lost in the way we develop the standard narratives of our experience and the standard accounts of what has happened in history. How is moving through an event in one's life like crossing a street? One gets to the other side without being crushed by its streaming forces, but getting to the other side safely is not the same thing as being truly in the event. Crossing a street is at most times a thoughtless undertaking as one's mind is engaged with other things. The point is that the kind of thought occasioned by the image is not at all well captured by the knowingness of someone who sees words as already in quotation marks, as bits of discourse. (And there is something fine in the notion of phenomenal time, rather than clock time, as like a fine dust that ages everything "into a characterization of itself," with the two opposed meanings of bringing out something's character and replacing the thing with an idea of it.)

Ashbery's phenomenology is in some respects Heideggerian, but instead of Heidegger's feeling that he has found an Ur-vocabulary in the wordplay that the German language offers, such that a new language sensitive to the Being of beings can emerge, Ashbery's attitude is that of coolness, flatness, and detachment. If there is often a sense of elegy and loss, of an emptying out of the terrain, of the passage of time, there is rarely a sense that despair is the proper response or that this emptiness might be filled up by anything the poet might do. Rather the poet accepts the flatness of language, the sense of skepticism about whether his experience, filtered through the cultural languages, is special. Instead of Heidegger's mystical talk of Language as the House of Being, there is a postmodern awareness that our self-consciousness about language is distancing ("The way / Is fraught with danger, you say, and I / Notice the word 'fraught' as you are telling / Me about huge secret valleys some distance from / The mired fighting" ["Variant," in *Houseboat Days,* 4]). Meaning occurs not through a Black Forest regression to the modes of experience of premodern Germany (or to those of pre-Socratic Greece) but through what happens to everyday language almost inadvertently. (To put the matter much too simply, Ashbery is a mix of Heidegger and Derrida: both an openness to the faintly appearing metaphysical character of what is real and a postmodern awareness of how invasive the effects of language are. Critics err in seeing only the Derridean side, but it is important that this side undercuts certain aspects of the Heideggerian one.) For Ashbery it is a matter of integrity to resist and frustrate what may appear to be moments of originality and inspiration, in favor of working with the admitted secondhandedness of the linguistic strings that we maneuver, a secondhandedness that is not a failure of poetic inspiration but belongs to the very character of language. Ashbery's stance is one of belatedly inhabiting a space in which certain experiences are no longer possible (though it is questionable whether they ever were).

Its scene drifts away
Like vapor scattered on the wind. The fertile
Thought-associations that until now came
So easily, appear no more, or rarely. Their
Colorings are less intense, washed out
By autumn rains and winds, spoiled, muddied,
Given back to you because they are worthless.
          ("Self-Portrait in a Convex Mirror," 81)

The pity of it smarts, Makes hot tears spurt: that the soul
   is not a soul,
Has no secret, is small, and it fits
Its hollow perfectly: its room, our moment of attention.
          ("Self-Portrait in a Convex Mirror," 69)

Instead of a space saturated with proliferating, disseminating signs (as in the description given of Rushdie as postmodern in chapter 2 and that will be given in chapter 8 regarding a memoir by Derrida), the space in which literature happens has an absence about it, a loss of what once entered it more readily. Thought associations that were easy now come rarely, are less intense, and are washed out, as the colors of a landscape might be by autumn rains and winds. They stabilize in the available field only because what once made them valuable has somehow detached itself from them, has allowed them to appear now as empty and worthless. The mind appears as gray and less vivid, with a muddying of boundaries and with shapes that seem to scatter easily like mist. Instead of the often grandiose investments of the romantic self, with its ability to transcend boundaries, we have a self that is small and "fits its hollow perfectly," the room made for it by forces that have produced this present moment of attention. The poetic self is not capable of the heroic gestures of meaning-making that once seemed available not only to the romantics but also to many of the modernist poets. But it can honestly and accurately describe the residues that remain when neither the world nor consciousness offers space for such gestures. It can capture the fading character of a world once believed in more intensely, and it can refuse to imitate, even through parody, the now-impossible gestures. (This is not an admission of cultural failure but merely a willingness to acknowledge both losses and gains in the forms of consciousness we have come now to inhabit.)

What is thus worth saying is not, as in Perloff's story, a kind of combustion obtained by rubbing fragments of language together. Ashbery is still dealing with patterns that are so fine as to disappear when we try to bring them forward, that we do not even know we have captured when we have done so.

> . . . Behind the mask
> Is still a continental appreciation
> Of what is fine, rarely appears and when it does is already
> Dying on the breeze that brought it to the threshold
> Of speech.
>
> ("A Man of Words,"
> in *Self-Portrait in a Convex Mirror*, 8)

I have given these extensive quotations from Ashbery to show that he fits only in a strained manner into Perloff's narrative. It is true, as she claims, that he is not a symbolic poet in the way that Eliot is. The idea of many poets in the 1950s and 1960s in America, especially of the New York School, was to present their experiences of the world straightforwardly without asking that they take on significance in a more abstract network of meanings. (The French poet Pierre Reverdy supposedly did this well and is praised by Ashbery precisely for this quality.) But if it is clear that Ashbery is not a symbolist poet and does not want to write poetry with all the religious, cultural, and historical references of *The Waste Land*, still he is not letting the scenes he describes simply stand for themselves. The physical landscapes that he moves through often play a double role; the space coming into view in them is not just their own but also the more abstract spaces of language, time, poetry, semantics, phenomenology, and epistemology. "Fertile thought-associations" are said to have colorings that are "washed out by autumn rains and winds, spoiled, muddied." Certain "abstractions" sift "like marble dust across the unfinished works of the studio." A message about human lives is learned "the way light at the edge of a beach in autumn is learned." A narrative is said to have "that flat, sandpapered look the sky gets out in the middle west toward the end of summer." It is difficult to talk about the ways in which language does its work, about how we take experience in, or about the workings of poetry. Just as Heidegger uses *lighting* and *clearing* to talk of what goes beyond the characteristics of physical space, so Ashbery's descriptions of the light and the landscape stand both for themselves and for more abstract spaces. That is why it is important, for someone who wishes to reflect on how language does its work in poetry, to remain connected with prelinguistic spatial and visual patterns of experiencing; these may still serve as a metaphorical scaffolding for attempts to comprehend more abstract realms. Without that scaffolding a crucial resource for our project of understanding language will have been lost. If we make the linguistic turn too thoroughly we defeat our purposes in making it. The energies in Ashbery's poems are clearly centripetal as well as centrifugal. There is not the convergence of meaning on particular symbolic items, as in Eliot. But there is a convergence of different spaces, different geographies, so that they come to occupy the same terrain simultaneously. "And then somehow the loneliness is more real and more human / You know not just the scarecrow but the whole landscape / And the crows peacefully pecking where the harrow has passed" ("Lithuanian Dance Band," in *Self-Portrait in a Convex Mirror*, 53). Perhaps the "harrow" here is the movement of the poetic lines. But then it is interesting that what the poem brings to our attention is the space that opens out once the harrow has passed; what the poem seems to be about is not the poetic lines but the experiential landscape that they move across and that appears briefly as an afterimage as one has followed the poem to its end. Great filmmakers have been able to capture that silent framing against which our gestures appear. Granted that often in recent films the sequences are moves within the language of filmmaking, quotations from earlier films, and so forth, and thus are intertextual. Yet one may wish, in viewing these, that there were moments that opened out toward aspects of the world that, in coming into view, made us equally as aware of the space the harrow has moved across as of the harrow's marks.

Ashbery may bring into his poems bits of cultural discourse, even what looks like a menu copied straight from a nursing home (as in "Grand Galop," in *Self-Portrait in a Convex Mirror*, 14). But he also gives us the moments of opening out to a larger vision, where an expansive unfilled space is present behind the words, even if we do not have the mental powers or the linguistic equipment to hold that vision steady or to articulate it.

> . . . To extend one's life
> All day on the dirty stone of some plaza,
> Unaware among the pretty lunging of the wind,
> Light and shade, is like coming out of
> A coma that is a white, interesting country,
> Prepared to lose the main memory in a meeting
> By torchlight under the twisted end of the stairs.
> ("And Others, Vaguer Presences,"
> in *Houseboat Days*, 48)

> A few black smudges
> On the outer boulevards, like squashed midges

And the truth becomes a hole, something one has always known,
A heaviness in the trees, and no one can say
Where it comes from, or how long it will stay—
A randomness, a darkness of one's own.
               ("The Ice-Cream Wars," in *Houseboat Days,* 60–61)

These passages are vintage Ashbery. First our stance is drawn back inward to the linguistic field by the use of language that calls attention to itself: "pretty lunging" or the pairing of "black smudges" with "squashed midges." But then the passages open out to a much wider field, to a feeling of distance, like coming out of a coma or becoming aware of a pervading randomness, a darkness of one's own.

Another writer Perloff treats as continuing the program of Stein is Samuel Beckett.[8] Perloff wants us to see Beckett as moving like Stein toward a view of language as compositional, where one arranges linguistic elements on a flat surface, with the semantic, referential world behind those elements becoming so insubstantial as to virtually disappear, except as a linguistic projection determined by the individual reader's perhaps idiosyncratic way of linking verbal elements. Language on this account will not follow the model of having older layers of prelinguistic articulation that are still in play, of being subservient to the givenness of what is external and earlier, of depending on ritualized forms and deep cadences whose basis does not emerge into full transparency. The stronger versions of the linguistic turn will try to present language as self-reflexive and self-moving, like the Cartesian system that has broken free from earlier gravities and can now maneuver by its own energies, fixing a world of objects for itself.

  Beckett fits quite poorly into such a narrative. Again and again (this is a characteristic postmodern move, as was seen revealingly in de Man) Perloff is willing to impoverish the rich psychological context of a passage and an often anxiety-ridden phenomenology of self-other relations in order to see a text as an autonomous realm of linguistic signifiers. She presents some evidence for her claims from Beckett's *Ping:*

All known all white bare white body fixed one yard legs joined like sewn. Light heat white floor one square yard never seen. White walls one yard by two white ceilings one square yard never seen. Bare white body fixed only the eyes only just. Traces blurs light grey almost white on white. Hands hanging palms front white feet heels together right angle. Light heat white planes shining white bare body fixed ping fixed elsewhere.[9]

"Beckett's white-on-white composition," says Perloff, speaking of this passage, "superficially resembles Stevens'. But here words like 'white' and 'bare' . . . have no definable meaning. Their value is compositional rather than referential, and the focus shifts from signification to the play of signifiers."[10]

Certainly there is an attention in this Beckett text to the compositional capacities of language as such, as if the words were notes joined in a musical work. But it does not seem that language is simply compositional here, that "white" and "bare" have no definable meaning; the bareness and whiteness of the body carry considerable semantic weight. There is an experiencing self that is here being reduced to a minimal environment, and we feel the pain of its attempt to comprehend the situation in which it now finds itself. In spite of Perloff's comparison this is different from the sort of white-on-white painting that an abstract painter forty years ago might have produced; the whiteness here has to do with the drastic impoverishment of the phenomenal world for a subject that has been stripped down, isolated, and severely limited in its range of activity. That sort of reduction is familiar from much of the rest of Beckett's work. In his trilogy of novels the world of objects and others, as well as the accoutrements of the self, are gradually reduced until one sees a minimal structure of subjectivity and world (rather than a free play of language). But this is also a controlled regression to a more reduced, not yet developed style of selfhood, to some of the primitive forms in which the child is aware of himself in relation to what is other, in which structures of aloneness and fears of dissolution emerge. One attempts to be self-supporting in that situation by producing language, by continuing a stream of words that keep themselves going by a metonymic inertia. But in Beckett there is never the apparent Cartesian escape from the forces of gravity. One feels always the gravitational pull of the earlier world, which threatens to take over the controlled regression and make it collapse too far backward, toward a complete loss of self.

That is the primary scene of *Molloy*. The narrator's movement across the surface of the landscape is the metonymic movement of language, its sideways progression from word to word in an attempt to be self-sustaining. But that movement is subject to the gravity of an earlier maternal relationship. He is always trying to get back to the place of his mother, however conflicted are his feelings for her. (Again, the great power in Beckett's writing comes from the tension between a threatening psychological world and the attempts to find in language compensatory structures. The literary weight is on that translational space and Perloff's more radical linguistic turn, precisely by losing one side of that translational space, is unable to show why Beckett's work matters so much.)

> And of myself, all my life, I think I had been going to my mother, with the purpose of establishing our relations on a less precarious footing. And when I was with her, and I often succeeded, I left her without having done anything. And when I was no longer with her I was again on my way to her, hoping to do better the next time. And when I appeared to give up and to busy myself with something else, or with nothing at all any more, in reality I was hatching my plans and seeking the way to her house.[11]

This regressive psychological space is, for Beckett, the space from which writing emerges. We know this because in finally telling his story the narrator has indeed arrived at his mother's place, and from there he is producing written pages, though she is no longer present.

> I am in my mother's room. It's I who live there now. . . . There's this man who comes every week. Perhaps I got here thanks to him. He says not. He gives me money and takes away the pages. So many pages, so much money. . . . Yet I don't work for money. For what then? I don't know. The truth is I don't know much. For example my mother's death. Was she already dead when I came? Or did she only die later? I mean enough to bury. In any case I have her room. I sleep in her bed. I piss and shit in her pot. I have taken her place. I must resemble her more and more. All I need now is a son. Perhaps I have one somewhere. (Beckett, *Molloy*, 7)

This is not the semantically indeterminate *linguistic* space of Perloff but a pre-Oedipal psychological space where individual boundaries and gender identities are blurred, where there is an oscillation between self and other, male and female, where one is trying with difficulty to set oneself in relation to objects. The narrator wonders whether the women he has been with might all have been men, whether he was deceived into believing he was putting his penis into a vagina rather than into a rectum (56–57). The identities of these apparent women blur into that of his mother: "And there are days, like this evening, when my memory confuses them and I am tempted to think of them as one and the same old hag, flattened and crazed by life. And God forgive me, to tell you the horrible truth, my mother's image sometimes mingles with theirs, which is literally unendurable, like being crucified, I don't know why and I don't want to" (59). Other individuals emerge in this space but are only half-real: "I watched him recede, at grips (myself) with the temptation to get up and follow him, perhaps even to catch up with him one day, so as to know him better, be myself less lonely. But in spite of my soul's leap out to him, at the end of its elastic, I saw him only darkly, because of the dark and then because of the terrain, in the folds of which he disappeared from time to time, to re-emerge further on" (11). The self is supposed to develop out of this minimal, blurred, transitional space until it has satisfying relationships with a world of subsistent objects and persons. But for some reason the narrator cannot reach that level, cannot attain that sort of engagement with objects, "in spite of my soul's leap out to him, at the end of its elastic." Reality can take on for him only the character of something blighted and emptied out, a world of ruins.

> But mostly they are a place with neither plan nor
> bounds and of which I understand nothing, not even of
> what it is made, still less into what. And the thing in
> ruins. I don't know what it is, what it was, nor
> whether it is not less a question of ruins than the
> indestructible chaos of timeless things, if that is the
> right expression. . . . But it is not the kind of place
> where you go, but where you find yourself, sometimes,
> not knowing how, and which you cannot leave at will,
> and where you find yourself without any pleasure, but
> with more perhaps than in those places you can escape
> from, by making an effort, places full of mystery, full
> of the familiar mysteries. I listen and the voice is of
> a world collapsing endlessly, a frozen world, under a
> faint untroubled sky, enough to see by, yes, and frozen
> too. And I hear it murmur that all wilts and yields, as
> if loaded down, but here there are no loads, and the
> ground too, unfit for loads, and the light too, down
> towards an end it seems can never come. For what
> possible end to these wastes where true light never
> was, nor any upright thing, nor any true foundation,
> but only these leaning things, forever lapsing and
> crumbling away, beneath a sky without memory of morning
> or hope of night.
>
> (*Molloy*, 39–40)

This could almost be a mourning chant for the failure of the modern Cartesian project, with no true light, no foundation, and no "upright thing." That raised up, self-sustaining world of ideas has been replaced by a regressive space where one hears a faint music of "a world collapsing endlessly." Molloy's inertial movement, which stands for the lateral progression of language across a textual space, is weakened by his injuries and illness so that he has to prop himself on a bicycle and then to crawl, and finally he is in a ditch and can no longer even propel himself. One reason why this particular space of literature is so powerful is that the stronger the regressive pull against the individual form and the self-moving activity of the self, the more enduring will be the linguistic architecture powerful enough, well-built enough, to survive it. So style in Beckett becomes both a matter of letting that centripetal pull be felt, and a satisfaction in the enduring quality of a line of prose that is able, by its very patterns, to resist it (in the manner of the steady movement of a caravan across an empty desert). Molloy keeps returning to the project of seeking a more primitive identification with his mother, of returning to that earlier space. There is a ritual repetition so profound that it comes close to a final dissolution and death. One space of selfhood (and of writing) that he finds is near a cave on a seacoast, looking out at storms, with a town behind him reachable by a swampy route that claims the lives of men every year. As his body is threatened with disintegration in that space, he finds a minimal standing in the positional-grammatical world by discovering a syntactic ritual, a testing of combinations and rules of arrangement as they apply to stones found on the beach, which he is transferring among his pockets (69–74). But this is an imperfect substitute for a genuine participation in the grammatical realm of cultural units and their allowable moves, for an advance to a more mature, strategic selfhood. So the literary space in Beckett is a staging of the psyche, very much along the lines of the psycho-metaphysical space of literature that I have been both describing and defending.

That space is very different from the flat, compositional, linguistic space that Perloff describes, in which the freedom from gravity is such that there is no challenge to the metonymic self-maintenance of language. (Whereas Molloy's momentum is dragged down by a deeper gravity, so that eventually he can barely pull himself along the ground, that frictionless postmodern linguistic space allows for unlimited linguistic momentum, as in Rushdie.) In Perloff's linguistic space there is no longer any sense of a lost world, of the attraction of earlier forms. But Beckett's textual scenes are scenes of the experiencing self; we see the structure of experience that remains in a reduction to a shape still able to keep a minimal selfhood going. The Beckett text, unlike that of Perloff's Stein, is what it is only over against the black hole of an even more regressive state that is threatening to dissolve all the articulations of the self forever. Perloff is concerned with a space that is already an articulated, linguistic, grammatical one, where an arrangement of words participates in metonymic energies and, in forming patterns, projects them onto a referential screen, so that a single poem can be taken to be about different and incompatible scenes. In Beckett language is submitting itself to the centripetal energies of a more primitive order, so that in many of the later prose pieces one feels the syntactic structure collapsing inward and one loses the normal structure of linkage. Grammatical articulations (the mark of what I am calling the positional, grammatical, triadic world) begin to dissolve just as individual boundaries do: "recorded none the less it's preferable somehow somewhere as it stands as it comes my life my moments not the millionth part all lost nearly all someone listening another noting or the same."[12]

In Perloff's narrative semantic indeterminacy is the sign of an advance into a more sophisticated linguistic field, where language has freed itself from its traditional duties of representing an already determinate world or of capturing states of the psyche and can now, maneuvering on its own, project several possible referential worlds at the same time. For Beckett, in contrast, the indeterminacy arises because of his access to a childhood space where an inchoate self remains frozen in its archaic and poorly formed state, so that semantic and individuational boundaries keep blurring. If in Perloff indeterminacy represents the power of language, in Beckett there is an indeterminacy of the self's experiential world that language is trying to get hold of, a world that is just beginning to form into something determinate enough to be nameable but that fails to arrive at a sufficient degree of grammatical articulation. Perloff treats her favored poets as like those painters sophisticated enough to see a painting as a nonrepresentational surface of colored bits that can be ordered in interesting ways. These poets are not caught within the dyadic structure of self-other representing and mirroring but rather allow language its full metonymic potential. Beckett shows that grammatical world threatening to collapse into the fragile space of a self trying, and mostly failing, to see itself across from a stably constituted other.

For Perloff the difficulty occurs in Beckett's texts because they engage in a particular sort of *linguistic* game. "To read enigma texts like these is rather like being sent out on a snipe-hunt, that popular children's game in which the players disperse in the dark, equipped with pillowcases, flashlights, sticks, and a set of rules, in search of birds they know are not to be caught. Not *product* as in the treasure hunt but *process* is the key."[13] The sophisticated writer supposedly sets up such a game in which readers go through the motions of figuring out reference while understanding that no referents are available, that the goal was just that activity of trying to project reference from texts where no such answers are to be found. Perloff several times refers to Beckett's work as *enigma* texts in which the difficulty offered is a linguistic one. "Rather, the enigma is created by the 'fragility' of the words themselves, words whose meanings are constantly eroded and reformulated."[14] This notion of an enigmatic text is taken from the French thinker Roger Cardinal, who speaks of different stages of poetry. In the most advanced of these the poet employs the gestures of mystery that have emerged in earlier poetic stages, but makes no effort to provide a content that those gestures are supposedly hiding. So the poem is poised between sense and nonsense, putting forth an inscrutable appearance that seems to require a solution without there being one. These enigma texts are sophisticated, reflexive moves that play with the gestures of poetry as a painter might play with conventions of representation; the sophisticated response to these texts will be an intellectual one that sees the moves that are thus being made.

But is that what is occurring in Beckett's texts? The difficulty in them does not appear to derive from an intellectual game with the gestures of poetry as such, from an attempt to bring those gestures into focus by frustrating our normal ways of working through them. It is not a postmodern fragility of words that is in question but a deeper fragility. Nor is Beckett sending readers on a wild-goose chase of trying to figure out referential meaning when there is not any, as in Perloff's allusion to the snipe hunt. (To compare Beckett's work to a childlike game of taking pleasure in going after referents that do not exist is to miss the entire tone of that work, the painfulness of what is at stake in it.) Rather we are dealing here with the difficulty of trying to give a description of spaces where the self is in a situation of extreme anxiety about dissolution, of inchoate, unstable forms of objectivity, of feelings of sadism and masochism. (One sees sadistic material especially in *How It Is*.) The problem is not, as Perloff claims, that words have meanings that erode and reformulate themselves, but that the translation of these inchoate, painful feelings into language, in order to test the kinds of compensatory stabilizing that language can offer, is a task of great difficulty if one refuses to settle for easy linguistic formulations. The problem is evidently much deeper than a linguistic problem. Or if it is a linguistic problem it concerns not the indeterminacy of language but the role of a turn to language in the geography of the transitional space of childhood. Such regressive states would have no use in themselves, simply as psychological phenomena. It is because they are deployed in the richer economy of the adult writer that they can have value here. They make it easier to see our worldly situation at a metaphysical and epistemic and psychological minimum, so that what is essential to these will stand out.

Perloff tries to back up her conception of the text as enigmatic by taking passages and pointing out how hard they are to make sense of. But in fact the passages in question are considerably clearer in meaning than are many passages by those poets, such as Eliot and Stevens, whom Perloff does not see as practicing the poetics of indeterminacy. For example, if Beckett writes, "I am not sleeping the wind blows tempestuous the little clouds drive before it the table glides from light to darkness to light," Perloff says: "The sharply defined images of this passage remain curiously enigmatic. 'The little clouds drive before it the table glides from light to darkness to light'—how do such things happen?"[15] If Beckett says, "my way is in the sand flowing / between the shingle and the dune," Perloff asks: "What does it mean to exist in the shifting sands between the shingle and the dune?"[16] One could say much about these passages, and there would be difficulty in doing so, but the lines do not appear especially enigmatic. It is easy to picture how clouds might drive before the wind while a table glides from light to darkness to light. And if "shingle" means the layer of stones that washes up on a seashore, it is no great feat to imagine being in the shifting sands between the shingle and the dune. One can see how great an investment Perloff has in her theme of semantic indeterminacy if she tries to locate it in such passages. But in fact the situation is far worse for Perloff's account, as can be noted immediately if the written context of the quotation about the clouds, the wind, and the table is examined. The quotation appears in *How It Is* (10–11) in the middle of a vividly imagined scene. The speaker is sitting at a table as the events referred to occur, and a woman sitting aloof fifteen yards from him is watching him while she sews. She might easily come over and touch him, he thinks, but her anxiety grows and suddenly she leaves the house and runs to friends. How can such a text seem so beyond decipherment to Perloff (in a way in which other texts more generally are not so)? Her reading of that passage can serve as an emblematic move of the linguistic turn: one is cutting off a world of circulating linguistic signs from the larger visual and psychological context that is needed to give it power and significance. Perloff's failure to mention the obviously relevant psychological context of the paragraph she quotes is a serious but representative one.

One item that shows how Perloff misperceives the space of Beckett's writing is her comparison of one of his poems to a painting by Magritte. The poem says: "my peace is there in the receding mist / where I may cease from treading these long shifting thresholds / and live the space of a door / that opens and shuts." Perloff says the door in the poem brings to mind Magritte's *The Field-Glass,* in which there seems to be a trick or paradox of representation: cloud shapes in the painting might be the appearing of a real sky or a reflection of the sky or a painted window shade, but then the other side of the window in the painting seems to violate the ordinary logic of perceptual space and to put those possibilities in doubt.[17] What-

ever the correct reading of Magritte's work is, Beckett here is up to something else entirely. There is a difficult-to-define truth of the self in the
claim that one prefers living the space of a door to a crossing of thresholds. Perhaps one meaning is that he wants to keep occupying a transitional space that can open itself to, without quite returning to, an earlier
regressive world. Perhaps writing can begin only when the self occupies,
with a calm persistence, that in-between space, that quiet space of opening
up and closing off, where one experiences both the enclosure of the self
and its riding on an earlier world where the unconscious spreads its patterns beneath and before the stage of well-formed individuality. Beckett is
not playing here in a reflexive manner with the conventions and rhetorical
moves of language, and he is not dealing with paradoxes of representation, as in Magritte. Rather he is trying to capture a subtle space of subjectivity in its relations to the world. Magritte does make something parallel to the linguistic turn. De Man would be perfectly happy with such talk
of the paradox and impossibility of representation; he too, like Perloff
here, dismisses psychologically painful states in Rilke in favor of linguistic
paradox. But Beckett moves elsewhere. He is trying to find a rhythm of the
line that will give him access to an earlier psychic space. He is attending to
a distant voice that in speaking through him is both self and not-self, that
presses on him unbidden because it keeps reliving, with ritual necessity,
the move into language from an archaic form of selfhood, and perhaps because it suggests a maternal voice whose presence in that space was both
wanted and avoided. Language in Beckett is built over and shaped by
older patterns of organization and musical rhythms, as well as earlier
voices.

> And if I went on listening to that far whisper, silent long since and which I
> still hear, I would learn still more, about this. But I will listen no longer, for
> the time being, to that far whisper, for I do not like it, I fear it. But it is not a
> sound like the other sounds, that you listen to, when you choose, and can
> sometimes silence, by going away or stopping your ears, no, but it is a sound
> which begins to rustle in your head, without your knowing how, or why. It's
> with your head you hear it, not your ears, you can't stop it, but it stops itself,
> when it chooses. It makes no difference therefore whether I listen to it or not,
> I shall hear it always, no thunder can deliver me, until it stops. (*Molloy*, 40)

Perloff may object that too much attention has been given here to *Molloy* and not enough to Beckett's later prose pieces such as *How It Is,* which
she pays more attention to. But the space of the latter continues that of the
former except that now it is more radically minimal; the regression to a

primitive phenomenology is more thoroughly made. The narrator is crawling through mud with only a sack, and he comes on another self lying in the mud and attempts to communicate, through a conditioned learning process that is a form of torturing the other. The sack may be treated as what object-relations theorists call a transitional object, something that is for the young child both self and not self and a stage on the way to a proper engagement with objects.

> no the truth is this sack I always said so this sack for us here is something more than a larder than a pillow for the head than a friend to turn to a thing to embrace a surface to cover with kisses something far more we don't profit by it in any way any more and we cling to it I owed it this tribute. (*How It Is*, 66)

In that space there is a confused coming together of movements and voices, without a well-articulated grammatical field to set things in stable positions relative to one another.

> rags of life in the light I hear and don't deny don't believe don't say any more who is speaking that's not said any more it must have ceased to be of interest but words like now before Pim no no that's not said only mine my words mine alone one or two soundless brief moments all the lower no sound when I can that's the difference great confusion. (*How It Is*, 21)

The narrating voice is struggling toward a conception of a more complex grammatical-positional field, so that matters can be more stably ordered and a distinction made between the self and its interchangeable position within a larger system of moves. The narrator imagines different ways the larger space it occupies might be syntactically constituted, with individuals moving in a systematic way to new positions, new pairings, different combinatorial possibilities. He theorizes about the various ways the different bodies might be circulating in order to end up in the different combinations. There is even, rarely, a suggestion that the alternation between one and two, between the self alone and the self in a couple, might develop into a triadic relation with the narrator lying between two other bodies lying in the mud, such that A has the relationship to B that B has to C. But these primitive attempts at a structuralist solution fail, and the narrator is either alone murmuring in the mud or in an ambiguous, often sadistic pairing. The questions and answers that appeared to go back and forth between two turn out ultimately, it seems, to be just a dialogue of the self with itself.

alone in the mud yes the dark yes sure yes panting yes someone hears me no
no one hears me no murmuring sometimes yes when the panting stops yes
not at other times no in the mud yes to the mud yes my voice yes mine yes
not another's no mine alone yes sure yes when the panting stops yes on and
off yes a few words yes a few scraps yes that no one hears no but less and
less no answer LESS AND LESS yes. (*How It Is*, 146)

It is worth recalling that two of Beckett's favorite philosophers were
Nicolas de Malebranche and Arnold Geulincx. Their conceptions of
human activity are perhaps more psychologically than philosophically interesting, in the way they make one's bodily movements seem so alien, so
disconnected from one's own mental life, and in the way God has to step
in to secure any sort of contact between oneself and others. In these
philosophies one does not even have power to make one's own body move
or to have physical contact with others; the feeling of experiencing such
contact must be implanted from a distance, by God. Someone today who
finds such philosophies attractive may be expressing distortions or even
pathologies in his sense of self and of others. With regular communication
impossible in *How It Is*, the narrator must attempt to establish a dialogue
with patterns of blows that, in the reinforcement necessary for learning
what they mean, turn quite sadistic. It rather goes to the painful core of
the attempt by a self, poorly equipped for the task for some reason, to establish itself in relation to the world and to other selves. So Beckett is
rather like Merrill and Ashbery, at least according to the general shape of
the narrative I have been developing. Perloff's narrative is insensitive to
what is going on in his work.

NEW HISTORICISM AND
CULTURAL STUDIES

In the schema put forward in chapter 1 the radical linguistic turn, after it had thinned out both the world and the space of subjectivity, might itself be trumped by the cultural studies turn, for which all significant determinacy is a projective effect of, in Foucault's terms, social regimes of discourse/power. Rather than looking at the structuring and deconstructing machineries of language itself, we will see all representations as having their meaning through the ways they circulate within, as well as expressing and affecting, the power systems of a culture. We will think of Shakespeare's work, for example, as a site of circulation and exchange where the power relations associated with various cultural representations are being negotiated and renegotiated. Every reading is then an acquiescence in, or a resistance to, those patterns of circulation and especially their harmful effects on those who are marginalized or powerless.

Before more general discussion of the cultural studies model, I want to look at some work by Stephen Greenblatt, one of the strong influences on the practice of reading literary texts in relation to configurations of social power. Greenblatt has called his work "new historicism" or "cultural poetics", and I will consider here some of his writings in *Shakespearean Negotiations.*[1] One of his essays, "Shakespeare and the Exorcists," is on *King Lear.*[2] Greenblatt is less interested in the intrinsic power of the drama and more in the way it gains power through its importing of parts of another text: Samuel Harsnett's *A Declaration of Egregious Popish Impostures,* an attack on exorcisms performed by English Catholic priests. Greenblatt sees that these exorcisms were a matter of social energy and conflict. The rite itself had great theatrical power, and the charismatic display of the priest, supposedly reflecting the supernatural power of the Catholic Church's hidden economy of saints and salvation, could easily be seen by Protestant England as disruptive and worrisome. Shakespeare in *Lear* has Edgar disguise himself as someone under demonic possession, and in that disguise Edgar uses some of the names and forms of activity that Harsnett had described in his attack on impostors who feigned such possession. So there is between the two texts a copying of the behavior described and a representation of it as fake; and the social energy attached to the rite can supposedly accrue to the play through that mimesis. Yet it is hard to see that Greenblatt has gained what he needed here. He wants to give us, as he says, "insight into the half-hidden cultural transactions through which great works of art are empowered."[3] Yet he seems to be employing a crude model of that means of empowerment: if something that has a certain social energy or charisma to it is transported across the border into the space of a play, then that play will take on a corresponding, though perhaps not equal, energy. Greenblatt gives, as one significant example of the "circuitous channels through which social energy could be circulated," the transport of objects "with a high symbolic valence," namely items and vestments taken from Catholic rituals and used in theatrical performances. (*Shakespearean Negotiations*, 9)

But even brief reflection indicates that this is not generally the way the economy of theatrical value works. Suppose we take an item that great social energies gather around, such as a movie star or celebrity or, in a different manner, the topic of abortion. It is likely that most efforts to transport that item into a drama would fall extremely flat, or at least would not succeed as drama. The social energy of what is imported does very little to make a play come alive; what matters is rather how the playwright puts things together, how he or she arranges linguistic items, the drama of confrontations, and so forth. One can take the most banal cultural item absent of social energy, such as a conversation after a dull faculty party, and turn it into a scene of stunning literary energy (if you happen to be Edward Albee).

Greenblatt, as one might put it, is a poor economist, even as the new historicists take over a wide range of economic metaphors. One might recall here Marx's claim, quoting Engels, that Adam Smith was the Luther of political economy.[4] What Marx meant was that both Smith and Luther replace a fetishistic, magical, externalist notion of value with one based on what the individual makes through his/her own labor. It is interesting that Greenblatt, who specializes in the Renaissance and has written extensively about Spanish exploration of the New World, seems to adopt what Marx considered a mercantilist and fetishist notion of economic value. The Spaniards, said Marx, thought that the way to a wealthy economy was to take what already had the marks of wealth, namely gold and silver, and to transport it from the exterior space of the New World into the interior space of Spain. That seems Greenblatt's model for an economy of literature: one imports into the space of the text what already has the markings of social energy. Marx congratulates Smith on seeing that it is the skilled application of labor to items not valuable in themselves that produces value. The same, of course, is true of the writing of literature: it is mostly a value-added economy whose value comes from the complex arrangements into which a writer puts items that may have little value on their own. As I argued in chapter 1, there are certain characteristics of literary space, when the writing is successful, that make it highly charged and that give energy to items that cross over the threshold into it. But the ideology of literary criticism today strongly favors an externalist account and Greenblatt's story does so as well. He does not deny that social energy, like economic value, may be amplified as it moves across boundaries, such as the boundaries of a text or play. But when he sets his guiding conception down, in the introductory essay of *Shakespearean Negotiations*, the talk is not of such means of amplification but of borrowings, lendings, crossings, and exchanges. So it is importation from an external source that matters for literary intensity, rather than an internal putting together or the compression of different phenomenological and ritual spaces into a single charged atmosphere.

Perhaps there are some phenomena today, such as certain art installations, that straightforwardly import cultural items already possessing a built-in cultural energy, because of political interest or shock value. Such installations may indeed seem sites where various cultural representations have happened to stick, with the energy generated by what those items are elsewhere, either in the social field of power or in the workings of academic theory, and with the artist doing little to make a semi-autonomous charged field where incidental items take on a vivid life. So Greenblatt's account actually may fit certain forms of art and theater, especially today. If an artist puts a crucifix in a vial of urine (an actual case), then surely the energy the art project has, if any, is due to the fact that the crucifix has great cultural energy elsewhere. But that is hardly what Shakespeare is about in suggesting an exorcism in *Lear*.

Greenblatt unfairly pictures his opponent here as holding a straw-man position that few would want to defend. He presents himself, in the introduction to the Shakespeare volume, as arguing for such claims as that "there is no expressive essence that can be located in an aesthetic object complete unto itself, uncontaminated by interpretation, beyond translation or substitution"; that "there can be no appeals to genius as the sole origin of the energies of great art"; that "there is no originary moment, no pure act of untrammeled creation."[5] But who could possibly occupy the opponent's position in such a debate? Who would ever believe in that degree of isolation and noncontamination by otherness? Who would want to support that magical account of artistic originality? If one wants to present literary space as a privileged arena where certain ritual transactions occur only because that space is intensified and differentiates itself from surrounding social spaces, one need hardly entertain notions of a pure creation ex nihilo by an autonomous artistic genius.

For Greenblatt, influenced as he is by Marx and Foucault, the circulating energies of most interest are those having to do with social and discursive power, with the ways that cultural representations play a role in its increase and decrease, its subversion and legitimation, its exchanges and negotiations, its changing constellations. For example, in the essay "Invisible Bullets," Greenblatt tries to use an external text, Thomas Harriot's report on the colonization of Virginia, to illuminate Shakespeare's Henry plays and the strategies of power they illuminate.[6] That report contains an account of the religious beliefs of the Indians, an account that is secular and disenchanting in that it sees Indian religion "as a set of beliefs manipulated by the subtlety of the priests to help instill obedience and respect for authority" (26). But once that explanation of Indian religious belief is in view, then one is not far, says Greenblatt, from the hypothesis that Christian religious belief is of the same sort. So the text threatens to undermine itself, as it presents both a story of the triumph of English Christian colonizers and the means to falsify that story. In addition the report talks of an epidemic disease that overcame the Indians as showing the power of Christianity, but the Indian chief also fears that further colonists will come, invisible and without bodies, who will shoot invisible bullets into the Indians and kill them. Greenblatt again sees this as a case of the text threatening to subvert itself. He says "that the theory that would ultimately triumph over the moral conception of epidemic disease was already present, at least metaphorically, in the conversation" (36–37), that is, in the chief's reference to invisible bullets, which to Greenblatt suggest germs. Greenblatt then goes on to find the same pattern in Shakespeare's texts: in seeming to defend the ultimate legitimacy of Henry V as King of England they generate a much more subversive picture and also contain that subversion.

How much does this comparison of texts teach us? Harriot's report and the Henry plays seem actually to have little in common. What Greenblatt takes to be the common feature, their movement of self-undermining, seems hardly present in the Virginia narrative. Greenblatt's hypothesis, when he argues that the text is self-undermining, is that whenever one gives a disenchanting view of another's religion one risks admitting that the same disenchanting view might apply to one's own religion. Yet the history of the world is a history of those who had not the slightest trouble giving a secularized, naturalizing account of the religions of others while feeling their own to be invulnerable to such an account. (The same is often true of nonreligious beliefs. To read anthologies of contemporary literary theory is to see critics remarkably busy at deconstructing the beliefs of others whose ideas are politically different, while remaining astonishingly smug about their own premises.) And it is far-fetched to suppose that the chief's image of ghostly colonists shooting invisible bullets makes the Virginia narrative self-undermining, simply because that image metaphorically suggests (to us!) not a religious or moral but a natural theory of epidemics. That reading seems forced on the text (the chief was not intending any such natural theory of epidemics) and was unavailable to English readers of the Virginia narrative then. Therefore it cannot be an example of strategies of subversion and containment within the text that are mirroring the strategies of monarchical power in England. So the external cultural narrative that supposedly illuminates Shakespeare's text actually does not possess the qualities that, according to Greenblatt, make it analogous to Shakespeare's. It can appear that Greenblatt had certain theoretical structures that were waiting for application and worked hard to apply them. He wanted in advance to locate in the text moments where opposites, such as subversion and justification, cross over into each other. He wanted to find the deconstructive model of the self-undermining text, and wanted also to discover some version of the Marxist reference to the self-contradictions of modern cultures, to their dialectical relations of domination and resistance, to the production of resistance as a way to justify dominance. He was determined as well to locate the structures we identify with Foucault regarding discourse and power. So he reads the Virginia narrative in order to find such patterns.

> In Harriot's text the relation between orthodoxy and subversion seems, at the same interpretive moment, to be both perfectly stable and dangerously volatile. We can deepen our understanding of this apparent paradox if we consider a second mode of subversion and its containment in Harriot's account. [35]

But why, we must ask ourselves, should power record other voices, per-
mit subversive inquiries, register at its very center the transgressions that will
ultimately violate it? [37]

Again, these lines show the patterns that contemporary theory will reward
Greenblatt for finding in the texts, but does the manner of thinking displayed in the quotations tell us much about Shakespeare's England? The
voices that were threatening to royal power then were either Puritan ones
or Catholic ones whose threat was clearly recognized as such, not the hidden messages produced by self-undermining texts about native peoples.
The Indian voices in Harriot's text were hardly very "subversive" to dominant forms of belief or "transgressions" that would ultimately "violate"
central power; the Indian chief's worry about invisible colonists with invisible bullets probably struck readers back home in England as a quaint
belief of a backward people, not as a dangerous forward-looking suggestion of a naturalizing discourse. Centuries later, after myriad instances of
explaining the religions of native peoples in secular, naturalist terms, the
British still had no trouble whatever in supposing that the God of their
own religion was real and was on their side. The mentioning of Indian
voices in Harriot had nothing to do with special strategies for the production and containment of oppositional energies; the oppositional energies
hardly appear here, and colonialism had more direct means of containment. Greenblatt's discursive need to find texts that contain operations
that would subvert them is shown, in a different essay, when he quotes
from a letter by William Strachey on what occurred when an expedition to
Virginia was marooned by a storm on Bermuda. In responding to the difficulty men of the better sort who had never worked much before "were
able twice forty eight hours together to toil with the best." The violence of
the storm, says Greenblatt in responding to this passage, "has turned Strachey's own language upside down" (149) because the lower classes have
now moved into the position of "the best," as the Romans called their aris-
tocrats. But this again is a forced reading. If one says that a certain well-off
politician can go into a working-class bar and "drink with the best," one
is hardly raising any threat to the class distinctions of society. To say that
the lower-class seamen on Bermuda were the "best" workers at building a
ship contains no ideological threat. It is rather that Greenblatt is looking
for a certain pattern of ideological subversion and containment, of texts
that seem to undermine their own values, and is willing to find such a pattern where there is little evidence for it.

Regarding Shakespeare's histories Greenblatt is not much more persuasive. He sees these texts as offering evidence that would seem to under-

mine authority and legitimacy; then this very subversion turns out to play a useful role in supporting the authority structure of England. The plays supposedly show Prince Hal's transformation from an idler with Falstaff into a legitimate king. Greenblatt claims, correctly, that Shakespeare gives us evidence that in some respects makes that ascent more questionable. In that sense, surely, Shakespeare is all about challenging and complicating our easily held beliefs. Hal can seem both genuinely friendly with the lower classes and yet also manipulative, in that he says he is learning their language in order to deal with them more effectively when he is king. Even later in his great triumph over the French, Shakespeare has a soldier mention how Henry has betrayed Falstaff, and Greenblatt shows that his excuse for slaughtering prisoners is invalid, as the order was given before he received the information that supposedly justified it. The fact that Hal might be psychologically complex, with mixed motives that he himself may not understand well, and the fact that his route to power and legitimacy might be similarly complex, with readings of that route differing as to the degree of legitimacy won, can hardly be a surprise to a reader of Shakespeare. That is precisely what he is about as a dramatist. But Greenblatt, with his grammatical model, has turned away from analyses in terms of the psychology or ethical phenomenology of the self. Rather he must find here pattern-generating grammars internal to cultural discourse itself, having to do with representations as counters in a strategy game of positions and moves, where one strategy deployed by this particular cultural grammar is to maintain power by appearing to subvert it. (For the literary theorist the most satisfying patterns generated by such internal discursive machineries will be those that seem to match structures of rhetorical tropes.) So it will turn out that Shakespeare's plays supposedly mirror the power strategies of the English monarchy. There is in both, Greenblatt says, a theatricalization of power, with the following important similarity. In the theater the audience is asked to make up, with its imagination, for the obvious deficiencies of the production: the stage may give the merest suggestion of a forest or of a shipwreck, and adolescent males may be playing adult female roles. In a similar manner, says Greenblatt, the theatrical performance of the monarchy has many weaknesses, and the audience, the citizens of England, must make up for that gap between real and ideal.[7] In doing so they become invested in that performance, so that its very weaknesses turn out to be a source of strength. Many moments occur in Shakespeare's presentation that would seem to delegitimate Hal's procession to kinghood. But those very subversive moments are generated in a manner that ultimately contains them, in a narrative that, with the help of the audience, is supportive of Hal's kingship.

Whatever may be the case with an audience's investments in Prince Hal, it seems doubtful that the English monarchs at the time were engaged in such a strategy. They would have preferred less attention to all the fragile contingencies behind their rise to power; they were not in the business of giving lots of evidence for their own moral weaknesses and illegitimacy as a way of forcing English citizens, thought of theatrically, to deploy their imaginative investments in supporting the given order. (That is what Greenblatt's analogy with Shakespeare on Prince Hal would suppose.) Monarchs want to appear as having their positions inevitably, not as the result of a contingent and problematic causal path, as if showing the latter were a way of releasing subversive energies that might then be contained. And it is quite complicated and risky to assume that an audience of citizens will use their imaginations to make up for any differences between real and ideal; they are just as likely, especially if influenced by the Protestant Reformation, to suppose that the gap in question is a reason for revolt—as in the case of the Pope, whose great theatricalization of power hardly convinced the European audience to make up with their performance-attending imaginations for the serious weaknesses in the church. (Here again we see a result of the theological model. It is quite possible that allowing oppositional structures in a society will release energies that might be more dangerously expressed. But just as God's relating to the world must become a self-relating, so for Greenblatt the text or the monarchy must be seen not as responding to oppositional energies but as generating them out of its own resources, in an internal discursive activity that projects otherness as a feature of its own logic.) Greenblatt's work here also shows the danger of supposing that the literary theorist's contribution to social history, instead of the patient investigation of causal processes by the historian, will be to look for an oscillating or crossing of literary phenomena over to the world and vice versa. It is far too tempting, and therefore dangerous as a matter of scholarship, to project those literary patterns, such as a play's theatricalizing of oppositional energies, onto the political scene, while letting that projection escape further empirical scrutiny.

There is a better way of stating Shakespeare's interests here. Recall the earlier description of Daniel Dennett's multiple-drafts model of consciousness. A good poet remains open to the work of those earlier drafts, to the linguistic possibilities that, in normal usage, have been erased by the final draft that appears. A culture as a whole might be thought of as going through such a continuous process of forming and revising competing drafts about itself. Like the good poet, Shakespeare is alert to that multiplicity and competition that the final cultural draft usually writes over and erases. The final draft here would be the one that celebrates unambiguously Hal's rise to a legitimate kingship. But Shakespeare keeps the other drafts alive as well. He is less interested in supporting or subverting power than he is in indulging his powerful intellectual curiosity. The history plays are not rituals of producing and containing subversion, not the working out of that particular discursive grammar, but rather explorations of the complicated nature of political legitimacy. To present here an analogy, when a tropical storm starts from the west coast of Africa it may turn out that extremely small factors determine whether it eventually heads as a hurricane across the Caribbean or, instead, goes up the Atlantic coast. For Shakespeare there are small factors that might have made the matter of Hal's legitimacy as king go either way. It is interesting to examine how his rule did indeed end up consolidating and legitimizing itself when, given his father's questionable route to power and certain points about his own character, matters might have turned out differently. It is not surprising that along the way there are fragile moments that might have become hinge points for a narrative with a different ending but did not. What is of interest here is a matter of a rich psychology, of a complex narrative of ethical self-formation. As different as Greenblatt is from de Man, he is like him in strongly devaluing that space of psychology and ethics, in favor of a space constituted by the projections of a grammatical-rhetorical cultural machinery.

Returning to "Shakespeare and the Exorcists," while it has some of the same flaws it also has important insights into why Shakespeare's plays are powerful. Yet these insights offer less support for Greenblatt's externalist, "social energy" model of literary space than for the psycho-metaphysical model of that space that has been defended here since chapter 1. Consider the way the exorcism rite mentioned by Harsnett is used in *Lear*. Edgar stages something vaguely like an exorcism when he sees his father, Gloucester, wandering blind and tormented near the coast. (Actually it is Edgar, not Gloucester, who has been exhibiting the symptoms of possession.) Gloucester wants to be led to a cliff where he can cast himself off. Edgar does not reveal himself but takes Gloucester to a flat space, lies about how the scene beneath appears, and lets his father leap to what Gloucester assumes will be his death. After Gloucester falls only a few feet Edgar, pretending to be still another individual, says that Gloucester has fallen from a great height and has been miraculously saved by God. The figure who had been with him on the top of the cliff, Edgar says, had flown off in the manner of a demon.

This scene is indeed a powerful one, but how much of its energy is borrowed from the social energy that exorcism might have had in the surrounding culture? We are profoundly moved because of the situation that

Gloucester has come to, the terrible reversal in his life, the emotional response of the son at seeing him this way, the willingness of the son to come up with such a theatrical performance to save his father, the contrast between the tragedy of the scene and the comedy of Gloucester thinking he is leaping to his death and falling only a few feet, and so forth. A theatergoer in Shakespeare's time might have been moved even if he had no belief whatever or interest in exorcism, if, for him, no social energy or charisma came along with its representation. (In the film *Tender Mercies* the Robert Duvall character undergoes a baptism by immersion. That the scene contributes to the power of the film is due to the overall arrangement of images and narrative in the film, not to the imported social energy of the ritual. Many viewers of the film might well have looked with irritation or condescension at similar baptisms presented on evangelist television shows.) Once again Greenblatt ignores the obvious, the rich psychological texture of the scene against a metaphysical backdrop showing the fragility of selfhood, in favor of an externalist account of circulating cultural items.

Nevertheless, Greenblatt is clearly onto something here when he speaks of the relations between theater and ritual, Protestant and Catholic. Shakespeare arranges the play as a whole as a ritual, a metaphysical one, where the rhythmic power of the lines allows us to hold steady as a space opens out before us that is extraordinarily bleak, where the chance events of a meaningless universe take human errors and inflate their consequences in pain and suffering, where decades of familial closeness break apart into hatreds. We are not, in watching this, hoping for an exorcism ritual that would magically cleanse this world and take away its difficulties; we want instead a linguistic, theatrical ritual whose containing forms give us the courage to let that bleak space open out, to comprehend it for what it is, and to accept it as the way of the universe. Many dramas will perform this function without their mentioning *within* the plot any particular religious or cultural rites, so as to borrow their social energy. If the ritual we want is of that sort, then the space of the play is metaphysical in the sense described in chapter 1.

Greenblatt is correct, surely, to insist on the intertextual nature and the social constructedness of any literary text. But whatever enters the Shakespearean space gets its power and value for the most part from what that space imparts to it, as with Vermeer and Proust. As a reader of literature or a watcher of films one has great interest in how that mysterious process takes place, how a space emerges that gives such moment to everything that enters it. Yet both deconstructionist and new historicist studies seem precisely designed to make it impossible to ask and answer this question, since doing so requires looking at a text or a film as having a certain internal integrity, as forming a charged space different from what surrounds it, such that the arrangement of words or images in just that particular pattern is what matters. Greenblatt's textual economics resembles the developing global economy that in circulating commodities across all borders makes differences between being inside a certain space and being outside it less significant. Having a literary text no longer form its own particular aesthetic space would then be like the sort of globalization that would eventually erase the Japanese cultural space or the French cultural space as having an integrity of its own.

Greenblatt does make the proper point that Shakespeare's plays can be powerful because of the feeling they give us of loss, of an acknowledgment that the rituals that once carried us have been emptied out. In that sense he is right to connect Shakespeare's theatrical space with a world in transition from premodern Catholic rituals to the more rigorous modernity of Protestantism, with the latter's stronger barriers against regression to those premodern forms of experience.[8] But in fact what the theater is thus capturing, even on Greenblatt's description, is less a matter of social conflict than of the psycho-metaphysical space of literature. Theater can have a special energy in such transitional spaces, as with the dramas of ancient Greece, when there was an increasingly demanding individuation from which the ecstatic power of communal rites tried to offer relief. Lear stands in some respects both for the world of Catholic England and for its Celtic past, and he is powerless against the more self-consciously strategic thinking of Edmund. The more modern attitude thins out those earlier worlds until they have little effective power and are ready to disappear. Greenblatt gives us the wrong sense of that loss when he speaks of the "intimation of a fullness that we can savor only in the conviction of its irremediable loss" and then quotes the Shakespearean lines that "we that are young / Shall never see so much, nor live so long" (128). Those lines refer in the play to a past of enormous suffering rather than to a fullness we profoundly regret losing.

I have claimed that it is the entire play as a ritual that is at stake here; and one is tempted by the idea that Shakespeare does not so much produce an effective metaphysical ritual for us as feign one, in the theatrical performance. Then like Edgar, with the audience (ourselves) in the role of Gloucester, he tells us that we have been miraculously saved when all along we have jumped just a few feet. We have come to a time when our culture, unlike many ancient ones, fails to offer ceremonies of vital, satisfying Dionysiac regression or rites, such as the Catholic communion, that supposedly join us in a magical way with Christ. Theater then becomes a performance that mimes such rites but cannot repeat them. It exists precisely in a transitional space where certain ways of being connected to the universe are being lost, and where an increased self-consciousness is offered as compensation. Greenblatt's model is too much a sociological one; when he discusses ceremonies, such as the exorcisms that Harsnett criticizes, they are moves in a power game among the Church of England, the Puritans, and some persecuted Catholic priests. So he is less sensitive to how Edgar's theatricalized ritual in the play has as its arena of operation not so much a territory of strategic negotiation as an empty psycho-metaphysical space opened out as the characters roam the desolate fields in a storm, where "unaccommodated man is no more but such a poor, bare, forked animal," where the regressive pull of death, the longing to give up the pains of individuation, is strong.[9] Shakespeare sees the metaphysical bleakness that must be the lot of the world, taken on its own, when its sacramental energies are radically withdrawn from it and concentrated in the inner self and its powers of construction. Eventually things can mean no more than what we make them mean, and our power to make them mean, in a world where natural and unconscious powers and the blind operations of chance swirl through us, is extremely limited.

Greenblatt is correct, then, when he uses *Lear* to describe a double space of both modern disenchantment and an elegiacal sense of holding back in a world that is being lost. (Chapter 1 speaks of the importance of literary space as transitional, regressive-disenchanted, and translational.) Shakespeare, he says, presents the orthodox view of the time, as in Harsnett, that exorcisms are theatrical fakes. But then Shakespeare places his sympathies with the character most closely associated with exorcism, Edgar, who might be seen as representing Catholic England over against the illegitimate (Protestant) brother who has usurped power. So Shakespeare seems to situate himself in such a transitional space, where one can no longer believe in the same way in the Catholic rituals but where one can still find satisfaction in weaker, theatrical versions of them. Various conflicts about social power and its distribution, about the social energies that express that power, will disappear over time. But insofar as a playwright stages the sort of space described here and in chapter 1, the play may have a lasting power through long periods of history. Greenblatt in some respects sees this, but the ideological paradigms of cultural studies badly distort his attempt to express it. As with the linguistic-postmodern model, with its radical linguistic turn, the cultural studies model flattens literary space into a site of strategic negotiation and loses its richer psychological context and its ways of being supported on less transparent, somewhat regressive forms of ordering.

Literary theory has recently tended to consolidate itself as a branch of cultural studies or sociology.[10] There is less work in graduate schools that might style itself as deconstructionist and more that presents itself straightforwardly as social history. Under the influence of Foucault and Greenblatt, feminism and Marxism, one looks at literary texts as social actions embedded in large social processes. One might study the circumstances in which the text was produced, the conditions for determining what got published and what did not, the social meaning of different publishing venues, the ideological effects of the work on readers, the history that led to a work's canonization or disappearance. Even more, one might see literary works as indicators of, and causal factors in, a range of social processes that have great extraliterary significance. Among these are the culture's ways of forming and habituating individual selves; the construction of gender roles; the conceptualizing of race; a training in styles of innerness and subjectivity; the formation of national and group identities; industrialization and consumerism; imperialism, immigrants, and globalization; and the articulation of space into public and private zones. The working out of these cultural matters can be seen in the literary works that we find exceptional, but it is notable that they will appear just as surely in popular but mediocre novels and poems, as well as in diaries, letters, self-help manuals, popular magazines, and court documents. Indeed the exceptional literary texts may be, from a social-sciences standpoint, poor choices in this sort of investigation. The story about the social construction of different phenomena may be skewed or hidden in these works by a higher level of intellectual complexity, by the writer's self-conscious manipulation of social ideas, or by the writer's idiosyncratic compensating for problems of self-formation. Additionally there is the model of Foucault, who said that issues about knowledge and subjectivity should be studied not by reading the works of great philosophers but by reading such materials as medical manuals; rules for the organizing of schools, hospitals, and prisons; guides written by experts to help ordinary people achieve physical, sexual, and mental health; regulations for disciplining bodies through exercise regimes, sleeping arrangements, organizing of the day; and so forth. So there will be little interest in the literary as such, or in the texts that express it most powerfully.

One might simply, as a social historian, investigate all these matters from an impartial standpoint. But in recent literary theory there are often political reasons for finding some social processes of more compelling interest: the ways groups are defined over against others who are then marginalized and delegitimated; the way a social order will generate energies and anxieties subversive to it and will also have means of defusing and containing those energies; the ways that groups oppressed by the social order find rhetorical and political sites for resisting it. It is crucial to this kind of interest that one sees society as a whole as having "multiple drafts." These different drafts, often incoherent, are competing to work their way into the culture's dominant speaking positions and into its self-definition. Instead of looking for the unifying forces that might form a culture into a larger "we" one looks for indications of conflict and contestation; one breaks down apparently unified groups and concepts into multiple competing versions. And one uses social-science techniques to show that what appear to be universal and necessary patterns of social life are historical and contingent; they become denaturalized as we see how they might have been different, how they depend on chance and on the circumstances of power.

With this destabilizing of larger wholes there is an interest in less organic and less unifying patterns of cultural formation. One sees the constellations that form in society as shifting and temporary, as involving many sites of negotiation, as showing how socially constructed boundaries are permeable, unreliable, and at risk. One might well get a better sense of these arrangements not by looking at the individuals and works most central to the dominant constellation, but rather by looking at those places where interesting negotiations of sameness and difference, belonging and not belonging, are being worked out. And so one will investigate individuals and works situated in more than one area, on both literal and metaphorical borders, where speaking positions are hybrid and polyvocal. If Hegel looked for processes that formed ever more complex self-maintaining wholes, where oppositions were both intensified and resolved, the cultural studies model is anti-Hegelian. Identity and resolution at any level are never innocent, it is claimed, but involve an implicit coercion and violence, a marginalizing or exclusion of what does not seem to fit, a training of individuals in activities of accommodation and assimilation. No reading or writing can ever be ethically neutral. These are social actions that intervene, positively or negatively, in the circulation of cultural representations as these express networks of power that privilege some and devalue others.

Described in that way, the transformation of literary study into sociology and social history has evident virtues that we should not wish to do without. If we care about social justice, then we should want both scholars and students to consider the issues raised by the cultural studies model of reading. Yet if I affirm the value of the model in some respects, I also have doubts about its influence. An adequate general treatment of the topic would require far more space than is available here, but I do want to suggest, very briefly, some of the ways this skepticism might be expressed in such a longer account.

The schema from chapter 1 spoke of four levels: world, subjectivity, language, and regimes of social power. The radical linguistic turn would collapse the first two levels into itself. The radical cultural studies turn would collapse the first three levels into itself. Then world and subjectivity are emptied out and count only as projections of social power; we can no longer take seriously the notion of the self's intentional activity as bringing the world into view. Calling a statement true, therefore, will appear as one more power move that tries to privilege the statements of some and disenfranchise the statements of others, in ways that express or resist the power grids of society. Such an impoverishing of the notion of truth is unjustified, as I argued in Chapter 3. Here I want to insist not so much on that argument as on the damaging effects on scholarship of the cultural studies reduction of truth. One comes to believe that one's own statements have their value by the effects they have on the flows of representations across the cultural grid. In an almost Darwinian fashion, one tries to assure that representations favorable to oneself or to one's group or ideology reproduce themselves successfully while those of one's opponents do not.

But then one has no incentive for learning the requirements of scientific scholarship. To form one's beliefs well is to learn how to evaluate evidence; how to investigate alternative causal explanations before settling on a favored one; how to be skeptical about one's own assumptions by looking for evidence to invalidate them as well as to support them; how to be especially skeptical about conclusions in which one has an emotional investment; and how to make one's abstract concepts more precise so that their logical links to the facts under investigation are tighter and clearer. The field of literary study today can seem an investigatory space where the constraints of scholarship are by no means rigorous. No matter how much material is unearthed from archives, it seems rather easy to make it support the ideological and ethical attitudes that now serve virtually as platitudes in the discipline. The literary-theory vocabulary is unusually lenient; practitioners will be able to take any text and find in it the favored phenomena of coercive identities, subversion and containment, the discursive production of selves, the repressive structuring of conceptual boundaries that yet undermine themselves, sites of contestation and hybridity, and so forth. Claims operate in such a frictionless space, virtually immune to contrary evidence and so fully in agreement with the mindset of the discipline, that they are not part of a process that complicates and qualifies intellectual and ethical expectations. But then one settles for work that is ultimately of poor scholarly quality, that is impressionistic and ideological. The literary theorist becomes a social historian poorly trained as such, with beliefs so strongly attached to certain goals and strategies that they are not compelling to those with a more open intellectual curiosity, with a capacity to be surprised by the patterns that emerge as one studies the materials of history. To let truth be reduced to the workings of power is to give up one's best hopes for getting a wider audience, even those quite differently situated in terms of their attitudes toward the world, to share one's beliefs. As so often happens (literary space is an analogous case) the impoverishing of epistemic space is a self-impoverishing. Of course most of us do not pay sufficient attention to the demands of good argument. But the cultural studies theorist has ideological support for not doing so, and for doing something else instead.

Perhaps literary theorists will carve out a space for themselves, and claim superiority to social historians, in the following manner. They supposedly understand the theoretical work that has gone to destabilize notions of reality, truth, representation, and subjectivity. So they are ready, as perhaps the social historian is not, to apply that theoretical expertise across the culture as a whole, to all the various ways that the culture raises up a realm of representations, especially its self-representings. And since they see the reading of a text as a far more complicated process than others do, they have an advantage if one sees all aspects of the culture, including the behaviors of those within it, as texts to be read. But if the argument in chapter 3 is correct, then what the literary theorist thus brings to the table will be of much less value than supposed. A proper understanding of metaphysics and semantic theory shows that there is less of this deconstructive destabilizing of notions of truth and representation than the literary theorist may argue for.

Or perhaps (in a different attempt at claiming a special role) the literary critic will seem well placed to perform a certain crisscross of vocabularies, so that the literary text is defined in economic or social terms while the social history background is defined in textual or rhetorical terms. One might suppose, for example, not only that such notions as debt, interest, the gold standard, inflation, deficit spending, counterfeiting, and the like have useful analogues in the actual operations of literary texts but also that drawing out the analogies somehow illumines both sides. Or one might hold that social-historical phenomena might be usefully described in terms of literary tropes such as metonymy or anaphora, or that Columbus-era expeditions to find lost cities of gold are implicitly commenting on the inability of language to achieve reference. But it is difficult to see how a strained attempt at such analogies will lead to an illumination of real causal relations able to augment the work of the social historian. (There is a way in which the literary theorist may have a special function in studying social history. Individuals will often perceive the world in terms of categories and schemes they have been trained in through the reading of literary texts. Presumably the literary theorist can show this happening better than others can.)

The cultural studies theorist is right to insist that our concepts often unify the phenomena being investigated more than they ought to. But we also have to guard against a fetishizing of difference. Consider how literary theorists often take for granted a notion of selfhood far too plastic, in the way the self is supposed to be a result of social construction. A form of subjectivity will appear as a temporary construct of quite local and narrow circumstances. But the radical turn that would support so strong a notion of social construction is illegitimate; there are richer, more stable notions of subjectivity that should not be reduced to the changing flows of social power in this fashion. In choosing the more radical conception the literary theorist loses hold of what makes literary texts matter over time, and also of what provides a useful site of resistance to regimes of social power. To explain further, it is easy to see, first of all, that some of our acts of supposing features to apply universally, of finding sameness across a field of differences, can be dangerous and coercive; for example the Spaniards' universalizing of their Christianity had dire consequences for native Americans. But after we recognize the force of that claim, we have to recognize as well that claims of sameness are also accurate. Humans are astonishingly alike in their genetic legacy, and it is more likely, we are told, that two randomly picked humans will resemble each other in this manner than two chimpanzees from nearby regions of Africa will be similar. Even though brain architecture is a matter not just of genetically programmed engineering but also of culturally influenced neuronal connections made after birth, future science is not likely to support a strongly parochialist, radically social-constructionist account of being a human self. It is not just that humans' brain architecture is so much alike. Humans share a knowledge that they will die; a long period after birth of intimacy and dependence that is unusual in the animal kingdom and from which we must eventually separate ourselves in order to move into adulthood; the need for strong attachments and the feeling of grief and loneliness when these are lost; emotions of shame and guilt as we understand the meaning of our actions; pleasure in the competence and power that language and intelligence bring to us; a need to employ certain cognitive processes in order to handle our surroundings; a rich array of activities of self-concern and self-awareness; and the special feeling of being a conscious human self maneuvering through the world. When Gen. William Westmoreland said regarding Vietnam that Asians do not experience the death of loved ones as painfully as Americans do, he might have been seen as acknowledging cultural differences, but he was foolishly and tragically and reprehensibly wrong. De Man may argue that our psychological states are simply linguistic projections, but that claim, we saw earlier, is nonsense.

Some of the experiences that literary texts make important are not shared universally, perhaps, but rather by those cultures in which development and reflection have made individuation and self-consciousness more intense and burdensome, and in which social training produces the sort of self for which linguistic and symbolic compensation takes over for more instinctual gratification. Such cultures are not just the modern ones of the West but surely also include ancient ones; see Horkheimer and Adorno on the Greeks in *Dialectic of Enlightenment*.[11] No premodern culture can any longer hope to resist that intensifying of reflection, individuation, and self-consciousness. So even if we have reasons to resist certain humanist claims about the universalizable character of being human, we are not wrong to expect considerable psychological sameness across different cultures. Social construction certainly produces great differences: the sixteenth-century Lutheran self is hardly the same as the Japanese samurai or the contemporary postmodern individual. But in spite of the great role of cultural differences there are biologically grounded and culturally reinforced aspects of human selfhood that allow for legitimate identifications across times and across cultures. These are crucial for the continuing value we assign to certain works of literature. (This point is an aspect of the larger claim here that a phenomenology of self-to-world relations does not reduce either to language or to practices of social power.)

This matter is crucial not only for literature but also for the ongoing hopes proper to the cultural studies model. One problem with cultural analysis in the style of Foucault is that the discursive systems seem so powerful (in what I have called a theological manner) that there seems no point that escapes them sufficiently to be a site of resistance to them. Therefore it is good news, rather than a discouraging surrender to determinism, to discover that the ways our brains were formed by evolution give them an already rich content when social systems attempt to program them. Fortunately for us that content is diverse enough that we have a sophisticated machinery for responding to the world flexibly, instead of being blindly driven by a few programmed responses. But one consequence is that there are some social systems that humans can never be satisfied within; that is a minimal starting point, then, for social change. Cultural studies practitioners make social construction so powerful that they remove the very condition that is needed to make resistance to social forms more than illusory. Only a less radical linguistic or sociological turn, one that keeps the structures of the experiencing, self-forming self in play, can show why we are not plastic projections of social power.

An example from Greenblatt shows how contemporary criticism tends to overstate the parochial character of our conceptions of the self. In speaking of the story of the return of Martin Guerre, he suggests that notions of self-identity were quite different at that time, that whether or not it was the same person who returned may not have been as absolute a matter as in our day, that modern legal and cultural forms of defining self-identity, of the sort that would lead to psychoanalysis, were just beginning then.[12] But that is a strange hypothesis to form about a culture that had strong Augustinian notions of sin and salvation and for which everything depended on what happened eventually to one's immortal soul rather than to someone else's, as no one else could replace one at the Last Judgment and one's sins adhered with absolute determinacy to one's own soul and not to another's. The villagers or magistrates in the Guerre case were very different from us, Greenblatt claims. None could even deploy the notion of a biological individuality that Guerre possessed in having a body, such that if they could have figured out the continuity of that body they would have known whether the individual in question was Guerre. Nor did they have, he says, the notion of a soul with an identity expressed in continuity of subjective experience, in the feel of being oneself that spreads over the passage of a life.

Greenblatt begins with plausible claims: that the sort of psychic life Freud was uncovering in middle-class Viennese depended on modern identity-formation and should not be read into Europeans of several centuries earlier; and that how we think of ourselves as selves is strongly shaped by how our culture trains us to think. Then he strongly exaggerates the degree to which psychic identity and body-based individuality for Guerre's villagers were different from our own. To the believing Christian of that time it made all the difference whose body the outward signs of the church's sacraments were performed on, and whether the self one was conscious of at the moment of death was the same self baptized many decades earlier. To feel the Black Death invading one's body was to know whose conscious life on earth would soon be ending, and one might at that time look back to a childhood seen unambiguously as one's own. The villagers may have been epistemically limited in treating Guerre, but they would not have doubted that there was an individuality and a psychic continuity to which God had access. (There are philosophy thought experiments, often outlandish, that would make psychic continuity less determinate, but they are not relevant here). We could go back to the ancient world as well and find ascetics and gnostics, heroes and Stoic slaves, whose concern with the continuing experience of the self, over a whole life, was richer than Greenblatt is willing to assign to the villagers around Guerre. One sees here that the new historicist's talk of historicizing cultural matters, against essentialist readings, is not seriously meant. Greenblatt is happy to apply to self-identity in Guerre's time, without friction, precisely those topics that are most valued in contemporary cultural studies: negotiations, bodies, strategies, the social construction of self, transactions, non-totalizing attitudes, shifting and constructed identities, institutions, economics. It is deployment today of these notions that matters, not their degree of fit with the lives of early modern villagers. It is today's academic discounting of phenomenology and subjectivity, in favor of external institutional and discursive relations, that controls Greenblatt's discussion here, not a curiosity about what those situated differently in history were like.

To talk about sameness in this way is not to deny important differences. For example, the model of literary space defended here is at least weakly linked to an object-relational story of self-formation, and self-formation in the human species seems closely tied to gender. It ought to make some difference whether the process of separation-individuation occurs between those of the same gender or not, and whether the transition to a positional-structural identification assigns a male or a female role in the triadic field. So perhaps this model of literary space does capture a structure that extends more widely across time and space than the cultural studies model would grant, joining Aeschylus, Shakespeare, Melville, Proust, Beckett, and Cormac McCarthy (and Li Po, Tu Fu, and Matsuo Bashō) in spite of the substantial differences among them. But perhaps it is also the case that this structure has been designed over time in relation to the psychic needs of males. Perhaps not all men but rather those men who were still obsessively working out issues of separation and individuation, because of some level of difficulty in achieving these, hijacked the sphere of culture and used cultural items, including literature, to work out those obsessions in a symbolically more satisfying way. It is quite possible that much of the work in literary criticism over the last three decades will come to seem empty since it is determined by ideological drives little controlled by considerations of evidence and inference. But the case with feminism is different. It is a genuine revolution in the history of thought, and we do not yet know how narrow and limited our previous conceptions of literature will come in the future to appear. It is certainly a plausible claim that the defense of literature in this book has serious gender-related limitations (and not just because the writers whose works are most familiar to me tend to be male).

The cultural studies model is also dangerous in its readiness to find rationality as something of a local construction in the interests of power. It is often said that Western rationality is a coercive power system colonizing the rest of the world or (strangely) that the National Socialists were somehow an expression of Western rationality. Reason may appear as one more social-power strategy game, one especially good at marginalizing the statements of those without power. It is true that there are processes of social rationalization that may have both good and bad effects, and evil people may use reasoning to do their evil work more effectively. But what do we mean by the demands of rationality itself? My goal of succeeding well from the point of view of reason will place strong requirements on me. I must be willing to challenge my beliefs, especially those that upbringing or self-interest or political or emotional sensibility makes most attractive. I must work in favor of a tolerant society, for in that sort of society I will most likely do well at an overall project of excellence as a believer, as I test out my own beliefs against those of others who see matters differently. I will be concerned with the quality of the evidence for my beliefs and willing to change those beliefs as the best available evidence changes. If rationality is understood as captured by these and similar kinds of desiderata, then it is difficult to see that it is the mere product of local configurations of power or is simply the expression of Western discursive regimes. It rather requires us to put pressure on such local configurations to see if they can be justified. In doing so we find that some claims escape their conditions of origin better than others do, as individuals try, sometimes but not always self-deceptively, to move to a point of view that leaves their more narrow interests behind.[13] Making glib statements about the parochial and dangerous nature of Western rationality, in the manner of the radical cultural studies turn, may make us less committed to those practices that we are most in need of to make a fairer world.

The appeal of the cultural studies model of literary space, to many theorists, is that it may be conducive to a society that is more reflective about its ethical failings and more attuned to matters of social justice, and to the ways that an education in reading literature might play a role in these matters. But such a claim has only a limited truth to it. There is an issue here of social recognition of those previously invisible; that is surely part of what justice requires of us. But matters are less clear once we move beyond this point. While granting that it is a moral duty of Americans to make those who are badly off better off, how this can best be done in the long run is by no means self-evident. An analogy is that goodwilled people may set up a series of flood control dams that eventually create massive damage to the environment and consequent damage to individual lives. This is a complicated world in which the unintended consequences of our actions are numerous and serious. It follows that we have to look with great care at which policies, in the long run, actually make the poor better off and which do not. The ones able to answer such questions well, to the extent that they can be answered well, will be those with a pragmatic, skeptical cast of mind. It can appear that the education encouraged by much of literary theory and cultural studies today will not likely produce that sort of mind. Rather one is surprised at times by the moral smugness of many practitioners in these fields, by the self-congratulatory reviews of recent trends in the field, the justified expectations that the audience will respond predictably to certain applause lines. Such attitudes can end up causing serious harm precisely to those who are in need of social justice. The ideological confidence that one is bringing about social justice, and that those whom one dislikes are not, has been far more prevalent in the past century than the actuality of bringing it about.

Recently another version of this model of literary space has emerged; it is called "postcolonial studies."[14] One of the strengths of this field is shared by cultural studies in general, in that we are asked to reflect more rigorously on the relation between representations and power. How one culture represents those outside it will affect how these others are treated; this is especially of concern when power is unequally distributed among different cultures, whether political and military power or, especially, the power to control the content and distribution of networks of representations. Over the past few hundred years the nations of Western Europe and North America have acquired great influence over what gets written and read and viewed by people throughout the world, and one needs to ask what the effects of that dominance are on the capacity of those not of the West to acquire dignity, recognition, and economic and cultural power. Here again, as with the cultural studies model generally, the investigation of literature will transform itself into a study of how representations of the "other" circulate through literary texts; how these are related to networks of power and dominance; how the dissemination of the canonical literature of the West may be another form of colonialism; and how choices about what to read in literature classes thus have political and economic consequences for poor people throughout the world but can also provide opportunities for an education in issues of social justice.

I strongly endorse that concern for justice, and share the postcolonial theorist's pleasure in seeing that new cultural configurations being formed across the globe are hybrid, polyvocal forms that fuse different cultural strands in new patterns while not homogenizing these sources into a unified culture. It is a pleasure to look forward to an America with many more Latino and Asian influences, for example, and many more people whose racial mixtures are a complicated enough question that racial categories weaken. But I have worries about some of the tendencies of postcolonial theory. First of all, one may be tempted by the error of confusing the desirable goal of a multicultural discursive space open to all with the notion that systems of knowledge should gather beliefs in a representative manner, that is, in the way a political party might produce a ticket representative of different segments of the population. But truth does not work like that, and thinking in that manner may make one underplay how the circulation of Western discourses around the world has often been a means of empowerment for others. In addition the nature of academic life will perhaps make the postcolonial scholar attend to the wrong sort of failures in the politics of representation. What is most important is to address those sorts of representations of others that lead to evidently harmful treatments, such as German persecution of Jews or American consigning of blacks to slavery or perpetual poverty. In fact the academic world is generally liberal, so in order to mark out a rhetorical position that has some power to it, the postcolonial critic may focus rather on the ways in which liberal stances, even when pluralist and fair-minded about cultural differences, fall short of some perfectionism regarding the representing of self-other relations. The opponent will not be the right-wing skinhead but the good liberal such as Charles Taylor.[15] So one will lose opportunities for alliances that might help those disadvantaged groups one supposedly cares for. And one's arguments may depend so much on vague deconstructionist concepts and on free-floating abstract vocabularies that it is hard to see how a rhetorical site earned in that manner can do much good for the poor of the Third World.

The postcolonial critic also tends to exaggerate, in the way that the cultural studies field generally does, the value of antiinternalist accounts of development. The claim is made, for example, that Western conceptual notions were determined over against non-Western others, so that only in the hybrid space of postcolonial studies can Westerners come to understand their own concepts. On the one hand, there is surely some truth to that claim; one should not underestimate the role the Islamic world played in the West's definition of itself, for example, and the effect on Europe of its global exploration is enormous. And it is likely that the future of global culture will be a hybrid circulating of representations from all over. But on the other hand, as one examines the Western discourses we still need to reflect on rigorously, one sees how to a considerable degree the oppositions that mattered were those internal to the West: Catholic versus Protestant,

Greek versus Latin, Germanic nations versus Romanic nations, enlightenment versus tradition, bourgeois versus aristocrat, liberalism versus con-
servatism. Much of the intellectual tradition of European modernity on
ideas such as individualism, freedom, innerness, empiricism, economics,
and political representation is a matter more of internal dialogue and development than of responses to non-Western otherness, even if Western
economic relations to (and exploitation of) the non-European world are
important. As central as Kant was to the Western notion of modernity, he
lived in a cultural backwater and was reacting far more to Descartes,
Hume, Leibniz, and Luther than to non-Western others. We have to be
careful that we do not place such a great emphasis on antiinternalist accounts, on hybridity and the border areas of shifting constellations, that
we lose hold of the kinds of intellectual and social developments that we
must understand in order to reflect on our form of life and its limits. Otherwise students may look at the circulating global representations the way
they look at clothing styles or music, and try either to be trendier than
others or to express a personal style, rather than analyzing the ideas themselves.

The final reason to worry about the effects of the cultural studies model
has to do with my purpose in writing this book. The present teaching of
literary theory, instead of providing resistance to the programming of late
capitalist culture, actually contributes to the erosion of cultural features
important to that resistance. Postmodern culture generally encourages a
thinning out, a shallowing, of any space that does not easily conform with
its own style of operation. But that is precisely why we should work at retaining those spaces that offer us complexity and depth and a quiet opening out to metaphysically and ethically richer experiences. Exceptional
works of literature offer us these experiences. But the cultural studies
model is proud of its power to dissolve all privileged textual spaces (those
in which the way particular words are arranged in a particular order matters greatly) in favor of large-scale social processes that show themselves in
all the texts of a culture. It has been one of the great hopes, and often one
of the great accomplishments, of literature that it immerses us in a space
requiring us to make our ethical identifications and investments more
complicated rather than less so. To read Conrad and George Eliot or
Hardy and James, for example, is to learn that one's readiness to make
easy moral judgments, or to identify with characters as vehicles of our
own ethical attitudes, may indicate only the naive or shallow quality of
those judgments and attitudes. By dissolving the space of literature as exceptional, in favor of discovering indicators of general social processes,

one loses the ways exceptional works of literature require us to form a more complicated selfhood. But that more complicated selfhood, and the literary spaces that train us in achieving it, are forms of resistance to the postmodern thinning out of the social world.

One might object to that argument as follows. There is a distinction that has dominated this presentation throughout. On the one side are those matters that the psychologists Winnicott and Bowlby investigate: attachment and loss; separation and individuation; grief and compensation; the requirements of self-formation and maturity; the setting of the self over against the world; and the complex identifications and investments that help form the self when one is young and that still shape the self when one is older. On the other side is the positioning of the self in the field of cultural grammars, with all the game-theory strategies and maneuvers that these grammars make possible. Obviously these two sides are not independent; the cultural grammars will affect how one handles attachment and loss. But it may seem a weakness that my treatment of literary texts has related them almost exclusively to the first of these patterns of investment. It can be a selfish luxury to ask that an important area of culture, its literature, be used to further those earlier needs of self-formation, especially when there are serious ethical questions to be raised about the consequences for social justice of the operation of our cultural discourses. An individual should eventually move beyond worries about individuation and dissolution, separation and loss, in order to look at larger social issues in an adult manner. The study of literature should move, in a similar way, beyond the areas focused on here and toward social issues of power and justice.

But one is in error in making that claim. Recall Williams's argument that seemingly regressive features of ethical life, having to do with self-formation, character, and shame, must form the larger context of a more "grammatical" form of morality if it is to make sense. A similar argument applies here. If we want to fight injustice, we need to have selves for whom things matter, rather than more shallow selves easily programmed by their culture. So a training in the use of language and literature to handle issues of self-formation and loss is crucial for any larger project of forming cultures of individuals whose lives matter to them. Notions of attachment, separation, and mourning do not apply only to private losses but also to the ways, for example, that we as a community must leave satisfying forms of premodern life behind. So one cannot easily split apart private and public functions of literature, matters of individual self-formation and matters of social justice, in order to defend a cultural studies model of reading. The kinds of selves we become through the identifications and investments allowed by exceptional literary works have important social roles to play.

More generally, the cultural studies theorist does not see how complicated the process is by which ideas develop and circulate that lead eventually to radical critiques of our forms of life. The recommendation is that we read and write with an awareness of how we are thereby supporting or resisting the role of representations in socially unjust practices. But consider how many of the ideas of cultural studies derived from Foucault and ultimately from Nietzsche. Yet Nietzsche was concerned in his reading and writing with textual energies closely associated with issues of self-formation, of private fears and archaic anxieties, of an aesthetics of self-making that could style itself as healthy and vital. He did reflect on and intervene in systems of social power and subject formation, as in his critique of Christian morality and its sense of innerness. But he did this not to increase the flow of representations less favorable, say, to sexism and colonialism, but rather to understand his own unhappiness, and his own self-formational needs, as culturally symbolic. A cultural studies theorist placed back in his day would have found him to be considering literature and art in an elitist manner, unconcerned with the marginalizing of the poor. Yet that was the manner in which emerged many ideas that cultural studies as a field finds significant. Another case is that of Melville, whose deeply personal, anxiety-driven meditations on his culture, because of powerful archaic materials in his patterns of self-formation, ultimately led to a richer critique of the patriarchy and subject formation of his time than did other works that intervened more obviously in public ethical debates. For someone interested in how representations circulate in culture, the cultural studies theorist has an astonishingly impoverished view of how representations emerge that will prove useful to ethical criticism. In teaching students to make only the more direct political readings one may be eliminating the future Nietzsches or Melvilles who might contribute novel ideas to cultural criticism in the future.

It might appear from the topics covered in the field that literary critics can play an important role today in national debates about globalism, cultural minorities, the media, and so forth. That cannot be the case in the present state of the discipline. It is not just a matter of jargon and bad writing; it is the poor quality of the arguments as such. The character of political discourse today is generally poor; politicians and reporters seem to have taken polls determining which stances are likely to be applauded and which are not, or interest groups use the media to propagandize for narrow ends. The great need is for those with a ruthless will to follow arguments through wherever they lead, to be sensitive to good reasons whether they favor one's position or not, and to look for actual distortions in the field of rational debate rather than those that ideology would identify. These are qualities, alas, that cultural studies and critical theory show little sign of developing in their practitioners.

LITERATURE AND REGRESSION, BENJAMIN, DERRIDA

One may object that the model of literary space defended in this book has the undesirable feature of encouraging regression, both psychologically and culturally. To address this issue I will further examine what I called earlier a regressive-disenchanted literary space, and then consider what might be the advantages for literature of that regression. Then I will look at arguments by Walter Benjamin that may appear, in the kinds of disenchanting and antiregressive tendencies they value, to challenge the conception of literature supported here. Finally, I will consider, in regard to these issues, a memoir by Jacques Derrida on the approaching death of his mother.

In chapter 1 a poem by James Merrill, "The House Fly," was briefly mentioned, and it is worth examining now in greater detail. A fly buzzing around the poet in late autumn reminds him of a fly that settled one evening, years ago, on the bare chest of a lover who has since left him. The final stanza reads:

> Downstairs in this same house one summer night,
> Founding the cult, her ancestress alit
> On the bare chest of Strato Mouflouzelis
> Who stirred in the lamp-glow but did not wake.
> To say so brings it back on every autumn
> Feebler wings, and further from that Sun,
> That mist-white wafer she and I partake of

> Alone this afternoon, making a rite
> Distinct from both the blessing and the blight.[1]

The poet now has only the fly to celebrate his ritual with, as the sun represents the communion wafer of the Mass. It is important that this rite, the poetry itself, is "distinct from both the blessing and the blight." One no longer has the real presence of the ceremony's initiator, the lover, and the forms of connection are getting weaker. Note how the delay of the expression "feebler wings" in its appearance in the lines of the poem suggests the weakness of those wings, their inability to bring back the original happening. We might consider here the contrast made earlier between an iconic, identificational style of experiencing and a metonymic, grammatical one. In the first stanza of Merrill's poem there is a metaphorical identification of the poet with the buzzing fly ("If I close my eyes, / A self till then subliminal takes flight / Buzzing around me"), but in the final stanza we have only weaker metonymic connections. The fly he is watching has, he imagines, a causal, linear linkage to an ancestor; that ancestor, in turn, is connected to the former lover only by the weak connection of an accidental touching of his chest. So the poem enacts that passage from the mirroring phase to the metonymic one; one is left with connections in a chain, ultimately a linguistic one, that can never bring back the original presence. It is as if the Catholic rite of communion has been weakened by one's more sophisticated beliefs. The believing Catholic employs the older identificational structure. Jesus has a real presence there in the host; it has truly become his body and blood, and the communicant truly becomes him in some fashion. But in the weaker version of the rite (Hegel, in treating Luther, would say the less magical version)[2] the host is merely a reminder of what once was present and is now linked to the self only through feeble chains of association extending into the past. (For a truly Protestant turn, the internal activity of the self would on its own be able to invest the host with significance, but in Merrill the poetic self still requires that the external forms retain a certain power of their own; the fly and the communion-wafer sun do not just trigger internal memories but are part of a semipublic ritual.)

So as the final line of the poem indicates, we are in a halfway state, no longer able to move in the identificational, metaphorical world of premodern ceremonies and of the pre-Oedipal self. But at the same time we do not simply reside in the "blight" of an emptied-out modern world. We are still able to activate the earlier ceremonies, the earlier identifications, in a cooler, more disenchanted manner, with weaker lines of connection. The poet can still celebrate a type of symbolic communion, one that is ultimately the poem itself, and it is only through the poem's linguistic connections, threatened as they are by their "feebler wings," that the metonymic connection to the lover has any lasting power. There is no hope that the real presence of the lover will, through this ceremony, return. There is instead a complex set of partial identifications and investments in the material of the ritual. The poet does touch the lover in some way through the identification with the fly, or through the even weaker identification with the words of the poem that mention the fly, so that it is not simply a case of loss.

Merrill makes a similar point in a poem about opera. He describes an old stagehand who sees very well the stage machinery, has heard the opera often, and knows that the lead singers come from the most ordinary backgrounds; they are "Two world-class egos, painted, overweight," and yet he finds himself weeping as he listens to a passionate duet.[3] The poet today sees very well the stage machinery of language and knows how its mechanisms produce certain stage effects. (Recall Ashbery's scene in the park where the clouds are merely stage machinery pulled along on invisible ropes.) Yet from that disenchanted stance the poet is still able, like the stagehand, to be moved by words put together in certain arrangements.

Yet how can we defend a stance that admittedly, in its need for such rituals, has elements of regression? One suggestion is from Melville, where he speaks of Jonah having gone deep in drowning and losing himself, in being swallowed up by a consuming, threatening watery world. He has also, says Melville, been privy to deeper things and patterns, so that on his return he finds "his ears, like two sea-shells, still multitudinously murmuring of the ocean."[4] The suggestion is that there is a kind of understanding, an access to experiential patterns, that is available in certain regressive states and is not available elsewhere. It may also be that as we leave behind cultural worlds that were more attuned to various aspects of our brain design, of its ways of ordering, we take pleasure in compensatory symbolic modelings of those more archaic patterns and investments, as a condition for finding that what we are about in life still matters, psychologically and ethically.

Perhaps we can see a process in Wittgenstein that is in certain ways similar. He appears in his investigations to have better access than others do to those initiating conditions that are required for meaningfulness to emerge, even in a minimal way, as in the primitive language games he describes. Then there are his repeated meditations about solipsism, as against being involved in a world of already meaningful practices with others. One suggestion is that Wittgenstein seems to have to convince himself, through obsessive rituals that he undertakes as a philosopher and as an adult, of a metaphysical and social framework that most others learned to take for granted from childhood on. His claims about learning to stop doing philosophy, about showing the fly the way out of the fly bottle, are then not just philosophical remarks but comments on that regressive, ritualized obsession in him. But while repeating those moves might not be healthy for one's psychological development, it may allow one to bring the full intelligence and complexity and ego strength of an adult to the project that both phenomenology and deconstruction are interested in: getting back behind the taken-for-granted structures of our world in order to see them coming into view as such. The adult access to those constituting moves by which a child ordinarily enters into a world of meaningfulness may be beneficial to a philosopher, even if the condition for that access is a regressive, repetitive tendency of mind, as if one needed to work out, over and over, the initiating moves by which one establishes a relationship to the world, rather than simply moving about within the world so formed. The obsessive return to an activity that reassures one's fundamental relationship to the world and to others, an activity most accomplish in childhood and then move on from, may allow one to see certain aspects of philosophical issues more clearly. So Wittgenstein becomes able to understand, better than others do, why we can be confident that we are connected to the world and to others. A similar claim might be made for literature. The transitional space described earlier can be seen as such a Wittgensteinian access to initiating moves of meaning-making, of self-formation, of world-constitution, all of which can give a more powerful intensity to the space of literature.

A certain kind of regressive tendency might prove useful in a different way. The move of maturation to a positional-metonymic field, from a pre-Oedipal mirroring relationship, will have the consequence of strengthening the self as strategic, as able to make moves and to find power-conferring arrangements within the grammar of cultural rules. But that strategic self will be sensitive to the world in some ways and not others, relative to its self-interest. That direction of sensitivity may make certain features of the world less visible. Recall the ending of "The Dead" where Gabriel moves from at first a self-centered view of his wife's behavior to a more generous sense of the shape of her life, in the ways it is not focused on him, and then to an awareness and acceptance of the movements of the world itself, the falling of the snow that, in being general over Ireland, is annihilating all distinctions. Note how in that story's last pages the annihilating snow seems to fuse a high-level metaphysical view with primitive fears of dissolution, as if those two quite different matters naturally supported each other. By entering states of controlled regression from our status as strategic selves, from our maneuvering within the positional grammar of culture, we may feel the boundaries of selfhood becoming less insistent; we may thus open ourselves to a clearer perception of the overall character of the world. There are times and moods when there is a self-relinquishing, when things are less determined by our interest in them and more by what they are in themselves, by how they appear against a more metaphysical backdrop. When a more weakly determinate self needs to identify with the self-sustaining wholeness of the forms around it, its own interest lies in letting the world be as it is, so that the world can serve as a self-sustaining object of identification. Then, too, a ritual reclaiming of a childhood transitional space may reenact the child's metaphysical hunger, his object-relational need to find himself engaged with a real world of objects that are not just projections of his psyche. One feels a satisfaction not just in such an engagement but also in experiences when the overall feel of reality is especially strong, its character as a real world that extends into a space well beyond our human manipulations.

Certain regressive tendencies might also serve a cultural engineering that enriches the world of signs. Consider the well-known scene in Mann where Aschenbach, while watching Tadzio, writes an essay that will repeat some of Tadzio's qualities.[5] But it is crucial that the essay is not about Tadzio at all, or even about eros, and it is likely there is little direct mirroring between Tadzio's movements and the textual movements of the essay. Rather Aschenbach must find in his writing a certain proportion and grace, a gravity-resistant play, a rhythm and energy of internal resonance, which will characterize the linguistic world as such, in accord with its own qualities and resonances and combinatorial powers. It is important for Aschenbach both that Tadzio, with his rich iconic, identificational, and musical connotations, remains in view, and that these find translation into a linguistic form that leaves that earlier world behind while yet retaining it.

The model presented here of literary space shows why, in the ways we are used by culture, we so willingly build up that symbolic world, as Aschenbach does. Even as we turn to a linguistic, grammatical realm we do not give up the dyadic, identificational way of experiencing. So the patterns of language can be an object of our self-other identifications. We want to find ways that language, through the development of its own internal resources, can come to have the qualities we need to identify with; the ways it can have (what we want to have ourselves) a well-formed, self-sustaining architecture secure enough to take in difficult material without dissolving. Without the more regressive patterns of engagement, having to do in Mann's case with a more primitive need for identifying with what is well formed and moves lightly over against the gravities of the world, one might not have the same investment in building up the symbolic realm of culture. The space of literature, with its more intense repetition of that compensating turn to language, is one of the richer spaces where such long-term cultural work occurs.

We lose our grasp of some of these possibilities as more and more in recent criticism the unconscious is rethought as a tame construct of language. This outcome follows the general trend by which whatever seemed external to language, a condition shaping it from without, is claimed to be instead a product that language has set out over against itself. One sees in quite different thinkers a tendency to take the symbolically rich unconscious of the modernists and to colonize it as one more outpost of linguistic or postmodern construction. Joel Whitebook argues that this project, which he sees in thinkers as diverse as Lacan and Habermas, threatens to cut us off from the very processes that might make liberating new visions of human life emerge, because of the rich possibilities for metaphorical novelty in a realm that is iconic, symbolic, and musical, that is, in other words, prelinguistic.[6]

A regressive tendency may also produce a certain useful movement of compression. In Beckett we noted a centripetal force, a drawing in of different configurations until their articulations matter less and they begin to collapse in on one another. But that centripetal gravity can bring about a natural metaphoric power. Events and individuals may compress in themselves different systems of meaning, and that compression creates a literary power. (That sort of force is very different from the endless dissemination and proliferation that characterize discursive space with the more radical turn to language.) Such overlapping may suggest patterns of thought that would not have come to us otherwise, or that would have been covered over by the winning out of conventional ways of seeing. And we saw in Beckett how language that must set itself over against the gravity of a more regressive space may have a special power to it. The movement into language that the text is implicitly about, with its gains and losses, acquires energy if it repeats, and calls to mind, our earlier experiences as children of painful loss and separation, and of cooler compensations.

By holding on to the distant music of earlier rituals and psychic phases one may get a more intense feeling of the prices we pay, and the value received, for being a modern subject. All in all the move into modern selfhood is surely worth it; we will reenact earlier forms only from the stance of someone who has moved away from them. But against the false modern picture of an autonomous self that determines its conditions for itself, the forms of experience favored by this model of literature may give us a more accurate sense that the world is not something we make, is not a blank field on which we project our meanings. We see instead that we are surrounded by a dense world that we cannot make fully transparent to our seeing, and by deeper patterns we are moved by unknowing. It is important for literature to give us this experience of a world we are being carried on instead of fully determining, a feeling for meaning as what emerges from the dark of history, a closer sense of fate and death, of the elemental structures of human existence. Literature lets us see that while we can reenact in literary space the childhood move (and the original species move) into the lateral metonymy of language, we do so only against the gravitational pull of still-powerful forms.

Followers of de Man might at this point raise an objection to the argument so far. Consider Merrill's poem about the disenchanted communion ritual, with its weaker, yet more sophisticated identifications and investments. The degree of disenchantment there, the de Manian might say, is still insufficient, as we can see if we compare ways of engaging with poetry and ways of using a voodoo doll. The user of the doll has a magical belief that what happens to the representation of something happens to the thing itself, but so too does the reader of poetry. His magical belief is that the qualities of the language, its self-ordering rightness and ongoing rhythm, somehow become qualities of the self as well. Now suppose that the voodoo practitioner rejects his religious beliefs and no longer accepts that sticking a pin in the doll will harm the one represented, yet he holds on to a weaker version of the ritual, still finding psychological satisfaction in its enactment. An observer might say that his process of disenchantment has simply not gone far enough. And the follower of de Man might make a similar claim. Once one becomes sophisticated about linguistic mechanisms, about the ways they undermine psychological mechanisms based on identification, projection, and reference, then the proper response is a far more abstemious one than Merrill, in his poem on the fly, seems to recommend. Proper critical hygiene requires resisting such identifications even in their weaker form; it requires an asceticism that withstands any temptation to mistake linguistic effects, magically, for psychological ones. Science, after all, requires us to give up the notion of any special mirroring between ourselves and nature.

But that degree of asceticism is not called for here. A rejection of magical thinking does not require giving up the kinds of identifications that Merrill is pointing to. The obvious analogy is that it would be foolish to base one's intimate emotional relationships solely on forms of engagement compatible with complete disenchantment, so that one gave up any more archaic, less transparent patterns of investment. We hope that such archaic patterns do not dominate us in ways that are pathological, but human relationships would be emptier without them. Throughout our lives we move through rich experiences of identification and separation, and many of the virtues we admire, such as loyalty and depth of character, will depend on our not moving easily, as a free-floating subjectivity, to new forms of investment that retain nothing of earlier identifications. This will be true not only in leaving individuals behind but also in leaving earlier patterns of experience, as when we move from the more intense metaphorical blurrings of childhood to the grammar of language, and in leaving styles of cultural life, as when a Mexican Indian leaves her village in Chiapas to attend a university. Suppose such an Indian gives up her religious beliefs but retains, with a complex and ambivalent attitude, her participation in Catholic ceremonies that have a strong pre-Columbian component in their rituals. We need not conclude that she is incapable of the full disenchantment that modern selfhood requires. Our goal in living out a human life is not a scientific abstemiousness in our attitudes toward the world. In finding a human life worth living, we engage the universe with the full range of the forms of experiencing built into the brain, and our proper awareness of fate and death, nature and chance, aloneness and belonging, may depend on kinds of experiencing the de Manian would be suspicious of, that have roots in more archaic, pre-Oedipal patterns of identification and disinvestment. The satisfactions the Chiapas woman finds in earlier ceremonies might be both archaic and sophisticated, and usefully so, as when we listen to music and feel moved by partly unconscious ways of enacting our lives that are not otherwise available.

A brief humorous poem by Merrill suggests that humans are more complex in their regressive-seeming identifications than de Man would take them to be. "Santo" tells of a Hispanic woman who puts a saint on a shelf and prays to him about problems in the household.[7] When none of her prayers is answered she takes down the saint and changes his identity from Saint Francis to Saint Martin, painting his beard black and giving him a red satin cloak. In just a week her prayers are answered: her son sends a photograph from his navy submarine; the baby starts speaking; the aunt gets a job; and the sick dog gets well. On the one hand this is a kind of magical, Catholic thinking stuck in iconic, ritualized practices. But on the other hand the woman is hardly trapped in the mythical; she engages in that world for her own purposes, with her own power to manipulate its effects.

Merrill here is making a similar point about poetry. The poet is like the Hispanic woman in remaining engaged with iconic, metaphoric, ritualized, identificational modes of thinking, but the poet is at enough distance from them now to use them for his purposes, instead of being trapped within them. The woman has a complex attitude somewhere between belief and unbelief, and so does the poet. The gods or saints do not really return in our rituals (as they once did for ancient believers), and the poet's rituals do not make early scenes exist again for him in a way that enables him to set them right. Yet they are symbolically brought into the architecture of the poem and made subject to patterns now more under the control of the poet, as the Hispanic woman is able to repaint the statue when one saint fails at his task. Both the Hispanic woman and Merrill as poet have interesting, multilevel, fruitful, and partly but not fully ironic attitudes toward ways of ordering experience that de Man would consider archaic. De Man's various renunciations, in contrast, seem a simplifying of the world, a Cromwellian readiness to destroy a ritual world of statues, images, and stained-glass windows, in de Man's case because of his radical religion of deconstruction. Merrill certainly does not believe that through writing certain well-ordered lines he has magically made his own life have that quality. Rather he has engaged a fuller range of his mental faculties, and not just the cognitive level of belief, in the project of setting his life in relationship to time and the world, as with the palm tree at the end of his poem, which is rooted in his childhood experiences. The qualities of the poetry may serve as a temporary scaffolding for, and modeling of, ways of being a self that must ultimately be achieved on their own terms, rather than through the magical effect of the model.

That there remain, however, serious worries regarding that treatment of the virtues of regression is evident from the work of Walter Benjamin.[8] He returns to the past not in a regressive manner but to find there forgotten fragments or glimmers of unrealized utopian or messianic possibility. Benjamin will of course be worried by the regressive tendencies of fascism, by its desire to reanimate German society through appealing to the archaic, mythical energies of the German people; and he will question any appeal to the revitalizing power of Dionysian, natural, deindividuating cultic energies. We need instead, he believes, to escape our entrapment in myth and the archaic, in a natural, imagistic order that still overwhelms our powers of reflective criticism. But Benjamin believes that such an entrapment in nature and myth is found throughout modern culture, even in the institutions of the Enlightenment. He finds it especially in the German idealist model of a reconciling of the ideal and the real, of an incarnating of the former in the latter. This naturalizing of modern political and social institutions makes us see them mythically, and modernity continues to throw up images and commodities that function like dream images in this partly unconscious mythical present. Benjamin, in walking through the modern city, is more interested in areas that cultural energy has withdrawn from, areas that once were fashionable and now are run down, or in cultural items that have a revealing air of outmoded fashion. For these indicate a lack of fit between ideas and the items that temporarily seem to embody them, and that lack of fit suggests that whatever might bring unity and spiritual energy to this natural and historical order lies elsewhere, in messianic possibility and in the not-yet. So one must read these signs in a cabbalistic manner, as offering faint hints of, and correspondences with, a realm we have no access to, rather than as having any self-organizing unity of their own, as in Hegel. In art and politics one looks to both the present and the past for cultural items suitable, not for bringing us back nostalgically or for aligning us with the present, but for providing moments of shock and provocation that break open the space of the present and show the possibility of the new and revolutionary.

Benjamin's worries are repeated in much of recent literary theory, for which the notions of the symbolic, the metaphorical, and the organic are often treated negatively, for reasons much like his own. Consider the transition described in chapter 4: from patterns of ordering that depend on iconic identifications and blurring across self-other boundaries to patterns of ordering that depend on a positional, grammatical field of differences. It is clear that the three notions in question here (symbol, metaphor, and the organic) will have a regressive aspect. A sense of organic wholeness, for example, will be desirable for a self that is still working out issues of separation and individuation, instead of issues of strategic deployment within the grammars of culture. The forming self will want to identify, as in ancient Greece, with other selves and with objects that have such a well-formed wholeness. Additionally a seamless unity and organic wholeness will be precisely what the best symbols and metaphors are supposed to have. They should accomplish their goal of compressing different semantic fields into the same pattern to such a degree that no force or coercion is apparent. The vehicle and the metaphorical meaning will seem so naturally one as to have an air of inevitability, so that there appears no way of getting at that meaning other than through that vehicle. De Man is a representative voice who claims that any such moves toward identification, reconciliation, and organic wholeness are primitive and cannot survive the difference engine that is language. Others echo Benjamin's fears that the habits of making such moves will lead one politically to repress otherness, difference, and conflict in the social order.

In examining German baroque drama Benjamin speaks of it as portraying a world where, unlike in the world of classical drama, meaning cannot be incarnated in everyday forms. God has withdrawn, and things show in their ill proportions and grotesqueness and damaged quality, in their profound unnaturalness, their failure to have an internal principle of form. (Again we may note the results of late-medieval theological voluntarism. God's will in its unlimited freedom can no longer be seen as embodied in any worldly forms. Aristotelian principles of form cannot survive in such a world, and things are left, now that God's willing is ever more arbitrary and distant in relation to them, in a meaningless and emptied-out state, such that only an external and arbitrary intervention, having nothing to do with their own character, can animate them and make them matter. Habermas sees how this sort of account, without its theological underpinning, multiplies in twentieth-century thought; he is deeply troubled by what he sees as "messianic" readings that devalue the powers of human reasoning and human politics.)[9] On Benjamin's reading, this absence is not to be made up for by a return to an earlier world, or by a regression to a space where the bothersome differences and gaps begin to blur in an overall unity. One simply must hold open those gaps, those absences, that sense of ruin and damage, in order to keep the way clear for the only kind of solution that could work, a messianic intervention from outside, unmotivated by any internal self-development of the system.

Allegory in Benjamin's system will thus be superior to symbol. The symbol joins the idea and the sensory image too seamlessly, as if a spiritual order could find such a perfect incarnation in nature and in the human, and as if force and oppression were not involved in bringing about the unity. In allegory the connections seem more forced and distant. In baroque allegory, says Benjamin, the links between sensory images and ideas proliferate so abundantly that eventually almost anything can stand for anything else. Instead of a natural incarnation of the ideal order, there is such an arbitrariness that the sensory world seems like a written language where the joining of semantic content with certain letter shapes is completely conventional, where there is no suggestion that some physical forms are more apt vehicles for incarnating meaning than others. Benjamin likes about baroque allegory precisely what many others dislike: its artificiality, its exaggeration, its arbitrary juxtaposing of one thing after another; its habit of accumulating fragments instead of building wholes; its sense of reflectiveness and of calculated effects; its refusal to let life-energies inhabit natural forms and its preference instead for masks of death, for processes of decay; its analogies with writing, commentary, and exegesis rather than with aesthetic presence. All these features express a consistent metaphysical conception: the world as a place of fragmented and ruined items that can no longer be natural vehicles for higher meanings.

Yet Benjamin, in spite of his brilliance, is often dangerously wrong in these matters. Certainly the lesson of the century just completed is that messianism in politics is a bad idea. Instead of Benjamin's desire radically to devalue cultural forms, because they are signs of ruin that do not embody rightness in any manner, we have to see how imperfect political forms and institutions are at least partial incarnations of norms of reason and justice. If the seamless unity of the symbol is a bad model for how modern societies work, so is the notion of the messianic. The best defense against authoritarians, totalitarians, and fascists is to strengthen legal and political institutions of the Kantian sort, to stabilize belief in the notion that certain constitutional rights are not to be violated, to support practices that distribute power across several institutions instead of centralizing it. To see all Weimar institutions, imperfect as they were, as worthless sites of ruin and arbitrariness, in need of an impossible messianic intervention from without, was to lose the best chance of stopping National Socialism. Because Benjamin sees the dangers in analogies drawn between the aesthetic and the political, he wants us to give up the notion of the aesthetic, instead of training us to recognize, as most of us do, that the political and the aesthetic spheres work by different norms. Totalitarianism is bad; having an artwork whose aspects hold together in a totalizing way may be either good or bad; having a symphony orchestra whose parts come together seamlessly is usually good. In a similar manner totalizing explanations are not good or bad abstractly; they are so only relative to particular theories and particular phenomena.

We are sophisticated enough that we are able to employ symbolic modes of organizing in literature without supposing that these modes are models for ordering political life. Whether at the level of the individual or the political community or the text, we have to ask whether an act of synthesizing hides differences and discontinuities and disruptive elements we need to keep alive instead of submerging. It is possible, of course, that a tendency to find regressive states useful in the making of literature may accompany politically regressive views; quite a few modernists found fascism appealing, with its staged rituals of social unity. But others were antifascists. Benjamin's account is dangerous because it encourages us to see literary style and political attitudes as joined, when we ought to discourage any such conjunction and to foster political beliefs that are justified precisely as political. One can like both well-made poems and sloppy, heterogeneous democracies. One should learn from Benjamin about the dangers of some kinds of psychological regression. Perhaps certain individuals who easily give themselves over to the musical and unconscious energies of literature, who feel moved by its Dionysian deindividuating effects, may on another occasion be moved by irrational political appeals such as the Nuremberg rallies. But, again, a policing of literature will not be as effective a solution here as ethical and political training in the styles of interaction, the goals of justice, and the habits of rational self-criticism of liberal communities.

There is another oddness in Benjamin's treatment of the symbolic in literature. He is worried in his critique of the symbol about any premature softening or reconciling of a culture's oppositions, and about any suggestion that an ideal, spiritual, rational realm has been incarnated at all in natural or human forms. But when we think of powerful symbols in literature, such as the whale in *Moby-Dick*, it is not so much that there is any reconciling of oppositions as that the psyche is working at a level where its understanding is primitive, where prelinguistic, unconscious forms of organization are at work that we do not understand, where the thought has not yet conceptualized itself as separable from that prelinguistic matrix. So the symbol is hardly a harbinger of political or social unities; it is a sign rather of an epistemic primitiveness that is itself quite powerful because of the kinds of psychic organization it activates. We are not trying to soften oppositions but rather to move to a level where they have not yet emerged as articulable. The reader of *Moby-Dick* seeing Ishmael floating on a coffin alone in the middle of the ocean is hardly likely to think that some conciliatory unifying of the divine and human realms has been accomplished, or that political conflicts in society have been overcome. The fact that the different symbolic meanings have not yet separated themselves out, so as to make analysis clearer, has nothing at all to do with a preference for organic human communities where differences among individuals and groups have not yet separated themselves out.

A better notion of the symbolic is available in another Merrill poem, "Up and Down."[10] The second half of the poem narrates an occasion after his father's death when the poet goes with his mother to the underground bank vault where a safety deposit box holds jewelry from his father to her, including an emerald given at the time of the poet's birth. She gives him the emerald and tells him to save it for his bride when he gets married, though her hesitancy suggests that she knows this will never happen. He places it on her finger and tells her to wear it "until the time comes." Perhaps one can see here a playing out of the transition point between a dyadic, metaphoric way of seeing things and a positional-grammatical one. If the transition is successfully made, then the ring enters on a structural circuit (as the letter in "The Purloined Letter") so that substitution is possible within the grammatical structure; a wife will replace the mother in the family triad, and the son will take over the father's position. But here the movement of the ring is evidently short-circuited. It remains in the oscillating dyad between mother and son. But does the poet genuinely regress here to the childhood identifications? No, the movement to the positional, grammatical form of ordering is indeed made; only it is made at the level of language, at the level of the poem with its well-formed patterns of position and exchange. But Merrill recognizes that this level of substitution and grammar is not the same as entering into the social grammar of society. "The little feet that patter here are metrical," he admits. The emerald, in the way its green light seems to pervade the poem, is a symbol of the symbolic: "A den of greenest light, it grows, shrinks, glows, / Hermetic stanza bedded in the prose / Of the last thirty semiprecious years." (230) Instead of being given up, the earlier image-world of childhood remains a mysterious, "hermetic" presence glowing through the lines of prose that make up the life. The descent into the vault is a regression to that image level, to the "sprung lid" of a box, to something that is symbolically "bedded" rather than really so. But the tone of the poem indicates that there is now some distance to the handling of this material. We do not give up the symbolic; if we did so, we would lose the hermetic presence and lighting, the semiprecious glow, that give a richer depth from beneath to the lines of prose of a life. A more radical move to the grammatical impoverishes us.

The issue of the symbolic shows how we are often caught between a commitment to older ethical and psychological forms and a more skeptical reflection about them. There is no determinate answer as to how the two commitments must be kept in balance. Literature may help in keeping alive a rich set of resources for thinking about these matters, though it will not do so if we let its space become impoverished by theory. It may be a matter of luck, a play of fate as much as of our making, that we find the right balance between skepticism toward our earlier selves and the activation of earlier features that bring a depth of meaning to our lives. To make this claim is not to deny the great political and ethical dangers of more archaic forms of sense-making. That is why the terrain on which these projects are engaged has to be that of the disenchanted, self-conscious self capable of reflective criticism about its undertakings. A sympathy to the role of regression in literary space should never allow us to support political attitudes adverse to social justice.

The criticism to be anticipated here, of course, is that one will find this style of thinking nostalgic. Perhaps some writings mentioned so far, and others that will be studied, have in them the sense of looking back toward

a world, idealized now, that one can no longer inhabit. The cowboy protagonist of McCarthy's *All the Pretty Horses,* for example, can seem to occupy a stance that, with his stoical notions of honor and his sense of the
ethical inevitability of his decisions, suggests an appealing earlier world
that perhaps never was that way to begin with. (There is no such nostalgia
in *Blood Meridian.*) Yet McCarthy's purpose here is not to get us to long
for a lost world we can never recover; he is looking for the kind of story
and scene and character that will generate the powerful rhythms of his
writing, and he is examining the forms of ethical life still possible for us.
But whatever McCarthy's purpose is, to appeal to a literary space that is
both disenchanted and regressive is by no means a search for a rosy-
colored past. Rather it is an attempt at a realistic survey of the resources
that might be brought into play, from past and present, in asking what it
takes to lead a human life well today. There is no automatic virtue in moving thoroughly into a postmodern world while attempting to jettison as
much as one can of earlier patterns of thinking and experiencing. A richer
life may be one that does not float easily amid the changing cultural vocabularies but rides on rhythms, and on patterns of commitment and identification, that have more enduring, less transparent, less reflectively chosen roots. To consider that possibility, even while being critical of its
dangers, is not to be nostalgic but is to look forward to a life whose shape
one finds worthwhile to occupy. To occupy it well is always to occupy it
self-critically, but that is not the only virtue.

Other issues regarding this dialectic of regression and disenchantment appear if we look at an unusual text by Jacques Derrida. The writing is a
memoir Derrida wrote from January 1989 to April 1990 during the long
final illness of his mother.[11] It is very much an example of Derrida's notion
of intertextuality: the idea that everything we write is, implicitly at least, a
citing of, or a writing between the lines of and within the margins of, other
texts. So Derrida, as in his other work, represents here the stronger, more
radical turn to the linguistic and grammatical. Derrida's writing occupies
the bottom-third, approximately, of the pages of a three-hundred-page
book; the upper two-thirds of the pages present a long commentary on
Derrida by Geoffrey Bennington. Derrida often makes references to that
commentary, both to its content and to its position on the page, but he is
writing between the lines of other texts as well. One of these is a notebook
he wrote in the 1970s that gives personal meditations on the notion of circumcision, and another is the *Confessions* of Augustine, which is quoted
extensively. Still other texts in the background include Lacan's and other
writings by Derrida, of which *Glas* is especially important.

The choice of Augustine's autobiography works well here. It is not just that Derrida's writing is in a confessional mode; the parallels with Augustine's life are unusually close. Both were born in North Africa, and Derrida lived for a time as a child on a rue de St. Augustin. Both crossed the Mediterranean for education and advancement, heading to the center of an empire they were raised on the fringes of, an empire in each case in its final stages. Both face the death of a mother who moved from North Africa to the European country of her son's education. Derrida also faces a pervading sense of guilt that seems to derive, as with Augustine, from an original sin he could not have been responsible for; in his case it has to do, it seems, with the deaths of two of his brothers at the ages of three months and two years. If Augustine worries about how the individual can will freely in the face of God's predestination and foreknowledge, Derrida worries about how it can be worth writing anything when cultural vocabularies, or one's commentators and interpreters, have given a place in advance to whatever one might say. His attempt to say something not yet determined in that manner may then be like Augustine's attempt to show that humans have freedom in spite of God's power. And so forth. Derrida is ingenious at finding parallels that only rarely seem forced or arbitrary. It is hardly surprising to learn that one part of this memoir, with all its references to his mother, is being written just one town over in California from Santa Monica, named for Augustine's mother.

The earlier notebook reflections on circumcision generally, and on Derrida's circumcision as a child in Algeria, turn into a more general study of castration or of any originary splitting that undermines self-identity. Derrida decides that circumcision is what he has been writing about all along in all of his texts, for circumcision involves a cutting off of the self from itself, so that it can never expect perfect self-identity again. This is just what Derrida has described writing to be in his work on Plato and others. Plato was worried that the writer is separated off from what he has written, and so cannot secure for the reader precisely what the meanings are. But that, Derrida has argued, is the condition of any use of language, as there is no meaning-conferring intention that can give a pattern of sound-shapes or letter-shapes a fully determinate meaning. In spite of what Plato may have hoped for, a speaker can never accompany his speech in a manner that guarantees what it means. So what one has spoken or written is torn away from one like a section of skin; to write is, as it were, to write on such a skin (animal skins were indeed used to write on) that is thus torn away. So all writing is circumcision, and all Derrida's work based on his conception of writing, of grammatology, of nonidentity of meaning is in that sense, so he says, a reflection on circumcision. (Derrida quotes Augustine: "Thou has stretched out the firmament of Thy Book like a skin" [230–31]). Circumcision also suggests the primary castration that some followers of Lacan talk about, the separation from the mother in the process of individuation. The earlier identification is a narcissistic one; one sees the other as a mirror of the self. So separation from the mother is at the same time a separation from oneself, from a form of the self that has been given an external existence and that suggests one's hopes for wholeness and integrity. But again that separation from an aspect of oneself that becomes externalized is what circumcision is.

In addition the cut or separation produced by circumcision is from the outside. Thus it stands as well for Derrida's externalism, which one might oppose to Aristotle's sense of self-actualizing wholes that articulate themselves by their own internally developing forms. In Derrida there are no such forms or wholes. What may appear a well-formed whole as a text is a tissue of fractures and arbitrary junctures. Derrida remarks about his memoir that even it will be cut off arbitrarily from the outside, by the unpredictable moment of his mother's death, which will itself then be a form of circumcision:

> The nonknowledge into which the imminent but unpredictable coming of an event, the death of my mother Sultana Esther Georgette Safar Derrida, would come to sculpt the writing from the outside, give it its form and its rhythm from an incalculable interruption, never will any of my texts have depended in its most essential inside on such a cutting, accidental and contingent outside, as though each syllable, and the very milieu of each periphrasis were preparing itself to receive a telephone call, the news of the death of one dying. (206–7)

Having the apparent unity of the text be essentially disruptible by the insertion of what is external and arbitrary is for Derrida the condition of any writing whatever and not just of a journal that is waiting for the death of the author's mother. Derrida also claims that he is upset by the attitude of Bennington, the author of the commentary on the upper two-thirds of the pages. Bennington says that he is going to try to summarize Derrida's work in a coherent manner, rather than quoting directly from Derrida's texts. Derrida (we are not surprised at this by now) pictures that practice as a circumcision, as a cutting off of the skin of Derrida's own texts, through editing and paraphrasing them rather than presenting them as they are (26–31).

Since I have used Merrill's poetry to bring out features of the conception of literary space defended here, I will use his work as a foil in describ-

ing the space that emerges in Derrida's writing. Both writers are sensitive
to the way meanings are suggested by the material character of signifiers.
But there is a different balance in the work of the two. The wordplay in
Merrill is more strongly in the service of patterns that are iconic, spatial,
metaphoric, and symbolic. There is consequently what might be called a
process of distillation, concentration, and editing; the poet chooses which
tiny percentage of his preparatory verbal play and experimentation actually does the different sorts of work that the poem needs it to do, given its
extralinguistic context. Most sound combinations will be irrelevant to the
patterns and resolutions that Merrill's psyche, in the space in which his
poetry is written, makes significant. Derrida, in contrast, seems to work
more strictly within the linguistic field itself. Linguistic shapes are taken
more on their own, as already counters in a textual space, and he employs
a principle of proliferation and exhaustion, as intralinguistic energies keep
producing further associations. Considerable textual play is generated by
manipulating the Latinate roots of the word *blood* in crude, crural, cruel,
and so forth, and there is a great deal of play with words beginning with
circum, triggered by the word *circumcision.* In just a paragraph we get *cir-
cumference, circumbygone, circumnavigation, circumfession,* and *circum-
pletes* (13–15). The first syllable of *circumcision* in French is close to the
word for *wax,* he says, and that suggests an often-used theme in his earlier
work (72). Derrida's mother was named Georgette, shortened often to
Geo, which could also be short for Geoffrey, the commentator. So Derrida
can speak of a "Geo-logic" that is attempting to determine the meaning of
his sentences (73). In his summary of Derrida's work Bennington is trying
to establish a "matrix" that will, if successful, make what comes out of
Derrida's mouth predictable, as the expected output of a certain theoretical machinery (32–36). That matrix, of course, suggests the way Derrida is
determined by his mother, by the happenings of his early life. And the
Geo-logic, with its suggestion of earth and the maternal, becomes a
"Theo-logic" as Geoffrey Bennington takes his "divine" position on the
top of the page and tries to "predestine" what Derrida can say.

Another section of Derrida's text is governed by *pr* words: *pris* (past
tense of *take*), *prier* (pray), *Proust, price* (62–63). Or the image of being
carried for his circumcision leads to plays on root words for *carry: porter*
in French and *fero* in Latin, yielding *port, porterage, preference, reference,
transference,* and *difference.* Or there are a number of plays on the sound
ci (212). We are in an already linguistic, already textualized universe, and
the wordplay is part of a machinery of an almost limitless generation of
linguistic combinations. *Circumcision* and *confession* join to form *circumfession,* as in the title. Derrida's Hebrew name Elie transforms itself into

the past participle of the French word for elect (84). The SA of Saint Augustine can suggest Derrida's references in earlier work to Savoir Absolu, Hegel's Absolute Knowledge. If he is in mourning then he will find a further dictionary meaning for *mourning* having to do with the coloring of butterflies, one of which is a "half-mourning satyr," which Derrida then becomes (167–69). If the letter *I* moves from capitalized to small *i* then that suggests a kind of circumcision or a simulated castration (72).

The difference here between Derrida and Merrill should not be exaggerated. Some of the combinatory logic of Derrida's text is iconic; the image of skin being cut off becomes linked with similar images, such as that of sheets of paper being torn from a pad. But in Merrill's "Santorini," for example, rather more of the mapping of meanings is built on the spatial, iconic scene of what is represented: the island's topography and layout. (Of course this is one of the things that de Man has warned against, this mapping of linguistic meaning onto the iconic, the referential.) The movement is not only from signifier to signifier but also across a carefully marked out and richly presented visual geography: the climb up the mule track, the island's rising from the ocean, the descent to the underground classroom where Greek was kept alive, the ascent to the high point devoted to Apollo, the descent again to the black beach. The spatial arrangements and images become metaphorical as they resonate with less easily visualizable patterns. The perceptual world continues to guide the conceptual. (It is an important condition of the notion of literary space defended in chapter 1 that it is built up on the scaffolding of a vividly described visual space, rather than becoming simply a textual space.) In Derrida there are some visually powerful scenes, but there is not a spatially and visually organized field that serves as a rich template on which other meanings are arranged. Perloff, one will recall, said that in Eliot, but not in Ashbery, there is an actual referential space, a locatable scene on which symbolic meanings are constructed. Derrida fits Perloff's narrative in that a play with language, with a similarity of syllables, moves with greater freedom apart from the confines of a concrete geography. He seems to be moving at all times through a textual universe. Derrida does not only treat phenomenology critically as a philosopher, in favor of looking at the machinery of grammar, writing, and language; he also reduces the role of the phenomenological in his own writing, in favor of the lateral, metonymic production of linguistic patterns. (The town of Santa Monica is not present as a visual scene but only as a reminder of the name of Augustine's mother.)

Derrida's use of that productive machinery seems not a means of having access to darker, more archaic regions of the mind, in the manner, say, of

Melville, but of a consciously strategic employment of counters in a linguistic game whose moves he understands in advance. (Constituting discursive space as such a strategic field of positions and moves was one feature, seen earlier, of the turn to the grammatical.) In other writings of his there is often a deliberate producing of textual effects against an opponent. Thus in his debate with Searle he uses the letters of Searle's name to talk of him as an "S.a.r.l.," a *Société à responsabilité limité*, a kind of corporation in which Searle does not really own his own meanings; and he makes sexual innuendo about noting that Searle's name, in the copyright notice, has moved from the top of the page in an earlier draft to the bottom in the final one.[12] But he is not thereby being carried to new insights by the mechanically generative power of the linguistic shapes of Searle's text. Rather he looks around to see which of those shapes and sequences he can use to make the points he already wants to make against Searle. He understood long before writing this essay his own ideas about the speaker's inability to control fully what his utterances mean; he just examined the field of Searle's text to find "graphic" occasions for deploying what he already knew.

Something similar is at work in this memoir. Derrida's text is by no means simply a matter of wordplay. There are images of his mother in her illness, of his expulsion from school as a Jew when the Vichy government controlled Algeria, of the body as pierced by a syringe or as shedding skin. But as clearly powerful as these images are to Derrida, they are like much contemporary visual art in that they transform themselves almost immediately into something textual or into discourse. One often sees today art exhibits or installations that present strongly visual imagery, but one's regarding of them is transposed quickly into a positioning of moves in a conceptual field, having to do perhaps with social wrongs or with the history of art. While Derrida does not press us toward those particular discursive fields, there is still a quick transformation of images into the familiar textual moves of his philosophy. Thus the picture of blood being taken from his body by a syringe becomes a familiar network of correlations: the play of inside and outside; confession as the inside of a life exhibiting itself outside; the gesture becoming one of writing as the syringe becomes a pen; the issue of whether labeling the tube into which the blood was placed can avoid the ways that self-identity is inherently misappropriated (10). These are all well-known moves to the reader of Derrida; they are already part of a well-articulated discursive field into which the image of blood and syringe is quickly imported, instead of its becoming, as images do in Melville or in Merrill, more richly productive of novel meanings generated by the image field working on a more archaic level. (It is important in "Lost in Translation" that there is both the grammatical level of puzzle shapes fitting together and the richly ornate scene that forms the puzzle's picture.)

This is not a questioning of the richness of Derrida's own psychology but rather comments on the flaws in the textual paradigm in which he believes he has to express it. In accord with that paradigm the energies directed toward the world, toward his mother's situation, divert themselves rapidly into lateral, intertextual associations. Seeing her bedsores, Derrida lets the French word for *bedsore, escarre,* generate a stream of linguistically associated words that guide his discussion (87–101) or he turns her name into various kinds of linguistic play. The case here is parallel to certain postmodern accounts of our apprehension of the world. What we are apprehending is quickly seen in such accounts to be already textual, so that we almost lose hold of the idea that we are bringing into view a world that is itself nondiscursive, that our ways of speaking light up in particular ways but do not create. In a similar manner Derrida takes our more archaic forms of sensitivity to patterns and turns them into the regulated machinery of texts, of language. One reason I chose this text of Derrida's for discussion is that in its treatment of his boyhood traumas and the coming death of his mother, it has to bring the referential world into view as one of extreme importance. And yet the Derridean habits remain even here in a text of that special sort: the seemingly limitless textual productivity based on the lateral energies of language; the desire, even if any speaking cannot help but be intertextual, to reveal such intertextual directedness ever more explicitly and self-consciously and without end.

Merrill, as we saw in "Santorini," suggests that in writing poetry one goes through a ritual regression toward pre-Oedipal forms of experience, a threatened loss of boundaries as one descends into a Dionysian play with words and then returns. One relives earlier, more primitive forms of investment and identification, of dissolving and fusing, before reestablishing one's status as stable and whole. In Derrida that more regressive, pre-Oedipal experiencing seems to have much less appeal. It is true that Derrida in a number of passages mentions his continuing identification with his mother, even to the point that a facial nerve problem makes him drip water from his mouth in just the way his mother is doing in the nursing home (98). Other examples of narcissistic identification occur as well ("and for 59 years I have not known who is weeping my mother or me" [263]). But for the most part Derrida treats circumcision, both real and symbolic, as a cut, a separation that one can never get back beyond. It is the originating move that makes one give up one's hope for a mirroring wholeness and turn instead to language, to a progression across a field of signifiers that cannot retrieve any earlier unity. Of course there was no such original unity for Derrida; that notion is itself a construct of our metonymic wandering. To the extent that there is a constituting move that establishes the space of writing and difference, it is by nature inaccessible, so it makes no sense to speak of a pre-Oedipal return to it. The exile from the Garden is permanent, unlike in Greek myths (Merrill's Empedocles) that allow various kinds of cycling returns. That exile is for Derrida once again a circumcision, a cut, the move that establishes difference and deferral as the basis of all meaning. We are granted instead a sign-to-sign movement, what Derrida sometimes calls a life of "destinerrancy" (199).

If there is not in Derrida a Greek-Dionysian regression to more archaic forms of experiencing, or a ritualized-Catholic version of that regression, there is instead at times an almost mystical reference to the originating move, the lost original language, that one can no longer get back to. Thus he speaks of "the other, nongrammatical syntax that remains to be invented to speak of the name of God" (199) and of "what happens in circumcision, what is done outside language, without sentence, the time of a proper name" (121). And he talks of Hebrew as the hidden grammar he is unable to speak and of his real Hebrew name, Elie, that he had no knowledge of in childhood ("for I'm reaching the end without ever having read Hebrew, see someone who multiplies dancing and learned circumvolutions in a foreign language for the simple reason that he must turn around his own unknown grammar, Hebrew, the unreadability he knows he comes from, like his home" [286–87]). But it is not at all clear, for reasons Derrida has given us, what such an originary, untranslatable utterance could be, before and behind the cut of difference, a seemingly mystical unreadability without any of the features Derrida identifies as universal in his notion of textuality. Still it is interesting to see how Derrida phrases the matter, to note that he defines circumcision, the cutting away that permanently disrupts self-identity, as what is outside of language, nongrammatical, without sentence. The move that constitutes the grammatical field of positions, combinations, and maneuvers is itself outside of that field, not because the grammatical space rides on an earlier iconic-mimetic one, but because anything pregrammatical can be treated only as something from negative theology, as something absolutely unpresentable. That is why Habermas can treat Derrida as following in the line of Benjamin's messianism and Jewish mysticism, where the "book written in God's handwriting never existed, but only traces of it, and even they have been obliterated."[13]

If Derrida will not offer us sacramental rituals of regressive return, he does suggest a different, more textualized function of writing. He makes rather much of the parallel with Augustinian predestination, only his concern is the predestination that makes what one says determined in advance. If Bennington's summary of Derrida's philosophy is successful, then supposedly what Derrida is saying down below on the page will turn out to have been given its meaning even before he came to write it. The reason this does not happen is, as before, that the material character of language, its shape as written, keeps pressing its meanings beyond what author or summarizer might have captured or predicted. Derrida keeps telling Bennington, across the boundary separating the top two-thirds of the page from the bottom third, that his verbal play beneath (in the manner perhaps of genetic mutation) is going to produce, through the aleatory play of the machinery, something that will not fit into the conceptual networks prepared for it (30–36). That is Derrida's freedom and why he keeps writing.

There is a difference here between what Beckett, for example, is doing and what Derrida is doing. In Beckett there is the pull of a regressive, centripetal energy that threatens to reduce complex articulations to more minimal ones, that compresses spread-out differences into less differentiated ones, that pulls against the lateral-metonymic energies of language until it is harder for sentences to keep their structure going. So Beckett's movement is toward greater economy, toward a simple self-maintenance of language and self on the brink, against dissolving forces beneath. The writing voice keeps itself going, especially in the trilogy of novels, but the pull toward more minimal, more primitive, less discursive structures is evident there and in the plays. With Derrida, on the other hand, the circumcision or cut has so thoroughly exiled one into the positional-lateral energies of language that there cannot be any going back; since return is impossible, there is no pull toward earlier, more minimal structures. (Molloy's regression allows him, in his opening lines, to see that he is writing from his mother's space, while in Derrida the separation from the space of his mother, as symbolized by his circumcision, remains fundamental.)

So in Derrida one gets instead writing as an unstoppable forward energy from signifier to signifier, sentence to sentence. There is no threatened opening up of a vacuum; one is able to fill in, with still more words, all the empty spaces that open up. This is another meaning of Derrida's intertextuality (or of the more radical turn to language and the grammatical). Every text he sees offers space between the lines and within the margins that the metonymic drive of his language can begin to fill in. He actually says that the basic principle of his writing is that of the virus (92). Supposedly he means that the structures of his writing insinuate themselves into other texts so that when these other texts reproduce themselves, the Derridean inscriptions get reproduced along with them. The earlier texts now get read as if they were, even if written long before he was born, Derridean texts. So if Beckett's writing tends toward economy and silence, Derrida's principle is one of multiplication; that is why a text on circumcision cannot satisfy itself until it has gone through as many forms as possible of words beginning with *circum*. Since most mutations fail at reproduction one needs to disperse oneself in as many textual mutations as possible. Beckett hopes to find increased semantic power through a centripetal implosion that does not quite go all the way to silence. One gets the feeling that the centrifugal advance of Derrida's writing is not weakened by the end of a book but can immediately keep itself going without stoppage. To make the linguistic turn radically, to articulate a textual space no longer setting itself over against (and limited by) more archaic spaces, is to set that textual energy free to move about by its own rules. So the space of discourse, instead of being responsive to the world, becomes a site of unlimited dissemination.

There might be some surprise regarding Derrida's strong insistence in this text on finding a writing that escapes the power of other texts to produce him as a result; he will turn things around so that more and more these other texts are read as *his* results. Derrida has all along spoken of the invisible intertextuality that takes up all our utterances no matter what, and he denies the notion of a meaning-conferring origin. Yet he works hard in this memoir to avoid textual domination, to avoid being "written" by others even as he makes their texts written by him. He is, again, upset at Bennington because the latter is not acknowledging the character of Derrida's writing as *utterance-events,* as having its existence in those unique events as such, exactly as they are, apart from commentary; yet Derrida's own work seems to deny the possibility of such unique events and to exalt commentary. Merrill, we saw, does not try to resist that surrender of self to a programming not his own. The long trilogy that begins with "The Book of Ephraim" uses as its occasion a playing with a Ouija board. In Merrill this gradually becomes a surrender to being used by an upper world that contains former poets and friends, historical individuals, and eventually complex levels of angels. For Merrill it is no problem, indeed it is an advantage, to be written through by others, to have their meanings intertwine themselves with his texts, beyond what he is aware of. (An otherworldly representative tells him, through the Ouija board, "A SCRIBE SITS BY YOU CONSTANTLY THESE DAYS / DOING WHAT HE MUST TO INTERWEAVE / YOUR LINES WITH MEANINGS YOU CONNOT CONCEIVE")[14] But in this text of Derrida's there is no such surrender, no such risking of the boundaries of the writing self, no regressive challenge to identity. He is extremely self-conscious and careful about his rhetorical strategies, deliberately complicating his moves so that others cannot dominate them, working to intertwine his own meanings with other texts in a way they cannot do to his ("that's what they can't stand, that I say nothing, never anything tenable or valid, no thesis that could be refuted, neither true nor false, not even, not seen not caught" [272]).

Derrida's writing becomes, though anti-Cartesian in its content, rather Cartesian in the sense of achieving a self-propelling, self-maintaining systematic drive, having freed itself from earlier gravities. The fact that it will never reach its destination is part of its energy. Again his notion of circumcision comes into play. One reason a therapist may assign for a regressive return to an earlier pre-Oedipal and maternal identification is to allay anxieties about castration. One supposedly wants to overcome the mother's lack by being the phallus for her, by letting oneself fill any gap in her, and one tries to deny that a primary castration or rift in self-identity is structurally necessary. (Again I believe, rightly or wrongly, that this is a Lacanian notion.) But to understand our status as language users at all, Derrida would say, is to understand that such a fundamental rift has already occurred; the process of separation and difference cannot be overcome, and it is not something to fear in the future. That is why he can, in the memoir about his mother's illness and about his own childhood, present what may seem odd items, such as the image of devotees of the Magna Mater throwing their severed sexual organs into the homes they pass (232) or the notion that circumcision is something demanded by the mother (188–90). In being expelled into a world where identity is always self-dividing, a function of difference, of separation, of cutting off, the self no longer needs to feel the regressive pull of the pre-Oedipal (because a primary castration has already occurred and the pre-Oedipal defenses against it thus serve no purpose) and can focus instead, as Derrida usually does, on moves within the positional-grammatical field of language and culture. Returning to a ritualized, metaphorical, transitional space with its weakened identifications will then seem hopeless as a strategy for reducing the anxieties of selfhood.

The moves to be especially valued for Derrida are not those that try to reduce the triadic field to a more primitive dyadic one (that is the pressure we feel in Beckett), but rather those that refuse to let that triadic field close itself off, that resist its predetermined system of rules as to how one can position oneself within the structure. One uses the mutating energies of language, as Derrida does against Bennington, to break open the rule-governed field, to violate its grammars, in order to allow new things to be said. Perhaps it can be said that if Beckett and Merrill are dealing with an oscillation between the number two and the number three, Derrida is dealing with an oscillation between three and four, in that he opens up another unsettling dimension by the way he writes between and around and within other texts. That opening up is important because the move from two to three is normally a move toward accepting the grammatical field of culture, with its constraints on licit or illicit moves within that field. Those constraints may be especially strong in the areas of cultural position and gender identity. So it is important to Derrida that the machinery of the cultural game not be allowed to work smoothly, setting items in their assigned places according to the given rules. Fortunately that machinery, simply by being linguistic, automatically engenders moves that unsettle itself. Messages mutate in transmission; the places where differences have supposedly been reconciled begin to show fractures; repetitions change what they repeat; any move of dominance or differentiation is already contaminated by what it tries to move away from or to dominate. The triadic field of culture, then, with its rules of positioning and movement, offers the means for new rules ultimately to form, so that no present arrangement can count as natural and proper.

If Merrill seems to see virtues in a controlled regression to an earlier metaphorical, symbolic world, Derrida's opposition to that view is shown in his remarks on what Hegel says about Egyptian hieroglyphics.[15] For Hegel the Egyptian mode of experiencing is symbolic, as reflected in its art and architecture. Because the structure that Hegel calls "divine" (certain patterns of self-relating-in-relating-to-otherness) is poorly understood by the Egyptians, says Hegel, their artistic representations of it express their inability to capture its essence, its (to them) distant and incommensurable otherness.[16] The grotesque combinations of bird and man, or jackal and man, show that the divine cannot yet be comprehended in terms of proportion, measure, or self-maintaining articulation. Primitive notions of quantity, such as the great size of the pyramids, are also expressed in this more archaic notion of the divine. The Egyptian pyramid can stand for the very notion of a symbol, the way meaning is entombed in a material structure where that meaning is not at home, as in a dark pit. Hieroglyphics carry for Hegel that sense of forms that are still too lost in nature, too external to the meaning they are carrying, as opposed to an alphabet, which in representing the movements of the voice supposedly captures something closer to the mental activity that confers meaning.

Derrida will question Hegel's valuation and find benefits in the hieroglyphic language that Hegel did not find there (Derrida's move is unsurprising if what he has said all along about writing is noted). Instead of seeing in the hieroglyphs the visible remains of a more iconic, mirroring phase of understanding, grounded in nature and in magic ritual, he sees in them a positional-grammatical language with rules for combining the elements in various complex arrangements, almost in the manner of formal languages foreseen by Leibniz.[17] It is precisely a virtue of such languages, for Derrida, that they are not linked to states of consciousness or to the phonic. It is noteworthy with what energy Derrida moves away from the symbolic understood in the manner of Hegel's description of Egyptian art. There are no longer the hidden, darker, archaic aspects, the boundary-blurring, the primitive modes of comprehending the divine. Rather he focuses on what hieroglyphics has in common with a formal language such as those developed in computer science; its most relevant characteristic for him is its distancing from the human voice, from that connection to consciousness. Derrida is, again, similar to those who reconstitute the unconscious as itself a textual arrangement of letter shapes, as something defined by and transparent to a linguistic circulation (as opposed to the biological, Dionysian, unconscious will of Schopenhauer and Nietzsche). He seems to resist, to the point of reconstituting as more purely grammatical, the archaic, symbolic, ego-threatening, death-world of Egypt that Hegel's treatment suggests. Merrill and Derrida both mention volcanoes but in a different manner. For Derrida his mother has become "a sleeping water in the henceforth appeased depth of the abyss, this volcano I tell myself I'm well out of" (80). Merrill as poet is an Empedocles who leaps into the volcano, into a pre-Oedipal world of blurring, fluent identities, and hopes to return with senses intact.

I should acknowledge that Derrida, besides the verbal play, gives us in the memoir a sincere portrayal of the painfulness of selfhood, such as one might find in other confessional texts. Here is a self still in tears for the young child's experience of guilt over an infant brother who died not long before he was born. Here is still the child who identified so strongly with the mother's grief for that lost son, who therefore could not be comforted himself. Here is still the schoolboy suddenly exiled, and not understanding his exile, when Vichy rules forced him out of his Algerian school. One might suggest that Derrida can present his own psychological states only in the indirect, intertextual manner of working through Augustine's *Confessions*. He can be confessional, as it were, only by breaking the rules of being confessional, that is, by quoting someone else and thus not presenting his own immediate feelings. But in fact Derrida's own feelings about his mother and about his childhood (and about his sons) come through clearly. Perhaps it has been true all along that Derrida's deconstruction of subjectivity and the first-person voice occurs not because he is an enemy of these but because he is committed to their value and wants to understand them, by putting them under pressure. (Bennington makes this point as well in the commentary he gives on the upper two-thirds of the book [145]). Derrida does seem to allow here occasionally a status for subjectivity, for the voice, for original meaning-making, and for a lost moment of privileged meaning-conferral—all of which the textual machineries he describes elsewhere would seem to make impossible.

Perhaps features of Derrida's text will be clearer if we compare him, as the writer of this memoir, to the Eliot of *The Waste Land*.[18] (It is a melancholy fact, but true nonetheless, that ethical virtues do not track aesthetic ones. Eliot had certain traits that everyone should disdain; and if I were powerless and my human rights were being violated, perhaps I would be better off with Derrida to assist me than Eliot, even if I have serious doubts regarding the usefulness of Derrida's discourse in such a matter. But on the other hand Eliot in this particular work marks out a richer vision of literary space than Derrida does in the text we are examining.) Consider first a claim that Perloff makes about Eliot's poem. In comparing him unfavorably to Ashbery and Stein, she says that with all the rich echoes in his work it is still the case that one finds there a straightforward semantic determinacy that is not present in the other two poets. He is weaker, therefore, on her account because he does not let the full play and indeterminacy of the linguistic realm emerge on its own, as in her more radical linguistic turn (which, it seems, would favor Derrida). She mentions, as specific evidence for her claim, the stability of the reference in Eliot to an actual London church, Magnus Martyr, and its physical neighborhood, and she says that we can easily recognize when Eliot is making a positive or a negative valuation. "No one would argue," she says, that the "Ionian white and gold" mentioned as part of that church's interior decoration "is to be feared and avoided."[19] The reference is, she believes, a clear, obvious, and positive one.

Yet notice how easily the words "Magnus Martyr" slip into "Magna Mater." Close to the reference to Tiresias in the poem we get a transgendered church that apparently has lived its earlier life as female, as connected to the rites of the Great Mother. Given the other references in the poem to Eastern mystery rites the slippage cannot be accidental. Then perhaps the "Ionian white and gold" is also less stable. Perloff says that the reference is "both to the liturgy and to classical Greece."[20] But Ionia is the section of the Greek world on the coast of Asia Minor, where Smyrna is also located, the origin of Mr. Eugenides with his shriveled grapes and his apparently homosexual invitation to a hotel. Also on the Ionian coast is Ephesus, where there was a temple to Artemis (and behind Artemis the Great Mother) over which certain features of Christianity were in a sense constructed. And in Eliot's description of the society lady there is reference

to a burnished throne, marble, a golden Cupidon, a seven-branched cande-
labra, vials of ivory and colored glass, strange synthetic perfumes, and hair
that is spread out in fiery points (*The Waste Land,* lines 77–114). Again
there seems to be a ritual in a temple to the Great Mother, and a threatening ritual at that, so that Perloff's "Ionian white and gold" seems ever less
stable, ever less secure in her description of its meaning as positive.

The point is that there is more semantic slippage here than Perloff acknowledges, and it is also probably true that Eliot is symbolically working
at issues of gender identity that he has, himself, a rather poor sense of. As
the competing, text-influencing homunculi in his mind try to impress their
own drafts on the poetic composition, a certain network of cultural references he is familiar with gets taken over by more submerged homunculi
expressing quite deep psychological and cultural conflicts, having to do
with hidden archaic levels of goddess-worship, maternal structures, and
threats of violence and loss of identity for young male selves such as Eliot
once was. The reference to the Magnus Martyr church then has little stability; Perloff is wrong in failing to see this, but in another respect she is
correct. The semantic indeterminacy in Eliot is due to the power of a regressive, compressive movement that releases iconic, metaphorical, and
identificational energies expressing earlier, nonlinguistic forms of ordering. Perloff favors instead the sort of indeterminacy that arises on the linguistic level. The linguistic level is there as well in Eliot, of course; otherwise "Magnus Martyr" could not turn into "Magna Mater." But those
connections are there to release other energies that are not linguistic; that
is why Perloff is not sensitive to them.

These remarks on Eliot are hardly original, but I use them to make a
contrast with Derrida. That contrast is motivated by the surprising con-
vergences in the reference schemes of Eliot's poem and Derrida's memoir.
The following themes occur in both works: Augustine, the Rome-Carthage
axis or Europe to North Africa relation (Derrida as an Algerian); the worship of Magna Mater; implicit references to homosexuality, as when Derrida imagines Augustine as a little homosexual Jew heading to New York
instead of to Italy (172); the Grail (256); the layering of Western cultural
discourses; the making of claims through an intertextual maneuvering
through the texts of others; and so forth. Yet there remains an important
difference between Eliot and Derrida in the way these schemes are worked
out. Even when Derrida's proliferating linguistic energy produces iconic
resemblances, the result may be to emphasize separateness and barriers,
not convergence. For example, he refers several times to his computer
screen and also, after mentioning the notion of confession and of whisper-
ing in a confessional, refers to "the partition between two absolute subjec-

tivities" (228). On the page prior to that reference we read of "the infinite separation" from his mother and "the infinitely postponed divorce from the closest cruelty which was not that of my mother but the distance she enjoined on me from . . . my own skin thus torn off." So the computer screen becomes also the partition of the Catholic confessional, appropriate in a treatment of Augustine, and Derrida's emphasis is not on a way in which the two subjectivities on different sides of the screen or partition might converge, as in Eliot, but on the infinite task of writing thus imposed by that partitional structure. The screen is also (the point is made many times) the torn-off skin that signifies the impossibility of any renewed identity, even self-identity, and that becomes the screen on which one continues to write, to produce one's confessional words, "where my books find their inspiration, they are written first in skin" (227–28). (He speaks of his own "skizzolatry," his worship of what has been split off in the manner of a page of a sketchbook on which one is writing [103].)

So again we see what Derrida finds to be a necessary structure: the attempted movement through the screen or stretched-out skin toward identification always gets diverted (this is the logic of circumcision for him) into a lateral movement of writing. A movement toward regressive identification with the mother always transforms itself, in Derrida's text, into a sideways movement of intertextual reference, of intralinguistic wordplay. One looks across at the other through a confessional partition or computer screen that no longer allows one to merge across the boundary but offers instead a flat grammatical surface for the lateral movements of language, in pursuit of an other that one is always separate from.

One might say that both Eliot and Derrida question gender identity, but in rather different ways. In *The Waste Land* there seems to be the possibility of a centripetal return to a more archaic stage before gender was fully differentiated, before Christianity separated itself out from Eastern mystery rites, a sometimes prelinguistic realm where images blur and overlap in the oceanic tiding in which the Phoenician sailor has drowned. (The hyacinth girl, for example, blurs into the male Hyacinth of the ancient fertility rites, the lover of Apollo accidentally killed by him.) In Derrida the questioning of gender is not by such a return but by remaining on the grammatical level, by pressing the grammars of gender until they begin to oscillate and destabilize, not under any centripetal, regressive power but under the power of a linguistic dissemination to resist closure, to undercut any way that language tries to stabilize its configurations once and for all. I can only suggest here, rather than develop adequately, a further point. Given Derrida's brief reference in the memoir to the devotees of the Magna Mater throwing their severed organs into homes they pass, and his thought that circumcision might be demanded by the mother, we might return to *The Bacchae* as one of the urtexts of Western culture. If Eliot in *The Waste Land* seems to be hiding a fascination with the threatening rites up in the hills, and even an urge to cross-dress as does Pentheus so as to get closer to them, whatever the threat may be, Derrida tries to control any maternal origin by seeing it as, what he claims all origins to be, a product of the linguistic patterns supposedly produced by it. The play of linguistic dissemination, like the Cartesian machinery, undercuts any Geo-logic (that of both Georgette, his mother, called "Geo" for short by an uncle, and the earth goddess Ge or Gaia) that would have grounded it from the outside. Pentheus has always already been decapitated, but that, if one is Derrida, is his freedom to write. So while Eliot in his poem creeps in transvestite dress toward the bacchanalian rites before and beyond the settled grammar of culture, fearful of the scene in which the tree that Pentheus sits at the top of is snapped down by the wild women, Derrida knows in advance that those rites are themselves already a linguistic product, the projected effect of the disseminating machineries of language. (Or perhaps he is only trying to convince himself of that, in the way that the Cartesian grammatical machinery tries to imagine itself as self-supporting, as engendering out of itself the earthly world that engendered it. Then the move to the grammatical in Derrida, instead of having the Rortyan "world-well-lost" character of postmodern space, would be covering over anxieties that are anterior to that space. The proliferating textual energies are then the symptom of a fear of death and dissolution, a refusal to acknowledge their sway, as opposed to facing and accepting their ultimate triumph as in Merrill.) Because the space of his writing has become an already fully textual one he is able to move too easily from, in his own words, a geo-logic to a theo-logic, from a world of maternal and earthly gravities to a divinized working of language.

LITERARY STYLE AND
TRANSITIONAL SPACE

Consider the way the narrator of Proust's *Swann's Way* recalls his own sobbing in childhood: "Actually their echo has never ceased: it is only because life is growing more and more quiet around me that I hear them afresh, like those convent bells which are so effectively drowned during the day by the noises of the streets that one would suppose them to have been stopped forever, until they sound out again through the silent evening air."[1] A literary style will often have that sense of an echoing music just beneath the lines, so that one has, in the style itself, a staging of the psyche, the laying out of a psychological space that both allows regression to earlier forms of experiencing and stabilizes the self at a distance from it. In this chapter and the next I want to apply the conception of literary space developed in chapter 1 to a range of literary texts. I will look at the way a style of writing, along with other textual features, may help shape a space that is phenomenological and metaphysical, ritualized and regressive-disenchanted, concerned with various kinds of translation and with loss, and expressive of a transitional space of object-relations.

It will be helpful on this matter of style to present Winnicott's account of that transitional space in some detail.[2] He claims that an individual's literary style is a replaying, at more sophisticated levels, of a particular stage in the child's development: his working through a transitional or potential space in which playing with objects is a way of testing capacities for separation and individuation. In this transitional space, says Winnicott, the play objects are to the child "self-objects," that is, extensions of the self, and also externally other, as the child learns gradually to set himself in relation to a world of determinate, independent objects and to be more clearly aware of his own boundaries. The transitional object is a symbol of union between mother and child but at the point where they have already become separate. One is re-creating the experience of that unity precisely from the point where one is leaving it, where one retains in a representational form the object left behind. During this transitional phase the continued availability of the mother is important, says Winnicott, her continuing presence somewhere in the environment even as the child separates from her. If the transitional object does not get renewed support from the dependably returning presence of the mother, then the child will experience trauma and anxiety, more primitive defenses, threats to the inchoate ego structure, confusion, a weakening of its feeling of personal continuity, and later on even madness.[3] The child who does not go through this stage successfully will later feel a need for a ritual repetition of those movements, or for compensating representations that diminish the regressive pull. The mother's presence in the background while the child is playing with the transitional objects should be just so much and no more, says Winnicott. For if that ritualized play space is too much invaded by the mother, then the child will not gain an experience of mastery over objects and self-mastery as well, but rather will be unsure of his boundaries. The child should gradually learn to find a middle ground between the belief that he has omnipotent control over objects that are his extensions, and the belief that his boundaries are weak and easily invaded by objects he has no control over. (Perhaps one might think of that middle ground as an Aristotelian pleasure in things that have their own integrity and rhythms, but that one can set oneself in relation to in predictable and satisfying ways.)

The first transitional object, say the Winnicottian theorists, is one's mother, thought of at first as both self and not-self. Then a space of play opens between mother and child in which a blanket and also dolls or toys may be the transitional objects. But finally and most importantly it is language that takes over this role.[4] We learn to manipulate mental and linguistic representations that are both self and not-self, that we can call up in response to our needs but that remain distant from what they portray. They are both the furniture of our own minds and presentings of what is other and different. For Winnicott one's future style in art or literature is determined by one's style of dealing with objects in this transitional space. In writing one returns ritually to that earlier space and again works out the issues of self and other that were determined there. And the writer's ongoing relationship with language will be a continuing remastery as well of that space, a reworking of the move to language as the most successful transitional object. (It is interesting that whereas a correct account of objects sets clear boundaries between what comes from them and what comes from the self, the correct account of language is to see it as retaining a certain in-between structure; it is both the appearing of the world and a putting forward of the self. So it has a peculiar intimacy, at a more sophisticated level, with the arrangement of Winnicott's transitional space.) Crucial to the psycho-metaphysical model of literary space I have described is the notion of such a dual, ambiguous space, where one's move to the grammatical-strategic field of culture remains partly in thrall to earlier metaphoric-identificational needs, to issues of separation and individuation, so that one looks, for example, for beautiful, self-sustaining patterns and not merely strategically relevant ones, in the ways that representational items are arranged. (It is likely that Winnicott's account is just a placeholder for a more developed theory that cognitive science and cognitive psychology will one day give us, but it picks out patterns that will remain relevant to a study of literary space. I have no intention here of endorsing all elements of it.)

In this transitional space we are dealing not just with stages of self-formation, but also with shaping an overall sense of the metaphysical character of objects and of the world. Whether we experience the world as emptied out or responsive, as malleable to our interventions or as reaching to a distance we have no access to, as solidly there for us or as a mere projection, will be affected by the style of handling both objects and language that we developed earlier. So the writer, like the phenomenologist who wants to expose the deep constituting moves that determine a world of objects, may try for a form of investigation, and thus a form of writing, that causes the features of that earlier transitional space (and of one's accomplishments or failures within it) to come more clearly into view, as they may not in ordinary life or ordinary speech. And this may not just be a move of self-knowledge but may express a continuing, even obsessive, need for such rituals in the face of feelings of aloneness or personal disintegration or a sense of the world as empty and barren. One of the cultural tasks we face now is to shape literary rituals that will train us in setting ourselves in relation to a universe whose operations are not designed to make a human life turn out well, or even to make it significant in the larger picture. For many centuries the Judeo-Christian picture has suggested a very different conception, but now we are closer perhaps to the more tragic outlook of the ancient Greeks, and literature can be one of our allies in facing up to that fact.

If Winnicott is even roughly correct then literary language, as intensifying that transitional space, will be in its very nature a response to mourning and loss, an acknowledgment of what is both left behind and held on to in a different manner. The writer's working through language will repeat and compensate for various kinds of necessary separations, both personal and cultural. The losses that may form the plot background of a work of fiction, or that are the occasion for a poem, have a peculiar affinity, then, with the character of the literary space that represents them, so that one thinks of that space as having required them, as having called them forth precisely to let the language do its sophisticated transitional work.

The question of style as just such a response to loss is the theme, to take one example, of Colm Tóibín's *The Heather Blazing*.[5] The lead character, Eamon, is a judge high up in the Irish courts. After several losses in his childhood, including the deaths of his mother and an uncle and his father's serious stroke, he has attained a certain control by his careful, unemotional arrangement of words in his legal opinions. Language and argument are important for him, even when that means making a judgment against the welfare needs of a family, and he had been especially disturbed as a child when his father's stroke caused a reduced capacity of linguistic articulation. Eamon has studied the more passionate times of Irish rebellions (the book's title is from the rebel song "Boolevogue") and recalls the political and religious rituals so vividly present in his youth. The fragility of what he has constructed, as well as the general fragility of human life, is shown by the fact that the area where he summers is being eaten away by serious erosion of the cliff underneath; soon enough the houses, including his own, will slip into the ocean. One might consider his careful movements through the language of the law, as a judge, to be the grammatical, metonymic stage he has matured into after the more vivid identifications and rituals of his childhood. There is in him, however, no nostalgia for a return to the more passionate and romantic Ireland that he knows of, the Ireland of "the heather blazing." Then his wife dies and his daughter has a child out of wedlock. He is shaken so much by the former event that all he can do is walk along the seacoast for many hours at a time, day after day. His walking across the landscape becomes metaphorical for the movement of the line of prose. In making that walk take on the self-sustaining rhythm that both character and author are trying for, Tóibín shows how the metonymic, lateral movements of language are asked to take on the burden of symbolically expressing and satisfying needs from an earlier psychic stage, one having to do with metaphoric identifications and the securing of individuation.

Even in the opening chapter, before Eamon's loss of his wife, the prose has a hypnotic cadence, a carefully composed tone of loss and elegy. (Note how in the first quotation the *n, d,* and *r* of Eamon's last name keep repeating in a manner that turns the sentence into a quiet chanting.)

> Eamon Redmond stood at the window looking down at the river which was deep brown after days of rain. (Tóibín, *Heather Blazing,* 3)

> They were close to the soft edge of the cliff, the damp, marly soil which was eaten away each year. He listened for the sound of the sea, but heard nothing except the rooks in a nearby field and the sound of a tractor in the distance, and coming from the house the swells of the music. He rested against the windowsill and looked at the fading light, the dark clouds of evening over the sea. The grass was wet now with a heavy dew, but the air was still as though the day had been held back for a few moments while night approached. He heard Carmel moving in the front room. She wanted everything in its place, the house filled with their things, as soon as they arrived, and he stood up now and ventured in to help her. (13)

We are dealing here with more than just a description of present events. In the ritual evenness of the tone, in the quiet steadiness of the cadence, there is a phenomenological stance: an acknowledgment that lets things emerge as they are, that is grateful for the way they arrange themselves over the eaten-away cliff, that grants them their metaphysical style as objects of the everyday world. They are independently determinate, and yet there is no loss or diminishment to the self in their being so; indeed one finds satisfaction in comprehending them as such. There is in the tone of the prose, in its rising and falling, a suggestion of inevitable loss, but this makes more valuable the capacity, for a time, to put "everything in its place," to fill a human structure with the things of a shared life, to fill the space of a sentence with words carefully arranged. The soft music of the sentences seems to maintain itself confidently just above the level where the articulation of a world would collapse into something less determinate, even if the self is as fragilely supported in its linguistic articulation as the cliff-side houses. Eamon, in the paragraph just quoted, moves to a certain distance from which he can see, and be reconciled with, that overall structure of loss and holding out, as observed in the fading light at day's end; then at the end of the paragraph he moves to enter again the space of the everyday world. The reconciliation depends in part on the evenness of tone, on a certain precarious balance between what is self and what is other, with no elements of the sentences pressing themselves forward too assertively or betraying a too forceful subjectivity that is shaping the sentences from the outside. Instead, as in the transitional space of Winnicott, there is a steady rhythm that is both the narrator's own self-sustaining movement and a deeper rhythm to things; it is important to style in Tóibín's novel that it be both.

An example of how Eamon's policy of steady walking along the coast, after the death of his wife, mirrors the character of the prose reads:

> He stood up and walked back to the strand, making his way slowly south. Earlier, when he set out, the air had been still, there was almost no wind, but now a thin film of sand was being blown northward along the strand. He could feel the wind in his face, but it was pleasant and warm as he walked along. He tried to move with an even step.
>
> There were gulls and a few other solitary sea birds lurking over the waves. The sea was calm. He was hungry already, even though he had eaten a boiled egg and some toast before he left the house, but he decided to go for another hour or so without opening the sandwiches. . . . Since he began to spend each day walking he had learned how to divide up the time. . . .
>
> He set off walking once more. He carried no watch or clock so he had no idea how long he had been on the strand, but guessed that it was one o'clock or two o'clock and that he had been walking for two or three hours. He passed a few people, but there was no one lying on the sand or going into the sea to swim; the wind was too strong. The sand was softer nearer the sea; he walked where it was wet. At low tide, he knew, you could pick cockles here, but the tide was well in and the strand grew narrower as he walked along. In a few miles it would disappear altogether. Then he would take to the road. (Tóibín, *Heather Blazing*, 206–8)

The loss of his wife has been devastating, summarizing all the losses of childhood as well. His need for that long, steady walking suggests how intimately bound the cadence of writing is to mourning, to a self-propulsion that retains in the background an earlier space of loss, where the child had to move away from its initial consuming identifications and accept instead a compensating but less satisfying linguistic movement. (Language, we saw, becomes the most satisfying transitional object.) The linguistic rhythm may be more appealing when it retains traces of the rhythm of what has been lost. The very simplicity of the sentences, their straightforward structure and movement, without complex subordinations, suggests a metaphysically reduced selfhood whose self-maintaining articulation is held steady over an oceanic flow the power of which will eventually dissolve it (as it seems to do at the end of each sentence). Note, for example, his references to moving with an even step and learning how to divide up the time. Again one can call that movement a metonymic one, from word to word, sentence to sentence, but this is not the proliferating linguistic energy of a Derrida or a Rushdie. The positional-metonymic world is astride an earlier, more primitive space that pulls strongly on it and that conditions a style of setting the self in relation to objects. Without that pull the sentences would become boring in their structure; what gives them energy is what they hold themselves up against, their remaining close to what would bring them under, as in the image of the house on the cliff whose support is being eaten away. And it is important that this quiet movement across the landscape, whether in walking or in writing, is a (metaphysical) training in letting the objects around Eamon emerge as they are, apart from how he might want them to be arranged (as he eventually accepts his daughter's pregnancy). The steadiness of the prose is an acceptance and a relinquishing, as well as a self-maintenance, and so links, as in Hegel, a structure of self-formation with a metaphysical attitude, a style of being a self with an attitude toward the world and toward death. One both holds the objects in view and acknowledges and accepts the fact that soon they will dissolve; but this fact makes us value the kind of integrity they have now, on their own.

There is a more complex relationship between earlier and later worlds in W. G. Sebald's *The Emigrants,* though here, again, there is a style that is working through a certain way of being related to the world, that lets a space open out behind objects, so that their metaphysical "feel" becomes evident.

> As for myself, on those Sundays in the utterly deserted hotel I would regularly be overcome by such a sense of aimlessness and futility that I would go out, purely in order to preserve an illusion of purpose, and walk about amidst the city's immense and time-blackened nineteenth-century buildings, with no particular destination in mind. On those wanderings, when winter light flooded the deserted streets and squares for the few rare hours of real daylight, I never ceased to be amazed by the completeness with which anthracite-coloured Manchester, the city from which industrialization had spread across the entire world, displayed the clearly chronic process of its impoverishment and degradation to anyone who cared to see. Even the grandest of the buildings, such as the Royal Exchange, the Refuge Insurance Company, the Grosvenor Picture Palace, and indeed the Piccadilly Plaza, which had been built only a few years before, seemed so empty and abandoned that one might have supposed oneself surrounded by mysterious facades or theatrical backdrops. Everything then would appear utterly unreal

to me, on those sombre December days when dusk was already falling at three o'clock, when the starlings, which I had previously imagined to be migratory songbirds, descended upon the city in dark flocks that must have numbered hundreds of thousands, and, shrieking incessantly, settled close together on the ledges and copings of warehouses for the night.[6]

The book's title indicates that it is about people who have emigrated from their place of origin to a different setting. (Sebald was born in Germany but spent most of his adulthood, before his tragic recent death in an auto accident, as a professor in England.) One of the four stories linked by the narrator's presence is about a Jewish painter in Manchester who left Germany as a teenager just before World War II; the rest of his family was later murdered in the camps. Connection to Jewish origins and the Holocaust is weaker in the other three stories. One man was a schoolteacher who lost his job in Germany for being one-fourth Jewish but who later fought in the German army. Another left Lithuania as a child in 1899 and settled in England, becoming a prominent doctor and changing his Jewish name, even hiding his origins from his wealthy wife. The fourth story is about a homosexual man who left Germany when young and eventually settled in America, and about his severe depression late in life. Two of the principal figures commit suicide in old age, and another willingly gives himself over to brutal electroshock treatments that seem almost a form of suicide.

The emigration the book is about is not just geographical but also the move from the space of childhood to that of an adulthood that has been emptied out. (So the literary space here can be seen as both translational and regressive-disenchanted in the way those features were described in chapter 1.) The transition from one space to another has occurred in a manner such that one cannot be at home in the new one, which seems an empty terrain of meaningless ruins. There is an obsessive return of features of the earlier world. Dr. Selwyn, the Jewish-British doctor, eventually reveals his heritage to his wife, though it is unclear that this is the reason for their divorce, and he claims that "the years of the second war, and the decades after, were a blinding, bad time for me, about which I could not say a thing even if I wanted to" (Sebald, *Emigrants*, 21). That sense of an obsessive return of what has been covered over is represented metaphorically by the story of an elderly Swiss guide whom Selwyn, as a youth, had become close to, so that "never in his life, neither before nor later, did he feel as good as he did then, in the company of that man. . . . Even the separation from Elli, whom I had met at Christmas in Berne and married after the war, did not cause me remotely as much pain as the separation from

Naegeli" (14). The guide disappears in the Alps shortly after that separation, and in the last lines of the story the narrator tells us that his body was released by the Oberaar glacier seventy-two years later. "And so they are ever returning to us, the dead. At times they come back from the ice more than seven decades later and are found at the edge of the moraine, a few polished bones and a pair of hobnailed boots" (23).

As those passages suggest, it is ambiguous in Sebald just what is the nature of the obsessive return from an earlier world. The schoolteacher receives his job back in Germany after the war and eventually retires to Switzerland, but he keeps a flat in the small German town where he had been teaching. As he becomes almost totally blind he tells an acquaintance that it is time now to sell the flat. He returns to the German town, lies down on the railroad track (he had always been fascinated by railroads), and is killed by a train. There is some suggestion in Sebald that the man is obsessively repeating the death by railroad that occurred to Jews who were taken east, but it is also possible that he is just elderly, depressed, and blind. Ambrose Adelwarth, who submits to medical experiments with electroshock given by a German doctor in America, may be ritually recalling earlier Nazi experiments, but again he may just be severely depressed and want some end either to that condition or to his life. The case is clearer with Ferber, the artist who lost his family in the Holocaust; he becomes a portrait painter but sees his work as a ritualized accumulation of ruin and dust.

> The entire furniture was advancing, millimetre by millimetre, upon the central space where Ferber had set up his easel in the grey light that entered through a high north-facing window layered with the dust of decades. Since he applied the paint thickly, and then repeatedly scratched it off the canvas as his work proceeded, the floor was covered with a largely hardened and encrusted deposit of droppings, mixed with coal dust, several centimetres thick at the centre and thinning out towards the outer edges, in places resembling the flow of lava. This, said Ferber, was the true product of his continuing endeavours and the most palpable proof of his failure. It had always been of the greatest importance to him, Ferber once remarked casually, that nothing should change at his place of work, that everything should remain as it was, as he had arranged it, and that nothing further should be added but the debris generated by painting and the dust that continuously fell and which, as he was coming to realize, he loved more than anything else in the world. He felt closer to dust, he said, than to light, air or water. There was nothing he found so unbearable as a well-dusted house, and he never felt more at home than in places where things remained undisturbed, muted

under the grey, velvety sinter left when matter dissolved, little by little, into nothingness. (Sebald, *Emigrants*, 161)

This description gives us a phenomenology of objects, one that focuses less on them than on the space or lighting in which they appear and by which they are given an overall character as real. But this overall character is one of a slow dissolution of things into ashes. This world is unable to incarnate the present meanings of an ongoing life because of the need for a ritualized return of what can no longer come back.

> He might reject as many as forty variants, or smudge them back into the paper and overdraw new attempts upon them; and if he then decided that the portrait was done, not so much because he was convinced that it was finished as through sheer exhaustion, an onlooker might well feel that it had evolved from a long lineage of grey-ancestral faces, rendered unto ash but still there, as ghostly presences, on the harried paper. (162)

If we think of style as reflecting modes of working through the Winnicottian transitional space, then Ferber's art would represent an obsessive attempt at establishing object relations with a world that has disappeared forever, with an earlier presence that can no longer be reliably in the background as an individual works out his separation, since that presence, rich as it was, exists now only as the palest of ghosts, "rendered unto ash," the ashes of the Holocaust. So Ferber must keep trying and failing at these iconic identifications (note that he is doing portraits) and cannot move on into a grammatical-metonymic world where he might reproduce the earlier world positionally, by substitution within a formal structure, that is, through forming a family of his own. Sebald's prose (importantly it is also the translator's, Michael Hulse) has the steady metonymic movement that links word to word in satisfying cadences. The book also makes references that give it an evident lateral, intertextual energy, as they seem to reproduce themselves across the textual field. Images of a butterfly collector, suggesting Nabokov, reappear, their presence unsurprising perhaps in a book about translation from one space of writing to another. One character stays in the house where Wittgenstein lived as an engineering student in Manchester, and there are curious Wittgensteinian parallels in the stories. Wittgenstein was an emigrant from the German-speaking world to England, as the narrator is, and the doctor in the book studied at Cambridge in 1913 when Wittgenstein was there and, like Wittgenstein, played down his Jewish heritage. The schoolteacher teaches in a small rural village where his efforts are unappreciated, as Wittgenstein did for six years, and he never marries. He also is a loyal enough German that he returns to Germany in 1939 and fights against Russia, as Wittgenstein was a strongly loyal Austrian and fought on the eastern front in World War I. Adelwarth, another of the book's central characters, is homosexual, again as Wittgenstein was. One notices in these people, and often in the narrator as well, the terrible aloneness of Wittgenstein, who made a hut for himself on the coast of Norway and later lived alone in a cottage in the west of Ireland. It is as if typical qualities of Wittgenstein were being distributed across the various characters. Other repetitions occur as well. Even a minor figure in the book, the woman who runs the hotel where the narrator stays, reappears later in a painting by Ferber, and her Salvation Army uniform in a photo repeats the dress of Selwyn's housekeeper in the first section. A Werner Herzog movie is mentioned, and one feels the mood of some of his movies in several of the narrator's descriptions. (Even the picture of a caravan in a small restaurant, the Wadi Halfa, seems to recall a scene, about a blind guide leading a caravan, in a Herzog movie. There could be, although this idea will not be pursued here, a direct German linkage between Heidegger's notion of a phenomenological-metaphysical space or clearing, the sense of cinematic space in many of Herzog's movies, and Sebald's shaping of a ritualized literary space. The differences among the three are evidently important as well.)

One certainly finds here in Sebald the intertextual, metonymic, text-generating energy that a Derridean might favor. But it is crucial that Sebald, or the narrator, does not move fully into that sort of space (as the linguistic-postmodern model of literary space would recommend). As with the painter Ferber, a lost iconic world is there in the background and he keeps trying to set himself in relation to it. Ferber's mother has left him a manuscript about the lost world she grew up in. It is filled with vivid images from her childhood, and that vivid imagery, when compared with the movement of Sebald's prose, can suggest the transition from an iconic mental experiencing to a grammatical, linguistic one; but here the transition is accomplished only symbolically, in the act of writing, and not in the life itself, whether that of Ferber or of the narrator. Indeed the book might be seen as examining the conditions under which that move into the syntactic, positional field of adulthood cannot be adequately completed, because of what has occurred in the world one is supposedly emigrating from. What ought to be a self-sustaining advance through a proliferating world of signs is haunted by more archaic forms; that advance seems instead a ritual repetition of a more primitive self-propulsion, one that still has access to earlier cadences and to an iconic world of painful images. This image world is sometimes that of the Nazi Holocaust, which Sebald did not experience (he was born in Germany in 1944). When he first sees Manchester from the air it seems "nothing but a faint glimmer, as if from a fire almost suffocated in ash"; it is a city "built of countless bricks and inhabited by millions of souls, dead and alive," a "necropolis or mausoleum" (Sebald, *Emigrants,* 150, 151). He finds himself attracted to the onetime Jewish quarter, where all that is standing is "one single row of empty houses, the wind blowing through the smashed windows and doors" (157). On one walk in Manchester the narrator passes "a long disused gasworks," a "bonemill," and a "slaughterhouse" (159). The city, he notes, was once "the industrial Jerusalem" (165). He repeats Ferber's view that the most impressive thing about the city was "all the chimneys that towered above the plain and the flat maze of housing" (168–69), making Ferber believe that he had found his destiny. Ferber describes as well his visit to Europe to see paintings by Grunewald, in which he notes "the monstrosity of the suffering, which emanating from the figures depicted, spread to cover the whole of Nature, only to flood back from the lifeless landscape to the humans marked by death" (170). As Ferber tells the narrator: "Throughout the nineteenth century, the German and Jewish influence was stronger in Manchester than in any other European city; and so, although I had intended to move in the opposite direction, when I arrived in Manchester I had come home, in a sense, and with every year I have spent since then in the birthplace of industrialization, amidst the black facades, I have realized more clearly than ever that I am here, as they used to say, to serve under the chimney" (192).

So the image repertoire of the Holocaust, of ashes and ruins and chimneys and slaughterhouses, keeps invading Sebald, as a German, as he moves into that textual, metonymic space of language, just as the movement to Manchester turns out to be a return in certain ways to the Germany that is the birthplace of both Ferber and Sebald. It would be a moral failing to move into that newer space cleanly and to leave behind the pervasive images, though this sense of a haunting by ritualized, half-forgotten patterns applies even to those of Sebald's characters who did not flee the Nazis. With Wittgenstein and Nabokov as frequent references we can see the theme of translation both in the physical emigration and in the move from one language to another. (Sebald was the first director of the British Center for Translation, and while fluent in English, he chose to write in German and to have the translation done by another.) We are dealing with a translational, transitional space where one cannot immigrate freely into the newer form of life but must find it a barren terrain, impossible to fill in with meaning. There are many separations in the book: the separation of Selwyn from Naegeli, of Adelwarth from the only person he could be intimate with, of Ferber from his family at the airport in Germany, of the narrator from his homeland. But death and loss occur in such a way that the earlier stage must be mourned for obsessively. The interesting suggestion here is that this is a proper reaction. Instead of acknowledging a duty to advance into what might seem a more mature phase, one sees that it is morally right, given the terrible nature of the loss (obviously so in Ferber's case), to engage in that ritual repetition of earlier moves, to let the grammatical-metonymic world be permeated by the iconic-metaphoric one. It is right for the German narrator not to be able to move easily in the world of England that he has been translated into, but rather to find it haunted by a general emptiness and by specific Holocaust images that repeat themselves in the landscape. The quiet power of the text does not express the self-determining energies of the linguistic realm but rather a holding steady that is ready to slip back into an earlier space of loss, such that the steadiness of movement seems an enormous accomplishment. There is an integrity in that very unwillingness to try to break free of the haunting earlier stage. The narrator refuses to play the role of the modern Cartesian, who supposedly will not care about the loss of earlier support because he believes he can make the new world self-sustaining on its own, can live within a self-propelled textual energy that constructs its objects for itself (as in the picture presented of Rushdie's work in chapter 1). Sebald instead keeps obsessively in mind the world being lost, especially through its effective power to empty out any present scene, to make it appear as bleak and exhausted, as nothing in it has the slightest capacity to replace what has been lost. The space of literature, again, is essentially defined here as a space of mourning.

In *The Rings of Saturn,* Sebald continues that combination of a linguistic metonymy with overwhelming loss.[7] The sideways, associative movement of language from one signifier to the next is mirrored in the movements of the self across the landscape, here a walking tour on the east coast of England. The intertextuality here is even more noticeable than in *The Emigrants,* with references to the writings of Thomas Browne or the memoirs of Chateaubriand, publications on the culture of silkworms or diaries of Roger Casement. But again the narrator is surrounded by a world whose capacity to retain its meaningfulness has disappeared. We see the decay of once-great family houses and seaside hotels, the decline of entire towns. He walks through an area where a great hurricane has wiped out millions of trees. As the narrator says on the first page, "I became preoccupied not only with the unaccustomed sense of freedom but also the paralyzing horror that had come over me at various times when confronted with the traces of destruction, reaching far back into the past, that

were evident even in that remote place" (3). The minimal but steady progression through the landscape of signifiers cannot be maintained, and the
narrator is taken to the hospital "in a state of almost total immobility."
The world falls loose from the ordinary network of meaningfulness that
holds it together; from the hospital window "it was as if I were looking
down from a cliff upon a sea of stone or a field of rubble, from which the
tenebrous masses of multi-storey carparks rose up like immense boulders"
(5). There is the image of Thomas Browne gathering burial objects (for
Urn Burial); he "scrutinizes that which escaped annihilation for any sign
of the mysterious capacity for transmigration he has so often observed in
caterpillars and moths" (26). Visiting an island once used for British military research, the narrator says: "the closer I came to these ruins, the more
any notion of a mysterious isle of the dead receded, and the more I imagined myself amidst the remains of our own civilization after its extinction
in some future catastrophe" (237). It is not only the landscapes but also
individual lives that have a painful emptiness to them. An unmarried academic acquaintance dies alone "in the deep and dark hours of the night"
(6–7). In one of the accounts in the book the poet Edward Fitzgerald as a
young man develops a deep passion for another young man. It cannot be
consummated, but they remain close friends for decades, and after the
other's death Fitzgerald withdraws increasingly within himself. He eventually settles alone in a farmhouse near Woodbridge and, dispensing with
the chore of cooking, subsists on little more than bread, butter, and tea,
assailed at times in his solitude "by what he called the blue devil of melancholy (205)."

So in Sebald as in Tóibín we have the steadiness of walking across the
landscape as a stand-in for the movement of prose. The world of language
offers us this lateral movement from one reference to another as texts keep
calling up variations and repetitions of themselves. But this is not a movement that can any longer hope by its own power to confer meaning on the
world or to tease out of the world an inchoate meaning just waiting to be
actualized. Given Sebald's background in German culture, we have to see
here an implicit claim that the Hegelian activity of spiritualization, the
raising of scattered elements into a meaningful and self-sustaining life, can
no longer occur. We have instead a world of ruins and absences, with no
features immanent to it that suggest any possibility of renewal. The narrator in walking might well be Benjamin's flaneur now transported to a
space much like Benjamin's description of German baroque drama, with
its sense of ruin and decay. We are left rather with the stoic momentum of
a linguistic movement whose hope is in that momentum itself, the ability
to keep moving, as in the narrator's walking tour, across a landscape that

may once have supported larger meanings but that is now a scene of traces we can hardly comprehend. Whatever once were the conditions for the full appropriation of a grammatical regime of signs, with the fertile, migrating energies of that regime, are no longer in place. In the landscapes of individual psyches as well, there are the remains of some earlier loss and devastation that we can no longer get back to, even if merely to comprehend it. The space of writing offers us a modest compensation, in the way its narrative and rhythmic momentum both moves us forward and lets the loss be felt, through what that forward movement has to hold itself out against. Instead of trying to fill up that absence with ever increasing gyrations and a forced energetics of language, one lets the language come closer to the reduced state that the gravities of that space are pulling it toward. One then shows how, even close to the edge of dissolution in that manner, to a solvent melancholy and sadness, one's linguistic articulation can remain self-sustaining. One's craft can hold itself suspended even over that unnameable loss.

There is a rather different view of the transition to a positional-grammatical space in *Seeing Calvin Coolidge in a Dream,* by John Derbyshire.[8] It is narrated by Chai, a Chinese immigrant to America who becomes one of the more convincing arguments for adulthood in recent literature. When he was very young Chai lost his father in the Korean War and then his mother died of tuberculosis. He went through poverty and hunger during the famine of 1959–61 and was sent to do brutal, freezing work in a northern rural area during the cultural revolution. His only comfort as a child, a small stray dog that, he says, was able to be satisfied with very little, was taken away and killed during a government program against dogs. He finally swam to Hong Kong, almost drowning, and fell in love with Selina, who left him suddenly because her family had determined that she would marry a man who had settled in America. So his world has been one of painful loss and suffering. But during his stay in the rural north he had determined to learn English and was finally able to purchase a paperback of *David Copperfield,* which he memorized during the long winter evenings. His English helped him succeed at a bank in Hong Kong, and then he was transferred to New York and became successful, marrying Ding and having a daughter by her. As Derbyshire gradually builds his story, language and the arrangements of it are brought to the fore, especially in the contrasts that Chai makes between Chinese and English. Chinese, he says, is an impoverished language, with an undeveloped grammar and mere onomatopoeia for items for which English has specific words (for example, *stridulating,* the sound crickets make by rubbing their legs against their wing cases). "English is just smarter," says Chai, "more sophisticated, and more powerful. Once you have mastered English, Chinese seems very second-rate and . . . I don't know, puerile. Volcano is *fire-mountain*. . . . Asbestos is *stone-cotton*. . . . Monday, Tuesday, and Wednesday are One-day, Two-day, Three-day" (41).

Chai is justly proud of his excellent English and can quote Samuel Johnson or play sophisticated games of Scrabble. But Derbyshire lets us see the irony in Chai's depiction of Chinese. Chai has memorized beautiful poems, from Li Po and Tu Fu and others, that he likes to recite, and he can feel excited when the single archaic character *zu* is used to express "died suddenly and unexpectedly" (Derbyshire, *Seeing Calvin Coolidge in a Dream,* 49). Chai may praise the life of capitalist democracy in America and denigrate China (he even defends Americans' appalling ignorance of history by saying they are a forward-looking people), but Derbyshire is setting up a more complex contrast. China becomes a more universal referent, standing for the losses and fears, the powerful images, passions and separations that one experiences in childhood. Chai's almost drowning in the swim to Hong Kong is a recognition of the pull toward dissolution, against secure individuation and form. America is the cooler world of Chai's adulthood. (One might recall here the images of glassmaking and cooling in Merrill.) It can seem that Derbyshire, in the way he focuses so much on Chai's linguistic abilities, is trying to present a model of what we have been calling the move from an iconic-mirroring phase to a positional, grammatical one. One learns with the latter to take up positions within a structural field, to recognize that if identity depends on structural position then one may find satisfaction with substitutes who fit those positions, instead of trying for the self-other identities, as with an irreplaceable mother, of the mirroring phase. So Chai has replaced his childhood family structure (both parents were lost when he was young) by putting himself in the father's position, taking a wife, and having a child (and even having a dog).

This may seem an obvious perception, but Derbyshire goes out of his way to emphasize how this is a move as well into a certain way of using language. The more image- and onomatopoeia-driven Chinese, with all its richness of resonance, is replaced by a cooler and more grammatically inflected language. Chai is even a bit pretentious in correcting others on their use of English, and because of his memorizing of Dickens and Johnson he possesses a slightly old-fashioned diction. The games of Scrabble he plays, with their interlocking words, become a metaphor for this new world of patterned linguistic arrangements, of moves within a positional grammar, that may no longer carry the punch of his Chinese. In praising

English for having the word *stridulating,* for example, he is praising it for a Latinate abstraction that distances one from the sound. And it is true as well that while he loves his wife Ding, the more passionate relationship was with Selina in Hong Kong. Chai's denigration of China and of the Chinese language is a defensive barrier against what must be still a strong pull toward going back to the earlier stage. (The novel is about the appeal of regression and about the virtues of staying instead within the "grammatical" model of adulthood.)

Derbyshire is in fact not making any point about the real relations between Chinese and English as languages; he certainly is not endorsing the view that Chinese is more impoverished, nor is he suggesting that Chinese culture somehow stands for a stage of childhood. (It is perhaps typical that the academic postcolonial reader will likely miss the subtlety and irony of what Derbyshire is doing and complain about the colonizing/subordinating attitude toward China.) Rather he is making a point similar to Merrill's in "Lost in Translation," where the translation of a poem from the "warm romance" of the French to the "rhyme-rutted pavements" of German, seen as a deserted ruin at twilight, shows what is lost in certain other translations: image to language, childhood to adulthood, passionate outpouring to the careful arrangements of words. Chai's Scrabble games with his wife and his frequent searches of dictionary and thesaurus, as well as his memorizing of the Dickens novel in English, stand, like the arranging of Merrill's jigsaw puzzle pieces, for the lateral, grammatical linkages of language that allow more primitive and traumatic experiences (and he has had many of these in China and Hong Kong) to be handled and ordered and accepted, even if a certain kind of power is lost in that translation of energy from one form to another.

Chai learns by chance where Selina is working in America, and he vows to see her. (It turns out, of course, to be by linguistic chance, as the palindromic spelling of her husband's name is a key to the discovery.) As readers we may now suppose that Chai is about to revolt against the world of positional arrangements he now resides in. We have seen him moving through the cooler, more abstract field of cultural representation: writing books on business, mastering the computer program that his boss cannot figure out, doing a difficult catalog of his boss's uncle's collection of Slavic literature (requiring translation from Russian), explaining nasal and lateral plosion in the pronunciation of English. But another interest of his comes into play here, his curiosity about and affection for Calvin Coolidge. The books in English that Chai reads tend to belittle Coolidge, but Chai studies his speeches and visits his birthplace. He comes to understand that Coolidge's taciturnity, and his emphasis on character and virtue as what the American system requires, cover over a life of pain and loss: the deaths of his mother (when Coolidge was twelve), his sister, and then later his son. Chai looks around at the bleak homestead in Vermont and wonders what it was like for Coolidge to spend the winter there after his mother's death. What might have seemed a quiet banality of Coolidge's speeches comes to seem a form of heroism. Chai decides that he might have an affair with Selina but then has a dream in which, when he comes to the hotel to meet Selina, Coolidge is in the room instead and persuades him of the wrongness of the affair. (Or perhaps it is not a dream and Chai's wife has hired the actor who used to play Coolidge in a small theatrical at the Vermont homestead.) By the end of the book Chai has decided that it is his duty to become more politically involved, as Coolidge was, and he decides to run for the school board in his Long Island town. He chooses, for what we can now understand are excellent reasons, the cooler linguistic and moral order of Coolidge instead of a return to his passionate youthful affair.

It is not easy to describe how satisfying reading *Seeing Calvin Coolidge in a Dream* is. Chai can be fussy about his knowledge of language ("I noted with approval, as a connoisseur of such things, that Uncle Sergei's English had practically no trace of Russian accent," 71). But his care about language comes to seem, like Coolidge's language, a form of heroism. The decision to run for the school board has a power to it that much larger decisions in other novels fail to take on. The steady advance of the prose both acknowledges and resists the earlier space that Chai still holds in view. Part of the sophisticated pleasure of the novel is the way writing comes to the fore in the parallels between what the author is doing in constructing the space of the book and what Chai is doing in ordering his life through language and through the languagelike field of his adult life. In the very mood of the prose, rather than in any mentioning of them, we are given a sense of the gains and losses in Chai's transition to the world (of both linguistic arrangements and adult commitments) that he now inhabits. But nothing is really lost, as Merrill says in "Lost in Translation." The palm tree's quiet growth is producing "shade and fiber, milk and memory." And so is Chai's world, as we leave him at novel's end well contented with his wife and daughter and with his life as a whole.

In both Derbyshire and Merrill, with their various images of the careful arrangement of linguistic items, there is a repetition perhaps of the Spinozist model mentioned earlier: what seems at first merely external, invading the self from the outside in an arbitrary and disturbing manner, is internalized as an aspect of the necessary arrangements of thought or language. There is, in Derbyshire and Merrill, a sense of a calm linguistic control, not one that has been forced on recalcitrant material but one that has truly gone over into the difficult events and objects, as they really are, and taken them up into the linguistic movement successfully. The dangerous character of the earlier moments remains: Merrill's memories of a time of parental divorce and Chai's memories of the crushing losses of his father and mother as a child, and then of Selina. But the poem and the novel are rituals that have tested the power of these internal linguistic energies to take in and handle difficult material and shown it to be sufficient. In that way these writers have replayed, now in a more sophisticated form, the satisfactions of the move into language in the transitional space of childhood. The slight stiffness and formality in Chai's English, even the occasional pedantry, call attention to the language as such, but in a way that makes Chai's ability to order his life quite moving. As he puts it: "Well, my pedant's cap came to me not from a life spent in libraries and lecture halls, but after suffering borne and suffering inflicted. I can wear it with dignity and humility, as it should be worn, not with the empty arrogance of the merely credentialed" (Derbyshire, *Seeing Calvin Coolidge in a Dream*, 96).

We can see in the very form of those two sentences something of what they are about. The rhythmic arrangement of words, the parallelism of formal structure, the contrasts that are both syntactic and semantic ("suffering borne and suffering inflicted")—all these bring out the Spinozist work of Chai's speaking. I have been discussing the linguistic turn in philosophy and in literature, and I have criticized more radical expressions of that turn located in de Man, Rushdie, Perloff, and Derrida. But here we can see that there is a partial truth in claims that make formal linguistic patterns primary and reference secondary. Writing does embody an excess of signifying power over the work of talking about the world. In Chai's (or Derbyshire's) language, as in the work of the historian Edward Gibbon, for example, one has the sense that formal repetitions and contrasts, the balances and structural parallels, are waiting around to fit what is to be said into their linguistic engineering, rather than merely being expressive of circumstances in the world. One reason for that excess of form over reference is, we have seen, the ritualized work that language as a transitional object is performing. But it is crucial, of course, that the psychic material being brought into a representational space is by no means a linguistic effect, as in radical versions of the linguistic turn (recall de Man). Precisely because the psychological is not already linguistic there is power, and gains and losses, in the translation into language.

By the end of the book Chai says that he is now going to master *Robert's Rules of Order* so that he may stand for the school board election in the spring. That sort of mastery seems a fussy project an American today would not undertake, and at the same time it stands impressively for the achievements of the cooler yet powerful orderliness that has allowed him to take in and master the pain of so much of his life, without falsifying it. The book is a tribute to grammar, it could be said, to the simple but deeply appealing craftsmanship of the sentences of Chai's narrative, to the cultural grammar of Chai's "new found land" that has allowed him his adult happiness, to the rules of discursive order he will try to abide by if elected to the school board. His wife is pregnant again, and he has put to rest the ghosts of his past. He has found his sister, still in China and doing well. "Between us we are planning to establish a memorial to our parents: a decent tomb, in one of the new cemeteries now permitted on the Mainland, with their names, dates, deeds, places of origin, and some suitable verses cut by a good calligraphist. I shall rest there myself at last: *luo ye gui gen,* as we say—The falling leaf returns to its roots" (Derbyshire, *Seeing Calvin Coolidge in a Dream,* 269). The linguistic ritual has allowed him to work through the transitional space of separation so that he can leave behind what must be left behind (as he gives up having the affair with Selina) and accept the satisfactions of moving through the arrangements available to him, of family and work and public service, while recognizing that his individuality will one day dissolve as he returns to that out of which he arose, to China. "So here I am: T. C. Chai, financial analyst for a New York investment bank. Son of Shije Zhai, engineer, soldier, and martyr, of the town called Willow Palisade in the province called Lucky Forest in northeast China. . . . Now living in great contentment with dear wife, beautiful child, and the hope of a second, in America—my new found land. Truly it is a strange road we travel, and what lies at the end of it only God knows" (273). As we have seen all along (this is why McDowell, Williams, and Wittgenstein were models in chapter 3) the turn to the grammatical would end in an arbitrary emptiness if one did not see that level of ordering in a wider context in which phenomenological structures of self and other, of self-formation, were still at risk and still in play. That is why the role of the grammatical in Chai's form of adulthood can be an *achievement.* Language is the most effective transitional object because of the sophisticated ways it both retains and leaves behind in representing.

A critic might suggest that *Seeing Calvin Coolidge in a Dream* is a slight work on which to be placing the theoretical pressure placed on it here. Or one might claim that all reconciliations implicitly employ coercion and a marginalization of otherness, so that even the sort of reconciliation Chai finally achieves with his life and with the world must be suspect, must fail to acknowledge, for example, the political failures of America in its oppressive treatment of minorities. The cultural studies theorist will surely find ways that configurations of power affecting otherness and immigration are not properly looked at here. But I find pleasure in the way that Chai's simple decision to run for the school board in his town, as Coolidge did, seems a more powerful commitment to the processes that might improve America than the work of the academic critics with their rhetorics of power and subversion. He understands, seeing what happened in China, that the impoverishment of the political sphere, of the very activity of ordinary politics, is a matter of grave concern. We should have more confidence in a future America populated by those like Chai than in one populated by cultural studies critics.

Another example of the moment of transition to language occurs in a literary scene in *Death in Venice* that was briefly mentioned earlier. Aschenbach, after watching the graceful movements of Tadzio, opts not to engage him in conversation but to work on his own writing, to produce linguistic movements that will quite deliberately match those of his beloved.

> He would write, and moreover he would write in Tadzio's presence. This lad should be in a sense his model, his style should follow the lines of this figure that seemed to him divine; he would snatch up this beauty into the realms of the mind, as once the eagle bore the Trojan shepherd aloft. Never had the pride of the word been so sweet to him, never had he known so well that Eros is in the word, as in those perilous and precious hours when he sat at his rude table, within the shade of his awning, his idol full in his view and the music of his voice in his ears, and fashioned his little essay after the model Tadzio's beauty set.[9]

It is relevant to the theme of literary style and regressive spaces that the youthful adolescent male can serve, for Aschenbach at least, as an obvious case of a transitional object. He is both self and other, both a mirroring of the self as a child and an other whose beauty and liveliness of form can, if identified with, allow Aschenbach to overcome feelings of disintegration and death. So he can form a pattern (recall Winnicott here) of what will become a way of setting oneself in relation to the world of others and, ultimately, a way of dealing with language. Aschenbach's dyadic, imaginary, identificational relationship with Tadzio can have the oscillating quality of an earlier structural phase. It will not be difficult to move from precisely this sort of model to language itself as an analogous and superior transitional object, one that is cooler and less immediately satisfying as an object for identification but is a more reliable long-term solution. Aschenbach is clear here about substituting language as one sort of transitional object for Tadzio as another. At least for Aschenbach this beautiful other already belongs in part to the field of signification. It is not just that Tadzio symbolizes various classical ideas of form, with form being one of those features that moves easily, as Plato argued, from physical instances to intellectual or semantic ones. The lightness and grace of his movements are analogues for the lightness and fluidity of the realm of signs, for their capacity to be easily embodied in different signifiers that may contain them only briefly, their responsiveness to the ephemeral shapes of subjectivity, their temporary capturing of the forms of a more abstract world, their lively readiness to embody pleasing rhythms and patterns. As Aschenbach turns to his writing he feels that the movements of language are spun off Tadzio's gestures and expressions, so that like a figure in an ancient myth, the boy captures a crucial moment of transition when one sort of transitional object, the mirroring other, is turning into a more effective one, language or representation, with Aschenbach deliberately choosing the latter instead of speaking with the boy. (In doing so he does not move simply into the grammar of language but remains at that moment of transition, where Tadzio still inhabits the earlier space of images, gestures, and music, and where his presence is still necessary for the project to work. That is why language, in Aschenbach's or Mann's writing, remains an object of metaphorical identification, so that its self-sustaining energy can become the writer's own.)

Death in Venice suggests that there are different ways language may serve as a resolution of that transitional space. One may use a rigid self-discipline, with its firm barriers against regression, in order to separate as fully as one can from the earlier maternal gestures and rhythms, and also from any halfway objects still belonging to both the earlier world and the linguistic-grammatical one. Then one's writing will show a staunch discipline of form, the steady progression of the line of prose from book to book, as an almost military labor, as a resistance to any slackening of adult commitment; Aschenbach reveals that he has made his reputation on just that sort of writing (Mann, *Death in Venice,* 8–15). Then there is a different writing, involving a partial regression to a space where identities are less rigid, where there are still oscillations between self and other, male and female, both a return to the maternal and a resistance to it, as in Aschenbach's travels to the Mediterranean, so that geography seems a staging of the psyche. The problem, as Mann sees it, is that this partial regression, while it might produce appealing art, leaves one at the risk of a further slippage, a negating of separate individuation so that one is attracted to a nihilistic dissolving. Tadzio as an object plays with that boundary, with that threat of regressive merger, in his frequent connection with the ocean as he both emerges from and points back to it, and also when Aschenbach, as a northern Protestant, spies Tadzio at the Catholic ceremonies of San Marco (the ceremonies of Holy Mother Church, with Venice female as La Serenissima). Then there are the forces of nature that threaten Tadzio, with nature represented here as a swampy origin of plague.

That psychological structure is represented at the end of the story when Aschenbach wants to run both toward Tadzio, in order to protect him, and beyond him toward the ocean to which he is pointing. In that small scene one sees how an intermediary object, as mirroring other, is unable to stop the strongly regressive movement toward annihilation of the self, toward a giving up of individuation and a return to oceanic rhythms. Yet in risking that dangerous regression toward a more image-laden and boundary-blurring world, one's writing may take on greater power than is the case with the other sort of writing mentioned by Aschenbach. The obsessive reenactment of the move into language may display the anxieties and resolutions of that move more clearly. Writing, then, may take on an urgency and power through its at least partial mastery over a gravitational pull that Tadzio, as identified with by Aschenbach, cannot protect him from. Another advantage of having language serve as a transitional object of that sort is that one can thereby purchase a prize virtue of literary writing: compression. Tadzio would be a poor choice if Aschenbach wants an actual human relationship, but he is a model of compressing different semantic, psychological, gender, and metaphysical registers into a single object. When writing takes over the place of that sort of object, it too must compress into itself such a range of different registers, so that meanings are necessarily multiple and oscillating.

The matter of literary style is one of Mann's themes in his novella. He joins Nietzsche in asking whether certain kinds of return to forms of experiencing that seem Greek or pagan can be signs of health, of a vital naturalness, or signs of an unhealthy decadence. Nietzsche in *The Birth of Tragedy* had praised what seemed a Wagnerian return to the Dionysian energies of Greek tragedy. By the time of *The Case of Wagner* it seemed instead that Wagner's attempted return was a sign of decadence, of an unhealthy need for artificial stimulants, for a kind of violence in music that prevented the overall Greek mastery of form, for the damp, blurry, sentimental feelings of the German soul instead of the sunny clarity of the Mediterranean, which itself remained for Nietzsche, as in his praise of *Carmen,* a place of healthy paganism.[10] Those alternative Nietzschean views of Wagner are the different poles that still mark out the field when we consider the value of a psychological and symbolic regression in writing. Mann, of course, emphasized the decadence of Aschenbach's return, as Tadzio's bad teeth and the plague of cholera are added to Aschenbach's highly artificial transformation at the barber's and his violent dreams, so that Aschenbach seems to repeat qualities that Nietzsche saw in Wagner. Mann's prose can be deliberately overdone, artificial, and mannered. Yet it is also the case that as he watches Tadzio, Aschenbach produces a wonderfully written essay, and his reaching toward beauty, even his dreamlike following of Tadzio toward the ocean at the end, seems not a betrayal of, but rather a continuation of, that which gave his writing its energy and form.

One of the strongest arguments for retaining as a writer some manner of access to Winnicott's transitional space is, of course, *In Search of Lost Time*. Proust was unusually attached to his mother, and after her death in 1905 he suffered serious illnesses and mostly withdrew from society to write. So one may suppose that the movements of his prose are an attempt to find something of a sophisticated object that will both replace her and let her go, to bring back her world but only as what has been lost, to have an extension of the self that will still seem, in its cadences, to be supported by her own. So the notions of memory and loss, time and language, mourning and a reconciliation to the passage of time are present from the start. There is a section, late in the work, that demonstrates how what is being worked out in this literary-psychological space is a fundamental metaphysical relationship to a world of objects, which is one of a child's projects from early on. The narrator is in Venice with his mother and decides at the last minute that he will not accompany her on the train leaving the city. The ambiguity of the transitional space is shown well in his talk of a desire to rebel against his parents, of "that defiant spirit which drove me in the past to impose my will brutally upon the people I loved best in the world, though finally conforming to theirs after I had succeeded in making them yield."[11] Few can mingle the movements of rebellion with those of surrender more complexly than Proust does in that sentence. The narrator is trying for a kind of separation, of self-willing, that will transform itself at the end into a yielding to the will of others. He remains at the hotel, determined to stay, while his mother leaves with the baggage. Yet he immediately feels desolate in her absence.

> My irrevocable solitude was so near at hand that it seemed to me to have begun already and to be complete. For I felt myself to be alone; things had become alien to me; I no longer had calm enough to break out of my throb-

bing heart and introduce into them a measure of stability. The town that I saw before me had ceased to be Venice. Its personality, its name, seemed to me to be mendacious fictions which I no longer had the will to impress upon its stones. I saw the palaces reduced to their basic elements, lifeless heaps of marble with nothing to choose between them, and the water as a combination of hydrogen and oxygen, eternal, blind, anterior and exterior to Venice, oblivious of the Doges or of Turner. And yet this unremarkable place was as strange as a place at which one has just arrived, which does not yet know one, or a place which one has left and which has forgotten one already. I could no longer tell it anything about myself, I could leave nothing of myself imprinted upon it; it contracted me into myself until I was no more than a beating heart and an attention strained to follow the development of *O sole mio*. (884)

The city that had earlier seemed magical now seems empty and meaningless. Without the dependable maternal presence in the background it is up to the narrator to invest the world with meaning on his own, and he has no power to do so ("I could leave nothing of myself imprinted on it"). This is a repetition of the condition of childhood separation and also a portrayal of the predicament of the modern self. If there is no capacity for this investment of self in things, one may shrink back into a vague unease; one feels powerless over against a bleak and empty world, a place that is metaphysically unfit to incarnate meanings, ideas, or any sort of larger significance, to be a place where subjectivity can, in Hegel's sense, find itself at home. An alternative for the child in that situation is to move closer to the dependable presence of the mother, a solution that in the long run, especially in its compensatory analogues, cannot be the best one psychologically, even if it was a good one for Proust's writing.

So we may feel a certain disappointment when the narrator runs off just in time to meet his mother at the train station. But we should note the temporary role the song "O sole mio" has played. It serves as a substitute formation so that while he is attending to its movements he does not feel the need to join her. He is afraid to make the more transparent psychological move of deciding not to join her, but that move, he says, "became possible in this indirect form" (886). He keeps telling himself that he is staying only to hear one more phrase of the song, so that his attention to it takes his mind off the need to join his mother at the station. But even at this level of indirection his separating off from her comes through, as the melancholy of the song "stabbed me to the heart" (Proust, *Fugitive*, 887). This sort of midway object, the singer's lament, is too weak to act as the necessary compensation for his loss. Its representation of loss and solitude does not have the power, as representational, to hold his separation in view in a manner that allows him to accept it as such.

> [The song], bellowed thus beside the insubstantial palaces, finally reduced them to dust and ashes and completed the ruin of Venice; I looked on at the slow realization of my distress, built up artistically, without haste, note by note, by the singer as he stood beneath the astonished gaze of the sun arrested in its course beyond San Georgio Maggiore, with the result that the fading light was to combine for ever in my memory with the shiver of my emotion and the bronze voice of the singer in an equivocal, unalterable and poignant alloy.

Proust will eventually try, after his mother's death, to find an artistic style that, in the way it is "built up artistically, without haste, note by note" like the song, will provide a more reliable object that will make less painful not only his mother's absence but also a range of other absences in his life. The song in Venice was unsuccessful for this purpose, but the long, intricate sentences of his novel that lovingly explore and describe the detail of the world will be a metaphorical substitute, at some level, for her presence when he was a child; at the same time control of their grammatical form and of their complex periods shows Proust's own mastery in such a manner, with such a fertile metonymic energy from phrase to phrase and sentence to sentence, that he need not fear a further dissolution and loss of identity, as a more profound identification with his mother would bring about. He can now accept her loss. Unlike with the song "O sole mio" Proust will not have to run off to the railroad station to join his mother at the last minute (or to join later substitutes) in a failure of the process of separation and individuation, of mourning. The music of his prose will be strong enough to bring Venice and any other scene back to life, to the magical meaningfulness it earlier seemed divested of. The writing will take on a self-sustaining life, an inevitability of form, that gives it greater power to hold out than was the case with the Venetian song, and that will confidently invest the appearing world with a significance that makes it substantial and vital. Proust in his emotional life will perhaps never graduate beyond that world of transitional objects, but he will discover one of them, in a style of language, that will have enormous energy and lasting effectiveness, as a way of substituting for his mother's presence that both loses her and does not, that both declares his independence and self-propelling selfhood and lets him give himself over to the patterns of an intricate earlier world, while metaphorically identifying with the qualities of the prose. In hearing Proust's narrator speaking of his defiant will that he would impose on others in order to surrender to them once they had yielded, we realize that Proust found a writing space with that same ambiguous quality of control and surrender. That is one source of the peculiar, complex pleasure of reading Proust, the sense both of irony and affection in his descriptions of the social world, of a world forever lost and of time regained. The prose expresses the distance of representation and of metonymic movement, of a working through grammatical patterns that, with their great complexity, activate the rich lateral energies of language in a self-sustaining advance. Yet the prose also retains something of a mimetic, identificational quality in the way its sinuous feel and rhythms, its loving intricacy, suggest the movements of the aristocratic social world he is describing the disappearance of. Again, everything has been lost in translation, and yet it is also true that nothing has been lost. In becoming representational things are leaving behind what they are and yet are becoming most truly what they are. (That is a conclusion in Aristotle and Hegel as well, so that Proust's style in some respects repeats the owl-at-dusk standpoint of Hegel.)

I have spoken here of the value for Proust of access to a transitional space where certain issues of separation, loss, and individuation, of orienting the self through language to a world of real objects, were still relevant. To make this claim is not to endorse, even for the purposes of literature, what can seem Proust's pathologically strong attachment to his mother or, by analogy, such a strong attachment to the past. The point is rather a structural one. That transitional space in Proust can be so crucial because the process of traumatic separation from what one was attached to occurs in many aspects of a human life and is intricately linked to such matters as consciousness and representation; time and memory; adulthood, loss, and death. At some level we are always working out a style of engagement with a world of objects that provoke our investments and attachments and then must be left behind. That process of separation will apply not only to people but also to a range of other situations: from the presence of the object to its representation; from premodern to modern forms of life; from magical, metaphorical ways of thinking to more analytic and grammatical ones; from childhood to adulthood; from ritualized relations to nature to disenchanted ones; from overwhelming passion to linguistic control; (ultimately) from living out a life to acknowledging its character as one dies. The goal is to find a mature strategy not merely of making these transitions but of holding on, in acceptable ways that still enrich us, to what must be relinquished. Such ways may be enacted in the space of literature, in the way it allows both intensity of presence and linguistic distance.

The point is not to return to an earlier stage, as if that were possible, but to acknowledge loss and to retain what has been lost in attenuated but still satisfying ways. Joyce's Gabriel in "The Dead" has no desire to return to an earlier Ireland; he rejects an invitation to travel to the west of the country with a Gaelicizing woman writer. But he can still feel the power of a distant music associated with the traditional ballad that his wife's long-ago boy friend sang to her in the rain before he died, and whose cadences we seem to hear more loudly as Gabriel, at the end, thinks of his own death. Amit Chaudhuri is glad to be at Oxford writing in English and studying Lawrence, but the music of traditional India remains behind his prose. Pynchon's prose is at its most powerful when a world in the process of being lost is held lovingly and elegiacally in view. Cormac McCarthy's cowboy protagonist hears the ghostly cadence of a Comanche war party from the past moving across the landscape. This is not a matter of nostalgia, of a romanticized past. It is a training in separation and loss, a training whose goal is not a looking backward but a patient acknowledgment of the value of the world as it is, given how fragile things are in the way they emerge into view, remain stably there for our seeing, and then dissolve. Ultimately what is at stake is the power of language to hold on to what it leaves behind. That is why, if Wittgenstein is the ghostly figure behind the contemporary philosophers treated here, Proust is the ghostly figure behind the contemporary authors. Modernism in literature was often especially good at articulating that sort of privileged space. With postmodernist fiction linguistic discourses often maneuver too smoothly, without any real friction from the world and in a manner that rejects the limits of consciousness and time, as well as the losses that come with representation itself. So there is no training in one of the most powerful ways that literature can enrich us.

Up to now this discussion of literary language and the transitional space has been gendered in unacknowledged ways. While object-relations theorists suppose that their overall structures apply both to males and to females, still there will be important differences in the way that separation and individuation are worked out.[12] For males individuation will typically be supported by an identification with someone whose gender differs from that of the person of primary identification. So a sense of secure separateness will be linked to gender difference from the mother. One consequence is that a regression that reactivates certain self-other identifications with the mother may be threatening to identity, since it will suggest a loss of the principal marker of one's difference. The female child, so the story goes, reaches a gradual differentiation from the mother where gender difference is not a crucial element of that separation. So there is more of a continuum on the path to separate identity. There will not be the degree of conflict and anxiety that in the male is associated with any regression toward a maternal identification, nor will the process lead to so radical a sense of aloneness as in the male.

I do not know if that general story is true; it has been pieced together from different sources. But it should be clear to the reader that the literature being explored here considers individuation and transitional spaces from a male perspective. Perhaps some of the patterns can be seen in female writers as well, for example in Anne Tyler, in novels such as *The Accidental Tourist* and *Saint Maybe*. In the former, one of the finest of recent novels, Macon Leary seems to demonstrate how the space of literature is translational and regressive. There is a deeply regressive tendency to return, after the death of a child, to the home where he grew up and to live with his siblings in an environment of comfortable family rituals. As both an aspect of that tendency and a resistance to further regression he turns to the grammar of language (he is a writer and sometimes corrects others on their grammatical errors) and to a systematic ordering of space and routine, a pleasure in repetition. His important discovery is that this linguistic inhabiting of the grammatical level is not enough. (Recall Merrill's acknowledgment that "the little feet that patter here are metrical.") Instead he learns eventually to reestablish his place in a social-grammatical order where other selves can now occupy the slots of partner and (step)son.

There is a different pattern in a writer such as Alice Munro, or at least in one of her stories, "Differently."[13] There is for Georgia, her protagonist, a slippage from a realm of clear forms and boundaries to a more oceanic realm of fantasy, passion, and play. A similar slippage occurred in Aschenbach, away from the more rigid life of Protestant northern Europe. What is interesting here is that there is no sense that Munro's character is under any threat of a dangerous loss of individuation, as in Mann. Munro signals the change by having Georgia take as a lover a deep-sea diver, while her husband is a decent, earnest, dutiful naval officer who clearly skims along the surface of oceans. "And Georgia herself, watching her children on the roundabout, or feeling the excellent shape of a lemon in her hand at the supermarket, contained another woman, who only a few hours before had been whimpering and tussling on the ferns, on the sand, on the bare ground, or, during a rainstorm, in her own car—who had been driven hard and gloriously out of her mind and drifted loose and gathered her wits and made her way home again" (204–5). She works in a bookstore and is pictured waiting expectantly within it (that is where the deep-sea diver shows up, on a motorcycle). The doors of the bookshop are described in a way suggesting entrance to the female body: "It was a long, narrow store with an old-fashioned funneled entryway between two angled display windows. . . . The store was a straight avenue of bounty, of plausible promises" (202–3). But if there is a loosening of the self to allow more passionate flows of energy and of fantasy, there is not the male anxiety that this may lead to further regression and a dissolution of the self, nor is there a sense that individuation involves anything like the radical separateness of the male loners that one often sees in literature. (Georgia divorces her husband but then takes a writing course and marries her instructor.)

So perhaps it is true that to the extent that object-relational structures may show themselves in more complex relationships later on, the effect on the language of female writers may be different from that on male writers. That is one of the claims of certain French feminists who speak of a "feminine writing" whose space of operation is fundamentally different from that of males. But this is a topic on which, both in terms of theoretical competence and breadth of reading, I am not qualified to take a stand. The next chapter, however, will explore the way the space of writing may be for the male writer not only a move of assurance of individuation, but also a move of assurance of gender identity.

JOHN UPDIKE AND THE SCENE
OF LITERATURE

Literary language may offer rituals that symbolically repeat, and also reassure us about the results of, the movements of an earlier space of self-formation. Such linguistic rituals, and thus literary style itself, may involve issues of gender identity. (Admittedly this discussion is from a one-sidedly male point of view.) The very access fueling the machinery that makes a certain literary style possible may also open the writer to other levels of experience, of a kind such that blurring and oscillation may destabilize the more determinate structures of sexual and cultural grammars. A controlled regression to an earlier transitional space may enable the intensities and satisfactions of a more energized style of language, a grounding in richer cadences, for the compensating power of language is a measure of what one must use it against. But that regression may also open up a psychic space in which there are greater anxieties about identity, as one reactivates something of the not-yet-resolved terrain of childhood. Our model, as before, might be Dennett's notion of the mind as a processing of multiple drafts, with the final draft that is expressed in speech or action often covering over other drafts that tried to impress themselves on the finished product but lost out in the competition. The writer, on this model, is one who retains access to a stage where the earlier drafts were still in circulation, before the final draft, or the finally established configuration of the psyche, made them invisible. So to find less rigid gender boundaries within or beneath the space of literature is not at all to discover something about the sexual preference of the writer in his or her actual life. Rather it is to discover something about the field of writing, about the process that, in some writers at least, gives a characteristic force and intensity to the prose or poetry.

In looking at John Updike's work I will focus on what determines that scene of writing for him. I want to keep in mind as well the richness of the phenomenon of subjectivity as it expresses itself in literature. (I argued earlier against impoverishing that phenomenon through a radical turn to language or to social power.) Updike is known as a writer of suburban adultery, someone who has spent much of his career describing adult women in great physical and psychological detail as they react to the men around them. Yet he has also given us writings in which there is a subtle exploration of earlier structures of self-formation: where separation and loss, selfhood and gender identity are still matters to be worked out. In *The Centaur*, for example, he takes the persona of Peter, an artist living now with a woman in New York, who is recalling a three-day period he spent with his father in a snowstorm.[1] That this period has a ritual and mythic significance is shown by the fact that characters appearing in the small Pennsylvania town mirror figures in Greek mythology. (Updike even provides a guide at the end of the book to match the novel's characters with the Greek ones. So as with Merrill one's now-disenchanted stance uses more self-consciously, but does not give up entirely, a range of re-gressive, ritualized investments.) The form of the ritual is not unfamiliar. Peter and his father leave his mother one morning to drive off to the town where he is a student and his father a schoolteacher. The sandstone farm-house they inhabit in the country belonged to his mother's parents and was her home when she was growing up. It is seen quite definitely as her world; the move back to the farm went against the wishes of both son and father, who prefer urban areas, and the guide at the back identifies her as Ceres, the goddess of agriculture. Peter is close to her, and in another story about the same sandstone farmhouse, written after the death of Updike's mother, the Updike character says that "he and his mother were regarded as having been unusually, perhaps unnaturally close."[2] During the three-day period of the novel Peter will have an opportunity for an identification with his father, however fragile, that will offer support for his status as a separate self, so that when the two of them finally return at the end to the farmhouse, trudging through the snow, with Peter following in his father's footsteps, he no longer needs to fear that too close identification with his mother, that identity-blurring connection to the chthonic forces out of which he emerged.

Peter's father, it appears at first, may not be equal to his task in the rit-ual. Since he is given the role in this contemporary myth of Chiron the cen-taur, with Peter in the role of Prometheus, we do know that he will eventually sacrifice himself for the sake of Peter's independence, as Chiron agreed to atone for Prometheus's crime in his place. The father can appear a figure of weakness and ridicule dominated by his wife, whom he fends off with self-deprecating jokes, and afraid of his supervisor at school. His weakness is indicated especially by the cars he drives. An automobile is symbolic here because its very name means to be self-moving, and so it represents the attempt to break free of the farmhouse, of Ceres and the earth, and to form one's own self-moving, self-maintaining (male) activity. We might think of Descartes as one figure behind these automobiles. He imagines a thinking activity that no longer needs to be grounded in the earth but can ground itself, that can set its own conditions for itself, initiate its own movement, and keep its own machinery going by a process of systematic construction. There is some anxiety that this whole self-sustaining system will collapse, but that fear is allayed by an identification with God the Father. In creating Descartes, God has given him, so the philosopher argues, an instrument (we may suppose it a phallic one) adequate to the task, provided he does not try to take over God's position but remains within his careful programmatic bounds and plays by the rules, especially for him the grammatical rules for constructing his system of thought.

Even from the start Peter and his father have difficulty getting this structure under way. The car (his father has never been able to afford a new one or even a dependable used one) will not start, and they have to push it down a hill to start it. It is a polished black car that, so Peter notes, once belonged to an undertaker and was used in funeral processions, so it is further weakened, at least symbolically, as a vehicle for achieving a self-sustaining life against the gravities of the land. Once on the road Peter celebrates their free movement toward the town and associates his mood with the radio: "and then a song came like a choo-choo, clicking, irresistible, carrying the singer like a hobo on top of its momentum, and my father and I seemed ourselves irresistible, rolling up and down through the irregularities of our suffering land, warm in the midst of much cold. In those days the radio carried me into my future where I was strong" (*Centaur*, 78). There we have the (Cartesian) identification with his father and with an irresistible and self-propelling motion and also a sense of the line of music as part of that momentum. Eventually the movement of writerly prose in Updike, from word to word, will be like that music, will be like the train carrying the hobo in Peter's image of the song. (And since the car Peter and his father are riding in once belonged to an undertaker, the suggestion is that the self-sustaining momentum of writing is ambiguous, both an expression of an ongoing structure of individuation and a regression to a dreamlike space where individuation would weaken. If the writer is carried on the rhythm of his writing the way a hobo is carried by a train, then he has temporarily sneaked onto a mode of transport where he does not quite belong, that is not truly his own. So his self-moving activity may really not be self-moving, may be a temporary simulation of true Cartesian activity.)

The exultant feeling does not last long, for his father stops the car to pick up a hitchhiker who, as Peter can see, is homosexual. He is already somewhat anxious in this regard: "I had once been approached by a shuffling derelict while waiting for my father in front of the Alton Public Library and his few mumbled words before I fled had scored me. I felt, as long as my love of girls remained unconsummated, open on that side—a three-walled room any burglar could enter. An unreasoning hate of the hitchhiker suffused me" (*Centaur*, 80). His father, unfortunately, turns off the radio that had given Peter his sense of strength and momentum. "The musical choo-choo . . . dropped over a cliff," so that Peter, who had been riding on the song's advancing motion, which is analogous to the rhythm of writing, suffers a similar collapse in his sense of self, a vulnerability of his boundaries. The hitchhiker seems already a return of earlier fantasy content, "snuffling and liquidly enlarging like some primeval monster coming to life again out of a glacier" (81).

Peter's father seems especially inept at helping his son through such rituals. Once when they visited New York, Peter, hoping to be an artist, had wanted very much to see original paintings by Vermeer. To see them would have been "to enter a Real Presence so ultimate I would not be surprised to die in the encounter. My father's blundering blocked it. We never entered the museums; I never saw the paintings" (*Centaur*, 85). (So the father has blocked the son's access to a desired iconic presence, a uniquely present entity that does not allow for substitutions within a formally defined structure, as the Vermeer reproductions can never replace the original. It will not be surprising that in the Updike story "Museums and Women" entry into a museum is compared with entry into a woman. Perhaps it is important that the father blocks this access through his blundering, not through his competitive strength.) Here the hitchhiker stands for all the lack of distinctness that Peter fears. His face is a "puddle," with a "smear" of a smile and an "emanation of muddy emotion." He seems attracted to Peter, who cringes and shuts his eyes "to prevent any further inwash of that unwelcome unthinkable ichor I had roused. Most horrible in it had been something shy and grateful and girlish" (86). Instead of helping him, his father tells the hitchhiker about Peter's skin problem ("In effect my father had torn off my clothes and displayed my prickling scabs") and then suggests that Peter might do better if he went off with the young man, who is heading to Florida. The father's easy suggestion that the son go off with the hitchhiker shows his inability so far to provide a structure that will support Peter's efforts at gender identity. As so often in Updike, the father is compared to an old auto: "Time to trade in on a new old man; I'm a walking junk heap" (89).

Peter's anxieties about homosexuality are by no means done with. The car breaks down in town after a basketball game (again the failure of his father to provide the model of a self-maintaining momentum across the available space). Peter and his father must seek a hotel to stay at. While they are walking in the cold a drunk accosts them, a man "smaller and further gone in degeneracy" than the hitchhiker (*Centaur,* 156). He accuses Peter's father of having picked Peter up for sexual purposes and tells Peter to go home: "He's not worth it. How much is he giving you? I don't care how much it is, it's never enough. When he gets a new pretty boy he'll throw you out on the street like an old Trojan" (157). And then: "Shall we call the cops, kid? Let's kill the old nance." Peter, attempting to form a clear positional-grammatical space here, with people assigned to their proper slots so that who can make what moves with whom is clear, keeps insisting: "But he's my father" (159). Peter then must take a room with his father in the very sort of cheap hotel that a prostitute might be taken to. Other scenes as well seem to reveal fears about his father's sexual identity. The father coaches the boys' swimming team and likes sitting around having conversations with one scantily clad boy, Diefendorf, with whom he seems to get on better than he does with Peter. Then too, in scenes that can be interpreted even without much of a Freudian background, the father, who fears he may have colon cancer and also has a toothache, is forced during the three-day period of the novel to go through a sygmoidoscope exam and to have a tooth pulled. The doctor performing the exam is identified in the index at the back, as Apollo in this myth, and perhaps coyly the index says that appearing also in the office visit scene is the character Hyacinthus, the beloved of Apollo who accidentally kills him with a thrown discus. Peter worries that his father, with little money even for basic bills, may have taken an illegal cash advance from basketball ticket sales; he has a dream in which his father is stripped and beaten for the crime.

The car is repaired. But the next evening, as they leave town after a basketball game, a snowstorm arrives and the car will not make it up one of the long hills on the route home. His father has failed once more to initiate Peter into the free, self-moving activity that Peter will need one day if he is to escape the gravitational pull of the sandstone farmhouse and of his mother. "A father who was half a man would have gotten you up that hill," he says to Peter (*Centaur*, 164). They have to leave the car by the side of the road and walk back two miles to the town through the fierce storm. Walking may not be the same as riding in the automobile, but Peter's father gives him his hat and tries to protect him from the wind. As they walk together there seems to be at least enough momentum transferred from father to son so that they can avoid giving in to the annihilating whiteness. With all of his weakness, his father has provided for Peter enough of an identification for him to go on into life without fear of regression into the mother-child relationship, into a blurring of gender identity (or even worse, as in *Death in Venice,* a regression into the whiteness of nonidentity, expressed in the swirling snow all around Peter and his father and in the cemetery they pass on the way). Before the storm Peter has been exploring the private area of a girl in his class, and we know from the frame of the novel as a whole that he now shares an apartment with a woman in Manhattan. Presenting the father as the centaur Chiron does introduce some complication here. The immortal Chiron, longing for death after an unhealable wound, takes over the punishment of Prometheus, letting him go free. So there is a sense that his father allows Peter to escape from the maternal pull on his identity by taking Peter's place there, masochistically giving himself over as a substitute sacrifice to a dominant wife. (Since Prometheus's crime can stand for a move of independence and initiative, it can appear that Peter at some level sees his own moves of separation and independence as matters to feel guilty about; and he sees that his father has sacrificed himself to the world of his wife, to her habits of denigrating him even as she loves him, in order to keep open a space for Peter's individuation, for his escape from the farmhouse.) After they make it through the snowstorm to a friend's house they are placed in the same bed. "It smelled of feathers and starch and was so like a hammock that my father and I, in underclothes, had to cling to the edges to keep from sliding together in the middle. For some minutes I kept tense" (271).

So there remains here some ambiguity as to just what sort of identification Peter will have with his father. His father might serve, first of all, as a transitional object in a self-to-other space that maintains at least some distance from the earlier mother-child relationship and so is partly a movement away from it. He can serve with this solution as a mirroring, partly differentiated object in a still-dyadic relationship in which Peter may work out anxieties and possibilities regarding individuation and boundaries (as when they share the same bed and Peter worries about sliding into the middle). Or his father might serve as one possible position in an already triadic, grammatical field of relationships; this structure opens up a second and a third possibility in the matter of identification. Sometimes he is almost the love object as Peter identifies with his mother and her position; that would be one strategy for moving into that grammatical field while still retaining certain aspects of the earlier mirroring relationship with his mother. Sometimes, alternatively, he is occupying a position that Peter may take over by coming to love a woman. In the novel the father seems to move unstably among these three roles, with the winning out of the third position being rather a close affair that could have gone otherwise. There are several references to the notion that Peter is sliding into his mother's role in feeling responsible for the care of his father.

Yet at the end of *The Centaur* whatever sort of identification with his father has occurred is sufficient to allay Peter's anxiety about a return to the maternal-transitional space in his making of art. Peter is back in his room, awaking from a dream that, suggesting a regressive world of boundary blurring, "seemed to take place in a sluggish whirling world that preceded" the figures in his life, a "shifting rootless flux of unidentifiable things" (*Centaur,* 290). His parents' voices below "seemed a grappling extension of my own," so that identities are blurring here as well, as his mother tries to persuade his father to become a full-time farmer ("It would make a whole man of you") while his father emphasizes his separation from that world of the earth-goddess by replying that he hates Nature, which reminds him of death. Peter looks from his bedroom window to a scene where the snow has covered everything with its annihilating whiteness. He sees his father coming out of the house, "an erect figure dark against the snow. His posture made no concession to the pull underfoot; upright he waded out through our yard and past the mailbox and up the hill until he was lost to my sight behind the trees of our orchard" (293).

That his father is erect and upright and able to hold out against the pull underfoot gives Peter confidence as he decides that he would like to paint the scene: "it came upon me that I must go to Nature disarmed of perspective and stretch myself like a large transparent canvas upon her in the hope that, my submission being perfect, the imprint of a beautiful and useful truth would be taken" (*Centaur,* 293). He has escaped the world of a shifting rootless flux, the experience he had when waking up, because looking out he identifies with the father's erect form that, in rising above a nature identified with death and with the white annihilation of the snow, allows Peter a strong self-assurance. Now he is able to reestablish ties with nature, even submit himself to it as in his image of a canvas, without fearing that the submission and regression that allow him to reoccupy a transitional space of writing will cause him to lose his identity. (Updike in other stories turns into a painter the character who stands for himself as a writer.) Updike's writing can at times seem a celebration of the distance he has gained in this ritual with his father, a distance that precisely allows him to return without danger to an earlier, more ambiguous space where the relationship to objects and to himself was more at stake. In this way the power of the turn to language and representation, with the consequent hypnotic power of the language, can be reenacted. Note that in his description of his future art, or his writing, Peter rejects the notion of having a "perspective" on Nature in favor of stretching himself out like a transparent canvas on her. In other words, he will move from the triadic-grammatical space whose triangulation allows a stable, positional, perspectival stance over against nature into a more regressive stance that is iconic, mirroring, and identificational. This move will give his writing greater power and is made possible by a confidence that the sort of regression in question will not dissolve his identity for good.

It is also the case that what makes up eventually for the failure of the automobile, for the father's inability to model a secure self-movement, is Updike's own ability to keep generating prose with the inevitable form, the irresistible momentum, that Peter identified with in the music on the radio as his father's automobile sped smoothly across the landscape. Indeed, Updike's very longevity as a writer of fine prose testifies to the effectiveness of the machinery that he put in place, exemplified in *The Centaur,* for translating those energies of self-formation into linguistic energies. That this machinery keeps itself going suggests that the psychic resolution reached by Updike in those early adolescent years is not of a sort that lets one then simply move on, leaving behind the earlier phases as one might adopt a new cultural paradigm. Rather he seems to find in much of his writing the ritual repetition of those earlier moves. He needs to relive that scene with its possibilities and to replay the turn to language and grammar that ultimately compensates for any fragility and instability in the psychic solution arrived at. Writing allows that ritual regression to earlier psychic spaces by giving the assurance that it can set things in their place in a linguistic pattern that holds itself firm against any gravitational pull, because of the order and intricacy of its internal, metonymic connections, an architecture whose complex and subtle engineering is a proof against destruction. In return the earlier instabilities and anxieties create a need for that linguistic structure to do its work, and so fuel its ongoing labor of compensation and resolution. Updike's energy as a writer derives in part from the fact that the three possibilities that Peter's father wavers among in Peter's psychic landscape have remained alive in Updike's own psychic landscape. This is not in the least to suggest that Updike has hidden homosexual desires. In fact the interest here is a very different one: not a writer's present sexual identity but the relation between the role of language in a writer's psychic life and the persistence of access to earlier psychic spaces where more possibilities were in play than one's adult resolution of them might indicate. It is important that in Updike it is the relationship between those earlier spaces and a more grammatical space of representation that is at stake, with both sides of that relationship still available as he writes. A more radical turn to the linguistic and grammatical, because one side of the relationship would thus disappear, makes one miss what is doing the work of generating literary style; one would never understand how the engineering works. It is true also that the transitional space Updike returns to is not simply one where gender identity is less distinct. Updike's great pleasure as a writer in describing the objects of the world recalls the young child's metaphysical work of setting itself in reliable relation to the world, from within a play space where objects seem invested with a special significance.

Some of Updike's other work will allow development of these points. After his mother's death he wrote about the sandstone farmhouse again, this time in a story with that title, as the Updike character (Joey this time) goes back to Pennsylvania to clean out the house and make it ready for sale. He had always found the house oppressive; it had worsened his asthma until breathing became difficult. (Under the pull of this chthonic world of Ceres he cannot breathe freely.) His reading, he felt back then, would eventually get him away from the farmhouse and from his family surroundings. Yet as he is doing the cleaning, "Joey had discovered himself talking aloud, as if in response to a friendly presence just behind the dry old wallpaper, within the thick stone walls. Weeknights, his own rooms, suspended above Manhattan's steady roar, . . . seemed to be flying somewhere. He felt guilty, anxious, displaced. He had always wanted to be where the action was, and what action there was, it turned out, had been back there."[3] There is something here of Proust's description of echoes from childhood that have never ceased, like "convent bells that are so effectively drowned during the day by the noises of the streets that one would suppose them to have been stopped forever, until they sound again through the silent evening air."[4] Updike gives us a clear sense of the doubleness of the transitional space: the maternal presence both as what one has been fleeing from and as what one has always been setting oneself in relation to. He also stresses its importance; for the writer that space is indeed where the action has been all along. (His "flying somewhere" above Manhattan, in that aeronautical Cartesian flight against gravity, for the sake of separation, now seems a displacement, where the anxiety about falling is greater because one's flight had never been self-sustaining to begin with. The return to the earlier space, the sandstone farmhouse, is less threatening now that his mother has died.)

Becoming more comfortable with distance and separation, Winnicott says, takes place successfully only if the dependable presence of the mother is there in at least the deep background of that space. That is the condition in which one discovers a characteristic style of engagement with objects, and thus a literary style as well. So a certain creative power in writing is enhanced if one can return, through what is opened up by the deep rhythm of writing, to a space recalling the child's working with objects in the mother's presence, a presence that is now much weaker ("a friendly presence . . . within the thick stone walls") and that is there perhaps for many writers only in the rhythmic cadence of sentences. (Merrill claims in one poem that his mother, while seemingly absent from his poetry, is always there in "the breath drawn after every line.")[5] One might imagine a more thorough transition to the structural grammars of culture, an advance that would strongly resist any return to such a transitional space with its more ambiguous maternal identifications, so that as a male one would simply have a woman as partner and not in any way be one. But that more rigorous separation, in its literary analogue, might deny the writer access to some of the powerful cadences, some of the more archaic presences, supporting his sentences from below.

The return to that transitional space, as Updike returns to it in *The Centaur,* will open up more ambiguous structures of self-formation, with possibilities of identification that are more various and unstable than in the psychic resolution that shaped one's adulthood. Updike plays with this possibility. It is, unsurprisingly, a motion of return that triggers it, his journey back to the sandstone farmhouse after his mother's death through the eyes of the fictional character Joey, who appears autobiographical in some respects but not in others.

> His first marriage took place in three apartments, his turbulent second in four, his short-lived third in only one, and now he wondered if women had been not quite his thing all along. He had always felt most at ease, come to think of it, in the company of men, especially those who reminded him of his quiet, uncomplaining father. But it was the AIDS-conscious Eighties by then, and his hair had passed through gray into virtual white, and he was content to share his life with his books, his CDs (compact discs, certificates of deposit), and his modest little art collection. (Updike, "Sandstone Farmhouse," 116)

This is a fictional character, one should grant, and the passage is meant to be humorous. Yet this is one of the most solemn of Updike's writings, a long tribute to his mother after her death. If he is playing with autobiographical elements here, it is quite serious play. That passage has a certain resonance with one in Updike's nonfictional recollection of growing up in Pennsylvania, in which he says: "Nobody has ever called me 'Uppie' except one boy, a boy I called 'Neil Hovey' in a short story. All my life, I have felt most at ease with other males of Neil's type—dark and stoical; and I suppose my father could be considered this type, too."[6] In that story, "The Happiest I've Been," there are again features of the shifting, hypnotic, regressive world that Updike sometimes makes present in his writing: the long, gliding trip by automobile; the sense of another's presence as that other falls asleep beside him; the switching of positions in the automobile; the automobile trip as a transitional space (as the narrator is driving with his friend to Chicago, where he will then join his girlfriend and drive back with her to Harvard). Neil Hovey is presented as someone who, in picking up the narrator in his father's automobile, performs the actions of picking up a girl on a date, joking with the narrator's mother in an adult way. "In everything that followed," the narrator says, "there was the sensation of my being picked up and carried."[7] In other stories as well Updike shows a willingness to play with the notion of a field of shifting psychological investments and identifications. In "Beautiful Husbands," Spencer's sexual activity is entirely with women, but he has affairs with these women because he finds himself attracted, in a much vaguer eroticism, to the masculine qualities of their husbands. ("His heart would flutter, his face get hot. It took a long time for Kirk's silvery magic to tarnish entirely.")[8]

A more fluid space of identifications is suggested as well in another story, written apparently after Updike's father had a serious stroke. The narrator, representing Updike, is driving back to Pennsylvania to visit his father in the hospital. Again in the story the father is compared to an automobile, to a used car about to be traded in. As the narrator is driving he picks up a sailor and lets him drive the car for two hours through Connecticut: "I trusted him. He had the full body, the frank and fleshy blue-eyed face of the docile Titans. . . . He had that instinctive optimism of the young animal that in America is the only generatrix of hope we have allowed ourselves; until recently, it seemed enough."[9] It seems that the illness and possible death of his father, with the earlier childhood anxieties that arise, require such a temporary replacement as a male identity figure, the "docile Titan" who can be trusted to keep the car properly self-moving, who is stronger than the father in that car-related capacity. (There is even a bit of regret as the sailor leaves to join other hitchhiking sailors at a rest stop: "They hailed him as if they had been waiting for him, and as he went to them he became, from the back, just one more sailor, anonymous, at sea. He did not turn and wave good-bye" ["Packed Dirt," 183]. The fleshy Titan may be a better transitional object than was sickly Tadzio for Aschenbach, though perhaps he is slightly feminized in the word *generatrix*. But he too returns seaward, leaving the narrator to proceed on his own, with certain anxious consequences: two paragraphs later, "I was nearly rammed from behind" by another car.)

It is also as if that self-movement in the automobile, as with the song on the radio as Peter and his father drove in *The Centaur,* must bring up the topic of writing. The narrator identifies himself to the sailor as a writer but admits he does not know why he writes. In the last lines of the story he talks of his father trading in an old car: "He would drive off in the old car up the dirt road exactly as usual and when he returned the car would be new, and the old was gone, gone, utterly dissolved back into the mineral world from which it was conjured, dismissed without a blessing, a kiss, a testament, or any ceremony of farewell. We in America need ceremonies, is I suppose, sailor, the point of what I have written" ("Packed Dirt," 192). The scene of writing has been from the beginning about loss and separation and mourning; handling these, regarding one's mother, was the child's first great project in life. Writing allows the ceremonial rituals, through language, that continue to hold in view what is being lost forever, what is dissolving back into the mineral world, with neither the original presence nor the full distance of disenchantment. (Merrill again: rituals that are "neither the blessing nor the blight.") So the connection between writing and the ceremonial is made by Updike as his father may be about to die, to dissolve back into the world from which he was conjured. His father, in leaving, deserves such a ceremony, and for the writer so does everything that emerges into visibility for us, holds there fragilely for a while, and then disappears.

In "The Rumor" a false rumor that an art dealer has left his wife for a young homosexual makes the art dealer in question, Frank, begin to think about men he is attracted to, repeating the formula Updike had used in *Self-Consciousness* and in "A Sandstone Farmhouse": "As an adult he was attracted, he had noticed, to stoical men, taller than he, gravely sealed around an unexpected sadness."[10] With men like this he became "a catering, wifely, subtly agitated presence." He feels that particular attraction toward Wes, his frequent tennis partner. Once when they slept in the same room on a golfing trip to Spain he had been unusually conscious of Wes and his snoring. Wes said the next day that Frank should have poked him; that was what his wife did. "But he wasn't his wife, Frank thought, though he had felt, in the course of the night's ordeal, his heart make many curious motions, among them the heaving, all but impossible effort women's hearts make in overcoming men's heavy grayness and achieving—a rainbow born of drizzle—love" (217–18). Wes was, it should be noted, the name of Updike's own father, and as in *The Centaur* there is the suggestion that beneath the stronger identification with his father that would have him take a wife there is an older and weaker identification with his mother that would have him see the father, instead, as a partner. As for Frank's mother: she "had given him an impression of women as complex, brightly colored traps, attractive but treacherous, their petals apt to harden in an instant into knives" (214).

In "His Mother inside Him" the Updike character finds his mother's eating habits becoming his own after her death. People keep telling him how much he resembles her. "She was in him not as he had been in her, as a seed becoming a little male offshoot, but as the full tracery of his perceptions and reactions; he had led his life as an extension of hers, a superior version of hers, and when she died he became custodian of a specialized semiotics."[11] He feels about land, "as about his mother, ambivalent, she having planted in him the idea that land was sacred, a piece of Mother Earth, endlessly valuable, and the last thing that the vulgar self-interest-seekers of the world would manage to take from you" (244). That ambivalence, we have noted, has not prevented him from remaining in touch with that earlier sacred space, so that writing has never been reduced to a utilitarian "self-interest-seeking."

Updike's descriptions often have a ceremonial raptness about them, a sense of the great pleasure of exploring the world in all its detail, the feeling that one moves in the text through a privileged zone of attention. Things still have for Updike a sacramental presence that a full disenchantment of nature, a complete and irrevocable separation from the maternal presence, as in the radical linguistic turn, could not allow. There are passages where the feeling of a ritual childhood space comes more evidently to the surface in Updike. The opening of "Museums and Women" reads: "Set together, the two words are seen to be mutually transparent; the E's, the M's blend—the M's framing and squaring the structure lend resonance and a curious formal weight to the M central in the creature, which it dominates like a dark core winged with flitting syllables. Both words hum. Both suggest radiance, antiquity, mystery, and duty."[12] Both the words *museum* and *women* and the places they represent form a radiant space of mysterious significance, like a child's absorption in a world of objects that hum in the mother's presence. (We also get the child's sense of letters, apart from the words they contribute to, as having such mysterious significance; that again connects this ceremonial space with writing.)

The first museum in the story, which the narrator visits with his mother, is "approached through paradisaical grounds of raked gravel walks, humus-fed plantings of exotic flora, and trees wearing tags, as if freshly dubbed by Adam" ("Museums and Women," 9). It is a fantasy space of strangely combined objects, of items from all over the globe, and "freshly dubbed by Adam" suggests the child's inhabiting of a world where he is first putting language to use. The boy's sense of rapt attention and the ritual, hypnotic movement of the language as it enters this space are evident. "An infinitely patient Chinaman, as remote from me as the resident of a star, had carved a yellow rhinoceros horn into an upright crescental city, pagoda-tipped, of balconies, vines, and thimble-sized people wearing microscopic expressions of pain." The infinite patience of the maker in his craftsmanship and the small size of the people suggest a world constructed by the imagination in childhood or the space of writing.

Then there were the "strange small statues":

> Strange, it may be, only in the impressions they made on me. They were bronze statuettes, randomly burnished here and there as if by a caressing hand, of nudes or groups of nudes. . . . Another statue bodied forth two naked boys wrestling. Another was of an Indian, dressed in only a knife belt, setting astride a horse bareback, his chin bowed to his chest in sorrow, his exquisitely toed feet hanging down both hard and limp, begging to be touched. I think it was the smallness of the figures that carried them so penetratingly into my mind. Each, if it could have been released into life, would have stood about twenty inches high and weighed in my arms perhaps as much as a cat. I itched to finger them, to interact with them, to insert myself into their mysterious silent world of strenuous contention—their bulged tendons burnished, their hushed violence detailed down to the fingernails. They were in their smallness like secret thoughts of mine projected into dimension and permanence, and they returned to me as a response that carried strangely into parts of my body. I felt myself a furtive animal stirring in the shadow of my mother. ("Museums and Women," 10)

There could hardly be a better literary rendition of the transitional space of object relations: the play figures, like dolls or toys, that are both extensions of the self and external objects; the narcissistic and homoerotic structuring of the space; the smallness of the objects that make them more subject to the child's control and yet their seeming distance and untouchability as independent things; the movements of identification and projection; the energies of eros and violence that become hushed and still in this specially charged scene; the shadow of his mother in the background. Eventually, of course, Updike will let words serve as these small objects that he will "finger" and interact with, that will project his secret thoughts "into dimension and permanence." Language will become the most successful transitional object. But he is first laying out the iconic, metaphorical, transitional world that will be transformed into a linguistic one and that will remain permanently in the background of that linguistic resolution. There is (necessarily) in that transitional space "the shadow of my mother." She is behind him in the museum as he watches, and "noticing how the small statues fascinated me, she said 'Billy, they seem such unhappy little people.' " Her gaze makes the narrator as well see the melancholy of the statues. They "seemed caught in a tarnished fate from which I yearned to rescue them. I wanted to touch them to comfort them, yet I held my hand back, afraid of breaking the seal on their sullen, furious underworld" (11). (The child must keep this unconscious realm as a dreamlike fantasy space instead of breaking the seal on it and letting its figures emerge into his everyday world. But they are clearly self-objects in Winnicott's sense, in the way the mother's gaze on these objects affects the narrator's perceptions.)

His mother's presence in the transitional space is to some degree intrusive and judgmental, and one might recall Winnicott's claim that this maternal intrusiveness will make it harder for the child to carve out the space of his own selfhood. The narrator's mood of dread in the museum, he says, "did not emanate from [the statues]; it seemed to originate above and behind me, as if from another living person in the room. Often my mother . . . was the only other person in the room" ("Museums and Women," 11). Again the matter of separation is difficult because her sort of presence is an enveloping, nontransparent one: "She had descended to me from thin clouds of preexistent time, enveloped me, and set me moving toward an unseen goal with a vague expectation that was more hers than mine." About the first girl he likes, in a group of schoolchildren visiting that same museum, he says that the decision to choose this girl "was as much my mother's as mine." As for this girl, "in the museum, a ruthless law propelled her forward to gather with the other bold spirits, tittering, around the defenseless little statues while I hung back, on the edge of the fountain, envious, angry, and brimming with things to say." Again the defensive little statues come into play as self-objects, this time absorbing the mocking laughter. In fact they keep reappearing, getting a brief mention in *The Centaur* (267) and in the story "Packed Dirt, Churchgoing, a Dying Cat, a Traded Car" in a reference to the "bronze statuettes of wrestling Indians that stirred my first erotic dreams" (186).

The narrator meets the young woman who will be his wife at a university museum (presumably Harvard's). Again it is a transitional space that reaches both backward and forward. The woman, even in winter, has sneakers so worn that they leave her toes bare, and the toes, in the narrator's concern for them, seem to echo "the exquisitely toed feet" of the Indian statuette that also gave off a sense of sorrow and vulnerability. That the scene remains somewhat a regressive, archaicizing, repetitive one is suggested by the observation that the museum is strongest in medieval and oriental art, and the two students develop their affair among such older art objects, these suggestions of an iconic unconscious. Another woman in another museum is imaginary, a beautifully carved statue who "was the size of the small straining figures that had fascinated my childhood, and as with them, smallness intensified sensual content" ("Museums and Women," 16). The layout of the various museums is a psychic space of object relations and gender identity, and the real and the imaginary women, as we can see by the descriptions, are taking over the place of the homoerotic statuettes and are becoming more resolutely other. Instead of a ritual return that strives for rigid repetition (one might think of Macon Leary in Anne Tyler's *The Accidental Tourist*), each entrance into a museum (or into a woman, as each statement here about museums is also a statement about women) is both a ceremonial return and a reaching for something new. "What we seek in museums is the opposite of what we seek in churches—the consoling sense of previous visitation. In museums, rather, we seek the untouched, the never-before-discovered; and it is their final unsearchability that leads us to hope, and return." A mature ceremonial repetition allows for newness in the performance. The more deeply regressive, and dangerous, return wants to restore the original relationship through the magical properties of an unvarying activity, as with neurotics who must perform actions in exactly the same way. (There are those for whom the other that is needed must be, magically and impossibly, the identically original presence of the mother, as in the movie *Psycho*.)

That more regressive sort of return still works at the dyadic level of self-other mirroring rather than in a field where objects, if they have the right positional character, are substitutable, with each substitution never quite a replica. In Updike's writing one can return to a transitional space in a way that allows for difference and replacement. The museum does not have to be the museum visited in childhood; the woman does not have to be his mother. "Museums and Women" is about these substitutions, these acceptances of difference that allow a new field to open up; it is important that the museum space in the story is successively associated with different women. One reenters in these museums the ceremonial scene of object relations in which even letter shapes and sounds have a mysterious symbolic significance, and at the same time one reenacts the movement into language as structural and grammatical, so that there is substitution among positions. The rapt, sacramental feel of entrance remains as the effect of a more archaic state, but the repetition is what it is only in not being quite the same as what it repeats. Updike keeps returning to recognizable themes in his writing. Story after story repeats the familial scenes in the small town of southeast Pennsylvania. But the space of the stories, as with the museums, allows for differences, for a more complex field of interaction and substitution. His writing, with all the words produced, is never an obsessive return to saying the same thing, so that his entrance into his texts is like the entrances he describes into different museums.

Many of the themes discussed here are especially vivid in the story "I Am Dying, Egypt, Dying."[13] We are signaled right away that the narrative space has something of a psychological-transitional quality by the dreamlike way the objects appear. Clem is an American taking a boat ride up the Nile.

> He fell asleep in deck chairs, beautifully immobile, glistening, as the two riverbanks at their safe distance glided by—date palms, taut green fields irrigated by rotating donkeys, pyramids of white round pots, trapezoidal houses of elephant-colored mud, mud-covered children silently waving, and the roseate desert cliffs beyond, massive parentheses. Glistening like a mirror, he slept in this gliding parenthesis with a godlike calm that possessed the landscape, transformed it into a steady dreaming. (96)

There is a hypnotic quality to this paragraph, with its chanted repetitions and reversals: "elephant-colored mud, mud-covered children"; "glistening . . . glided. . . . Glistening . . . gliding"; the repeating of the *d, t, p,* and *r* sounds in "date palms, taut green fields irrigated by rotating donkeys, pyramids of white round pots, trapezoidal houses." There is the semantic repetition of "asleep," "immobile," "silently," "slept," "calm," and "dreaming." The reference to parentheses suggests that this is a writing space as well as a dreamlike space of regression, but unlike in the world of *The Centaur* or "Museums and Women" the regression here seems more extreme, to a level of psychic organization with greater anxiety and fewer resources for developing complexity. It is notable, first of all, that Clem's gliding along is an image closer to death than to life. Indeed, Clem is described in a way that makes him a figure from an Egyptian burial chamber ("His posture was perfect but he walked without swing") (95). Clem, as it happens, brings up the analogy himself. The Egyptians, he is told, fear being unprovided for not so much in this life as in the journey beyond the grave; that is why the tomb must be stocked with supplies and with wall images that instruct the person how to maneuver in that next life, how to complete the journey. Clem, speaking to another passenger, advances "the theory that he was a royal tomb, once crammed with treasure, that had been robbed" (109). He feels an inner emptiness. "Into him, he thought, groping, peering with difficulty into that glittering blank area which in other people, he imagined, was the cave of self, religion had bred a dislike of litter" (109).

Here the transition in question is not between this life and the next one but between childhood and adulthood. Somehow that interior space of self was not properly stocked in childhood; the guidance as to how to make one's journey in the new life was not provided. So now he is gliding along in a trancelike state just as the Egyptian who has died travels along the river of the new world in a boat provided in the tomb, except that Clem does not have the psychological equipment necessary for adulthood, for engaging in the complex grammatical rituals of the new form of life. So he must enact a version of death-in-life, a return to a world that hovers close to dissolution and that cannot provide the strengthening, the revivifying, that he needs. Falling into the unconsciousness of sleep across from another, as a substitute for having sexual activity, is a sign of that regression. Here Clem's attempted sexual activity with a German woman instead becomes a deep night-long sleep alongside her. When he speaks with her on the boat, "languorously she shifted her long arms and legs; the impression of flesh in the side of his vision disturbingly merged, in his sleepless state, with a floating sensation of hollowness, of being in parenthesis" ("I Am Dying," 106). Again we see the notions of merger, floating, parentheses. When she asks him if he will sleep better after dancing, he says, "I'm sure I will, I'm dead" (110).

We are given certain clues as to the difficulties in Clem's self-formation. He goes to a small shop to have a caftan made. "In the flecked dim mirror, Clem saw himself gowned; a shock, because the effect was not incongruous. He looked like a husky woman, a big-boned square-faced woman quick to blush and giggle" ("I Am Dying," 112). The size of the caftan may not be correct, but Clem says: "I'll take it. The fabric is lovely. If it turns out to be too tight I can give it to my mother." In thinking of the cheapness of the caftan, his own cheap suit, Clem recalls the guide's hint as to how to remember the name of the ancient Egyptian queen Hatshepsut: *Hat—cheap—suit.* She was a powerful queen who showed herself in statues wearing a false beard and without breasts, and she refused to give up power to her brother or, later, to her nephew. When she finally died the nephew smashed all her statues, and where her name had been written on the walls he had it erased and replaced with his own. Clem, it appears, has not been able to break free of his mother's world; he does not have the necessary aggressiveness to write over the transitional objects still identified with her world, so as to impress his own identity on them. (One might suppose that Updike for much of his life, when he writes, is describing his earlier familial world in a way that makes it more and more his own, a place his language has etched itself in and given meaning to, as Hatshepsut's nephew wrote over the queen's name, while Updike's mother's semantic control of that space becomes ever less.)

Clem's object-relational response to that situation was a temporary success but a long-term failure. His childhood solution was a version of what Hegel called the Greek model of beautiful individuality, of form that is invulnerable in its self-regulating perfection. That is why the Greek gods, says Hegel, seem to withdraw from the world of everyday interaction. A young child who feels his boundaries threatened by the mother's overwhelming presence and intrusion may be tempted by that solution, that attempt at an invulnerability of formal perfection, though of course his own maintenance of boundaries will not have the ease about it of the Greek gods but rather will require constant policing. Clem is described as follows: "His perfection revealed no flaw" ("I Am Dying," 95). "The girl's green eyes, curious, pressed on him like gems scratching glass" (103). The German woman tells him: "That is your flaw. . . . You must always be beautiful" (109). He has a dream in which the wall cartouches of the tombs become "sharp-edged stamps trying to indent themselves upon him" (110). He is surrounded once by street vendors: "Something warm and hard was inserted into his hand, his other sleeve was plucked, his pockets were patted and he wheeled, his tongue pinched between his teeth flirtatiously, trapped. It was a nightmare; the dream thought crossed his mind that he might be scratched" (99). Hegel believed that the Greek stage of beautiful individuation, of identifying with a perfection of form, did not allow subjectivity or innerness to develop fully, so that Greek statues, Hegel says, show the eyes of the gods as blank.[14] That solution also does not allow a sufficiently complex relation with otherness. Clem too recognizes in himself no warmth of interiority. The level of psychological or cultural energy invested in that phase of beautiful form may reveal an anxious resistance to the gravities of nature or of the earlier mother-child structure. But to become frozen at that phase, out of great anxiety over the possibility of regression to an even earlier form, is to surrender too much of an adult life, is to be unable to adopt the complex self-other relations necessary for maturity.

The thought of penetration becomes more threatening. When he goes to the tailor's shop to be measured for the caftan we are brought back to the sort of transitional space we saw in "Museums and Women." As with the statuettes in the museum, smallness is the sign of this transitional region. "He felt oversize in this shop, whose reduced scale was here and there betrayed by a coarse object from the real world" ("I Am Dying," 108). Later he remembers the shop, "its enchanted smallness" (113). In it "a young woman was helping a small child with homework, and a young man, the husband and father, lounged against some stacked bolts of cloth" (107–8). But as the tailor is fitting him he begins caressing Clem in offensive ways. "Shielded from his wife by the rectangular bulk of Clem's body, the young man, undoing his own fly with a swift light tailor's gesture, exhibited himself. 'I can make you very happy,' he muttered" (108). When Clem goes back for the caftan it has a slit in it instead of the pocket he requested. The tailor "put his hand in the slit and touched Clem until Clem protested" (112).

The enchanted transitional world shows that as one returns to it in writing, positions and identities may become more shifting and unstable. The slit in the caftan, which Clem did not want, makes him vulnerable as feminized, as enterable by others. The apparently stable triadic model of father, mother, and child, as with the scene in the tailor's shop, takes on a more disturbing form, regressing into much less stable dyadic oscillations. Egyptian children are said by Clem to be proportioned as miniature adults. So perhaps the writing self, in regressing to this scene, is shifting its identification between Clem's position and that of the child, the adult self made miniature. Why then is the father in the shop presented as propositioning Clem? The situation is not helped when Clem brings with him for his protection a father-figure from the boat, an older man who has done a lot of journeying in Africa. This man nudges Clem too closely and asks him if he has ever tried it with a man. Clem gets the caftan and wears the feminizing garb for the party on the last night aboard ship. He goes to his room afterward and wants to open the window, but it is "sealed shut." As he tries to sleep Clem thinks of the German woman and says "You bitch" over and over in a rage. "He remembered nothing about his dreams, except that they all took place back in Buffalo, amid aunts and uncles he thought he had forgotten" ("I Am Dying," 118). To be back among these relatives is to be back in childhood, in a psychic landscape that feels "sealed shut," a protective measure perhaps but also the cause of a feared aloneness; his rage and his earlier description of himself as an Egyptian tomb emptied out by grave robbers reveal how much that structure, at least in his conception of it, was forced on him in his childhood.

Yet there is some complication here if our topic is writing rather than simply psychological development. Clem's situation in the story is compared with that of a Russian couple. The story takes place after the Russians have replaced the Western nations as advisers in Egypt. One Egyptian says that the Russians have no style, that they are people who appeal to the Egyptians only at the level of satisfying basic appetites. But while Clem is unable to have sex with the German woman, the Russians audible in the cabin next door have loud, grunting, satisfying sex and then fall asleep peacefully, leaving Clem to hear the man's snoring through the wall. In the last scene of the story the boat has arrived at the Aswan Dam.

> And the makeshift roads were ugly, and the graceless Russian machinery clanking and sitting stalled, and the styleless, already squalid propaganda pavilion containing a model of the dam. The dam itself, after the straight, elegantly arched dam the British had built upriver, seemed a mere mountain of heaped rubble, hardly distinguishable from the inchoate desert itself. Yet at its heart, where the turbines had been set, a plume like a cloud of horses leaped upward in an inverted Niagara that dissolved, horse after horse, into mist before becoming the Nile again and flowing on. ("I Am Dying," 122)

The stocky Russian couple beams proudly at the scene.

So the symbol in the story of passionate sexuality and flooding vitality is at the same time marked as vulgar and appetitive, without style or grace. But Clem's own model of beautiful form is sterile because its self-sufficiency depends on its being closed off to the world. Where do we find here a characterization of writerly energy? The writer wants the graceful style and sense of form that occur in the rebound from a regressive state where dissolution threatens, where individuation is at stake. But the "beautiful form" solution, as with Aschenbach's fascination with Tadzio, while it may provide a useful impetus to writing, risks freezing the self in a particular object-relations solution, one proper to an earlier mirroring phase, that in the long run may be inimical to full development. If that is the Greek moment, then the Egyptian moment in the story is that of the more regressive pull of death, of an unconscious dreamlike existence. Yet the Russian couple's more mature solution is in some ways unappealing. They have vitality and a more stable adult sexual life, but they have no Greek sense of beautiful form, as a writer must have to at least some degree, and they do not have access to the (Egyptian) dreamlike, hypnotic transitional space that is so useful to a writer. (Perhaps this is forcing a connection that is not there, but one is reminded of the progression of Hegel's art history from Egyptian symbolic art to the Greek art of beautiful form to modern art expressing the movements of subjectivity.[15] The lesson of the short story might then be that while the Egyptian and Greek stages are regressive or death-threatening, they make available a space of writing that the writer should not want to give up; while one must surely advance beyond them, one should not advance in such a way that one no longer has access to them. The entire scene of the story, then, can be seen as articulating the space of writing, with the moments of beautiful form and hypnotic gliding still available to the prose while the narrator, within the story, is examining the successes and failures of those moments as aspects of psychic life. Again, the space of writing must be both disenchanted and regressive.)

The poor Russians seem to be treated the same way in Updike's story as in Mann's. One will recall the attractively aristocratic manner in which the Polish Tadzio looked scornfully at a Russian family who were eating and drinking and talking loudly. In *Death in Venice* there is also, as here in Updike, a gliding death ship (here the boat along the Nile, there the black gondola in which Aschenbach is rowed across the water). Like Aschenbach with the Protestant self-discipline of his earlier writing, Clem comes from a Protestant background where, he says, he never learned to dance, and the German woman sees him as having come from "a stern childhood. In a place of harsh winters" ("I Am Dying," 105). Both journey to the Mediterranean to find an environment of greater warmth. But while Clem does put on feminizing dress for the costume party at the end of the cruise, and while he tries to dance with the German woman, he never descends to revitalizing Dionysiac energies. That the story has been a regressive ritual of some sort, suggestive of a preparation for dying, is signaled in its final sentence: "Gazing into the abyss of the trip that was over, he saw that he had been happy" (122).

I do not want to suggest, through this account of Updike, the notion that homoerotic investments will generally be a mark of regression to an earlier transitional space, one whose transitional objects have now been replaced by, or should have been replaced by, more full-fledged *others,* namely (in the case of men) women. I do not believe that; my intention has been to describe a certain scene of writing that may be found even in writers whose sexual preferences are heterosexual. The structures we thereby uncover, while they are clearly relevant to literary space as such, do not tell us much, if anything, about the psychic lives of adult homosexuals living out their intimate lives with others. In reading Updike I have been interested not in sexual identity but rather in the engineering of the space of writing in which he works. We saw earlier that Greenblatt tried to explain the power of literary space through seeing it in the context of circulating cultural representations and the regimes of power associated with them. I argued that this was a poor explanation. Here I have tried to describe other factors that might be more significant generators of literary power.

My readings have supported the view that literary language is intimately associated with processes of self-formation. But I do not want to suggest that through some magical identification with linguistic properties we are able to take on, in the sequence of our lives, the seeming inevitability and rightness that we may find appealing in good prose or poetry. That conception of art is a central theme in Sartre's *Nausea*. Sitting in a cafe, Roquentin is prey to various anxieties about boundaries and wholeness: "The bottom of my seat is broken . . . I have a broken spring . . . if I turn it [my head], it will fall off" (Sartre, *Nausea,* 19). Time is too expansive. "Everything you plunge into it is stretched and disintegrates" (21). Definite outlines begin to weaken: "there was a whirlpool, an eddy, a shadow passed across the ceiling and I felt myself pushed forward. I floated, dazed by luminous fogs dragging me in all directions at once" (18). Everything changes as a jazz record is played in the café, a recording by a woman whom Roquentin takes to be a negress. Suddenly all the descriptions of softness and puddles and blurring are replaced. In just a couple of pages we are told that the vocal chorus is like "a cliff against the sea," that the duration of the music is a "band of steel," a "ribbon of steel" that "transpierces these vague figures and passes through them. . . . It seems inevitable, so strong is the necessity of this music: nothing can interrupt it, nothing which comes from this time in which the world has fallen" (21–23). Music, fiction, and art return in the novel as the only ways to overcome the bleak, accidental thereness of existence. This overcoming can occur, supposedly, because artifacts emerge that have the qualities existence does not: necessity, inevitability, a lack of anything superfluous, a momentum that determines itself instead of being determined by something external. As Roquentin would have it, musical works or well-formed narratives have a proper beginning and end, a development that fixes their own sense of completeness. By identifying with these various qualities of works of art Roquentin feels invigorated by a feeling in himself of such an inevitability, such a rigorous necessity, as if he could repeat those qualities in his movements, as if he could give his life that sense of completeness.

But there is a double aspect to literary space, and the moment of disenchantment remains as important as the symbolic reoccupying of an earlier space of mirroring identifications. We recognize that these reoccupations are due to linguistic rituals that are merely symbolic and only temporarily effective, though they may provide a scaffolding and modeling for ways of being a self that one must achieve on one's own. They may give us a more confident sense of being able to assimilate painful experience, but they do not change the metaphysical character of being a self, in a way that would reduce its radical contingency. Unfortunately for Roquentin, we can no longer participate in practices that would grant us such magical identifications. But the rewards of our more disenchanted stance, as seen in Merrill, are subtle and many.

I began this book with the idea of defending an attitude toward literature that others would take to be naive and outdated. I hope it now appears less naive. We have to be wary of claims that we are entering a new paradigm, that we are leaving old ways of thinking, and old ways of being a self, behind. Those claims can often be shown to depend on a wild exaggeration of the consequences of otherwise valid philosophical arguments. It is true that a certain conception of authorship, for example, can no longer be accepted. Arguments in the philosophy of language and the philosophy of mind show that we cannot defend the picture of an author formulating a determinate idea and then giving it an external form in language, so that we could discover the true meaning if we could only get back to that original authorial activity of meaning-conferral. Matters do not work that way; one is spoken through by language as much as one speaks through it. Yet an author is hardly passive and hardly disappears. There are reasons why a writer fights so hard day after day to put linguistic items in certain precise formations and not in others. Those formations are templates that readers can follow so that certain patterns of information they have not previously grasped, but that were comprehended in an original way by the author, come into view. They are also recipes for linguistic rituals that readers can engage in and, in so doing, form themselves in a more complex way in relation to the world and to themselves. We remain selves who care, as Aristotle supposed we did, what kind of selves we are becoming, over a whole life. Literature can play an important role in that sort of reflection, not just in the characters that it presents but also in the rituals of self-undermining and self-formation that we go through in taking over the readerly stance that the author has designed for us, whether intentionally or not. Some authors do this much better than others do, and good readers are grateful to them. The exact ordering of words in an excellent literary text matters more than their deconstruction, even if the latter is useful as well, and we often do well to read aloud and to encourage students to do so. Aesthetic space, indeed the notion of the literary as distinct from the social, remains legitimate and valuable and marked off from other social spaces; beauty is still a goal, if not the only one. My findings are limited, to be sure, especially regarding the matter of gender, since the engineering specifications of the space of literature as described here clearly do not take gender sufficiently into consideration. But the role of the academic literary critic is, as most of us have thought all along, much inferior to that of the writers who matter.

NOTES

1. The Space of Literature

1. I am thinking here of Bernard Williams's *Ethics and the Limits of Philosophy* (Cambridge: Harvard University Press, 1985) and *Shame and Necessity* (Berkeley: University of California Press, 1993). Friedrich Nietzsche's attack occurs throughout his work but especially in *The Genealogy of Morals,* trans. F. Golffing (Garden City, N.Y.: Anchor Books, 1956).

2. The expression was popularized by Richard Rorty, *The Linguistic Turn* (Chicago: University of Chicago Press, 1967).

3. A longer description of these matters and of the discussion of Aquinas that follows here is given in my *Subjectivity, Realism and Postmodernism* (Cambridge: Cambridge University Press, 1994), 1–15. Readers should also consult Hans Blumenberg, *The Legitimacy of the Modern Age* (Cambridge: MIT Press, 1983), 125–226, 549–96.

4. This is a view that Stanley Fish defends throughout his *Is There a Text in This Class?* (Cambridge: Harvard University Press, 1980). See my treatment of his work in *Subjectivity, Realism, and Postmodernism,* 262–69.

5. Willard V. O. Quine, "Ontological Relativity," in his *Ontological Relativity and Other Essays* (New York: Columbia University Press, 1969), 26–68.

6. See, for example, the essays throughout Richard Rorty's *Consequences of Pragmatism* (Minneapolis: University of Minnesota Press, 1982). My debate with Rorty appears in my "Rorty and Antirealism," in *Rorty and Pragmatism: The Philosopher Responds to His Critics,* ed. Herman J. Saatkamp (Nashville: Vanderbilt University Press, 1995), 154–88, as well as in Rorty's "Response to Frank Farrell" in the same volume, 189–95.

7. Jürgen Habermas develops an extended version of that argument in his *The Philosophical Discourse of Modernity,* trans. Frederick Lawrence (Cambridge: MIT Press, 1987). In that volume he considers what he finds problematic with the Hegelian

subject-object model on pp. 23–44; the Marxist version of the model is treated on pp. 60–69 and 75–82.

8. See especially Ludwig Wittgenstein's *Philosophical Investigations* (Oxford: Basil Blackwell, 1953), secs. 147–242.

9. As Rudolf Carnap's student Willard Quine would put it, to be is to be the value of a bound variable; there is an argument for this claim in Quine, "Existence and Quantification," in *Ontological Relativity and Other Essays* (New York: Columbia University Press, 1969), 91–113.

10. See Martin Heidegger, "The Origin of the Work of Art," in his *Poetry, Language, Thought,* trans. Albert Hofstadter (New York: Harper and Row, 1971), 17–87. Also see Heidegger, "What Are Poets For?," in the same volume, 91–142.

11. Ernest Hemingway, *A Farewell to Arms* (1929; New York: Simon and Schuster, 1995), 3.

12. Winnicott's theory will be examined in detail in chapter 9. The reference here is to D. W. Winnicott, "The Location of Cultural Experience," in *Transitional Objects and Potential Spaces: Literary Uses of D. W. Winnicott,* ed. Peter Rudnytsky (New York: Columbia University Press, 1993), 3–12.

13. James Merrill, "The House Fly," in his *Selected Poems 1946–1985* (New York: Alfred A. Knopf, 1995), 306.

14. The reference to distant music is in James Joyce, "The Dead," in his *Dubliners* (New York: Viking, 1961), 210.

15. A rather different account of the social and political role of the aesthetic is given in Terry Eagleton, *The Ideology of the Aesthetic* (Oxford: Basil Blackwell, 1990).

16. Steven Pinker, *How the Mind Works* (New York: W. W. Norton and Co., 1997), 99–131.

17. Daniel Dennett, *Consciousness Explained* (Boston: Little, Brown, 1991), 101–38.

18. Ibid., 227–52.

19. Charles Altieri argues for this conception throughout his *Painterly Abstraction in Modernist American Poetry* (University Park: Pennsylvania State University Press, 1995).

20. For just one of the texts in which Husserl develops what he means by "transcendental phenomenology," see Edmund Husserl, *The Crisis of European Sciences and Transcendental Phenomenology,* trans. David Carr (Evanston, Ill.: Northwestern University Press, 1970).

2. Literary Space in McCarthy and Pynchon, Rushdie and Chaudhuri

1. Cormac McCarthy, *All the Pretty Horses* (New York: Alfred A. Knopf, 1992), 301.

2. For a richly positive treatment of postmodernism and fiction, see Brian McHale, *Postmodernist Fiction* (London: Routledge, 1989).

3. See, for example, his reading of Proust in Paul de Man, *Allegories of Reading* (New Haven, Conn.: Yale University Press, 1979), 57–78.

4. Cormac McCarthy, *Blood Meridian* (New York: Vintage International, 1992), 157.

5. See, for example, Simon During, ed., *The Cultural Studies Reader*, 2d ed. (London: Routledge, 1999).

6. Salman Rushdie, *Midnight's Children* (1980; New York: Penguin, 1991).

7. See Jonathan Culler, "Paul de Man's Contribution to Literary Criticism and Theory," in *The Future of Literary Theory*, ed. Ralph Cohen (New York: Routledge, 1989), 271–72, for how Culler lists, as one of Paul de Man's lasting contributions to literary theory, this preference for allegory.

8. Thomas Pynchon, *Gravity's Rainbow* (New York: Viking, 1973), 111–12.

9. Thomas Pynchon, *Mason & Dixon* (New York: Henry Holt, 1997).

10. That phrase is from the title of Richard Rorty's essay "The World Well Lost," *Journal of Philosophy* 69 (1972): 649–65.

11. Hilary Putnam has defended his account, which he sometimes calls internal realism, in *Reason, Truth, and History* (Cambridge: Cambridge University Press, 1981); in *Realism and Reason* (Cambridge: Cambridge University Press, 1983); and in *The Many Faces of Realism* (LaSalle, Ill.: Open Court, 1987).

12. Amit Chaudhuri, *Freedom Song* (New York: Alfred A. Knopf, 1999), 216. That work is a trilogy of novels: *A Strange and Sublime Address*, *Afternoon Raag*, and *Freedom Song*. This quotation is taken from the middle novel, *Afternoon Raag*.

13. The literature on modernism is, of course, enormous. Let me mention here just a few texts that I found helpful: Michael H. Levenson, *A Genealogy of Modernism* (Cambridge: Cambridge University Press, 1984); Louis Menand, *Discovering Modernism: T. S. Eliot and His Context* (New York: Oxford University Press, 1987); Malcolm Bradbury and James McFarlane, eds., *Modernism: A Guide to European Literature, 1890–1930* (London: Penguin Books, 1991); and Christopher Butler, *Early Modernism: Literature, Music, and Painting in Europe, 1900–1916* (Oxford: Clarendon Press, 1994).

14. James Merrill, "Press Release," in *A Scattering of Salts* (New York: Alfred A. Knopf, 1995), 55–57.

3. The Philosophical Background

1. Williams, *Shame and Necessity* and *Ethics and the Limits of Philosophy*.

2. John McDowell, *Mind and World* (Cambridge: Harvard University Press, 1994).

3. Extensive reading on my part in literary theory is summarized here, but I should grant that in regard to the discipline I am, as a philosophy professor, an outsider. Without being part of the everyday back-and-forth activity of graduate schools and literature conventions surely I miss out, even with such extensive reading, on some arguments and interests familiar to insiders. And my reading has been concentrated in some areas and not others; to take just one example, I am poorly read, as most readers will be able to make out, in feminist literary theory.

4. In my book *Subjectivity, Realism, and Postmodernism* there are long sections on what I mean by the disenchantment of subjectivity and the disenchantment of language in philosophy. I will not repeat those treatments here but do refer the interested reader to them. Some of my claims about Davidson are given in much longer form in that book.

5. See Donald Davidson's account of interpretation in his essays "Radical Interpretation" and "Belief and the Basis of Meaning," both of which are in his *Inquiries into*

Truth and Interpretation (Oxford: Clarendon Press, 1984). See also "A Coherence Theory of Truth and Knowledge," in *Truth and Interpretation,* ed. Ernest LePore (Oxford: Basil Blackwell, 1986), 307–19.

6. See Donald Davidson, "On the Very Idea of a Conceptual Scheme," in his *Inquiries into Truth and Interpretation,* 183–98. He argues that claims about how others differ from us must assume, as justification for those claims, a wide basis of shared belief about a world that both we and they count as directed toward.

7. A condition for interpretation is that I not only attribute beliefs to you but also see you as relating those beliefs in inferential networks where the truth of one belief depends on the truth of others. But then there must be a roughly shared rationality between us. If I read you as over and over accepting truly odd inferences from your beliefs, that would be evidence that I have not translated your words correctly.

8. See, for example, two essays in Stephen Schwartz, ed., *Naming, Necessity, and Natural Kinds* (Ithaca, N.Y.: Cornell University Press, 1977): Saul Kripke's "Identity and Necessity," 66–101; and Hilary Putnam's "Meaning and Reference," 119–32.

9. David Pears, *The False Prison,* vol. 2 (Oxford: Oxford University Press, 1988), 525–26.

10. See Donald Davidson, "Knowing One's Own Mind," *Proceedings and Addresses of the American Philosophical Association* 60, no. 3 (1987): 441–58; and "First Person Authority," *Dialectica* 38 (1984): 101–11.

11. These claims by de Man, which he defends in his *Allegories of Reading,* will be considered in detail and rejected in chapter 5.

12. I believe that both Quine and Davidson exaggerate the difficulties of reference. It may well be that odd ways of dividing up the world into units and sorts could be made epistemically equivalent with what we think of as the proper way. But I think that the world shows a preference for some ways of articulating units: whole rabbits rather than rabbit time slices, as in Quine's example. But that argument will not be made here.

13. Donald Davidson, "Reality without Reference," in his *Inquiries into Truth and Interpretation,* 215–26.

14. For someone interested in this issue I strongly recommend Peter Lipton, *Inference to the Best Explanation* (London: Routledge, 1991). In his final chapter Lipton shows how the scientific realist has difficulties using an approach based on inference to the best explanation to argue that theories are true. But he remains a realist and does not offer any support for the literary critic who believes that evidence for a theory reduces to what those holding the theory or those in power generally are willing to count as evidence.

15. A good account of these issues in the philosophy of science is a dialogue intended for a general audience: Larry Laudan, *Science and Relativism* (Chicago: University of Chicago Press, 1990). Laudan is a pragmatist but argues strongly against relativist readings of scientific theories. See also Richard Boyd, "How To Be a Moral Realist," in *Essays on Moral Realism,* ed. Geoffrey Sayre-McCord (Ithaca, N.Y.: Cornell University Press, 1988), 188–99.

16. See, for example, John Dupré, *The Disorder of Things* (Cambridge: Harvard University Press, 1993). "The metaphysics of modern science," he says, "as also of much of modern Western philosophy, has generally been taken to posit a deterministic, fully law-governed, and potentially fully intelligible structure that pervades the material universe" (2). He rejects precisely that metaphysics. But he also says, "I place myself

firmly in the philosophical tradition that sees empirical, often scientific inquiry as providing the most credible source of knowledge of how things are" (1).

17. Reference here is to McDowell, *Mind and World.*

18. Ibid., 3–23. McDowell sets up this issue of the spontaneity of thought versus friction from the world.

19. Ibid., 14–18, 129–61.

20. "I have been talking about a pair of opposing pitfalls: on the one side a coherentism that does not acknowledge an external rational constraint on thinking and therefore, I claim, cannot genuinely make room for empirical content at all; and on the other side a recoil into the Myth of the Given, which offers at best exculpations where what we need is justifications" (Ibid., 46).

21. Ibid., 142–43.

22. This debate is often framed as involving humanist versus antihumanist conceptions, with the former supposedly naive. Christopher Butler, in being concerned with the apparent victory of the antihumanists, speaks of the debate as follows: "It is a debate in which the avant-garde of theory has aimed to dislodge the notions of intention as predominant for interpretation, of the author as origin and authority, of the humanist subject as controlling the discourses a writer 'uses,' and of the presence of 'character' within fiction" (Christopher Butler, "The Future of Theory: Saving the Reader," in *The Future of Literary Theory,* ed. Ralph Cohen [New York: Routledge, 1989], 229). He describes the antihumanist position in the following way: "Persons are the functional supports or effects of social processes, and misrecognize themselves in believing in their own autonomy and subjectivity" (231).

23. For a slightly different version of the thought experiment, see Ned Block, "Troubles with Functionalism," in *Perception and Cognition: Issues in the Foundations of Psychology,* ed. C. W. Savage (Minneapolis: University of Minnesota Press, 1978).

24. In my *Subjectivity, Realism and Postmodernism,* 217–44, I consider some of these sophisticated structures of subjectivity (such that many discussions of intentionality in philosophy of mind seem to miss the point).

25. See, for example, Dennett, *Consciousness Explained,* 101–38.

26. Daniel Dennett, *Elbow Room* (Cambridge: MIT Press, 1984), 50–100.

27. That is the central argument of Colin McGinn's *The Problem of Consciousness* (Oxford: Blackwell, 1991).

4. James Merrill and the Making of Literature

1. James Merrill, "Lost in Translation," in his *Selected Poems 1946–1985* (New York: Alfred A. Knopf, 1995), 278–84. For an excellent general treatment of Merrill's poetry see Stephen Yenser, *The Consuming Myth: The Work of James Merrill* (Cambridge: Harvard University Press, 1987).

2. James Merrill, "Santorini: Stopping the Leak," in his *Selected Poems,* 332–39.

3. I do not wish to attach myself here to any specific psychological theory. In what follows I have been influenced by patterns suggested by Merrill's poetry but also by a range of outside readings. My primary source for different versions of object-relations theory is Jay Greenberg and Stephen Mitchell, *Object Relations in Psychoanalytic Theory* (Cambridge: Harvard University Press, 1983). They describe the views of such

thinkers as Sullivan, Klein, Fairbairn, Winnicott, Hartmann, Mahler, Jacobson, Kernberg, and Kohut; and they compare these accounts to the drive/structure model of Freud. I also found useful N. Gregory Hamilton, *Self and Others: Object Relations Theory in Practice* (Northvale, N.J.: Jason Aronson, 1992). On mourning and loss I turned to John Bowlby, *Attachment and Loss:* vol. 1, *Attachment* (New York: Basic Books, 1971); vol. 2, *Separation: Anxiety and Anger* (New York: Basic Books, 1975); vol. 3, *Loss: Sadness and Depression* (New York: Basic Books, 1980). A secondary text on Bowlby is Jeremy Holmes, *John Bowlby and Attachment Theory* (London: Routledge, 1993). One book that reads literature in terms of psychological theories of mourning and loss is Neal L. Tolchin's *Mourning, Gender, and Creativity in the Art of Herman Melville* (New Haven, Conn.: Yale University Press, 1988).

4. The reader may recognize a Lacanian tone here, and I want to confess to some degree of influence without claiming that I have read extensively or reliably in his texts. My reading is limited to Jacques Lacan, *Ecrits: A Selection,* trans. Alan Sheridan (New York: Norton, 1977) and "Seminar on 'The Purloined Letter,'" trans. Jeffrey Mehlman, *Yale French Studies* 48 (1972): 38–72. I have also tried a few secondary sources that turned out to be in some places illuminating but that in others made me more confused. Among them were: Mikkel Borch-Jacobsen, *Lacan: The Absolute Master,* trans. Douglas Brick (Stanford, Calif.: Stanford University Press, 1991); Malcolm Bowie, *Lacan* (Cambridge: Harvard University Press, 1991); and Gilbert Chaitin, *Rhetoric and Culture in Lacan* (Cambridge: Cambridge University Press, 1996). So while the readings given here, say, of Davidson or McDowell or Merrill are ones that, however misguided, I am willing to defend as a result of long and careful work with the relevant texts, I make no such claims for the occasional ideas that have been influenced, well or badly, by a less well-informed reading in Lacan.

5. Clearly this way of speaking goes back to structural linguistics and structuralism generally in Europe and then to various forms of poststructuralism. I am using these notions quite generally so that one can still see them at work, for example, in the ways that a new historicist such as Greenblatt speaks of a circulation of cultural signs through various spaces of representation.

6. Pinker, *How the Mind Works,* 59–131.

7. Clearly there are important questions of gender that are brought up by an analysis such as this. I do not feel sufficiently knowledgeable to discuss such questions and so refer the reader to Nancy Chodorow, *The Reproduction of Mothering: Psychoanalysis and the Sociology of Gender* (Berkeley: University of California Press, 1978); and Dorothy Dinnerstein, *The Mermaid and the Minotaur* (New York: Harper and Row, 1976). Barbara Ann Schapiro considers these issues and also applies object-relations psychology to a number of literary readings in *Literature and the Relational Self* (New York: New York University Press, 1994).

8. While Roman Jakobson and structural linguistics are clearly influential on this usage, I am thinking especially of the way Paul de Man, for one, uses metaphor and metonymy so broadly in his sections on "Tropes (Rilke)," "Reading (Proust)," and "Metaphor (*Second Discourse*)" in his *Allegories of Reading.* There are many in literary criticism today who feel that de Man is now an outdated fashion, and it is true that much of what takes place in so-called cultural studies goes very much against his tendencies in criticism. But I think his continuing influence remains strong precisely on what can now be taken for granted, almost without mention, regarding the illusory

character of the referential energies of language and the devaluing of subjectivity. For this reason his work will be confronted in some detail in chapter 5.

9. Peirce's account of categories changed over the course of his career as his explorations in logic developed. What is mentioned here is referred to by Murray Murphey as Peirce's "Fourth System," from 1885 on. See his essay on Charles Sanders Peirce in *The Encyclopedia of Philosophy*, ed. Paul Edwards, vol. 6 (New York: Macmillan, 1967), 70–78.

10. For Donald Davidson's notion of triangulation see his "Rational Animals," in *Actions and Events*, ed. Ernest LePore and Brian McLaughlin (Oxford: Basil Blackwell, 1985), 480.

11. "It is not the *speaker* who must perform the impossible feat of comparing his belief with reality; it is the *interpreter* who must take into account the causal interaction between world and speaker in order to find out what the speaker means, and hence what he believes" (Donald Davidson, "Empirical Content," in *Truth and Interpretation*, ed. Ernest LePore [Oxford: Blackwell, 1986], 332).

12. Michel Foucault, *The Order of Things: An Archaeology of the Human Sciences* (New York: Vintage Books, 1973), 17–213.

13. James Merrill, "The Book of Ephraim," in his *Divine Comedies* (New York: Atheneum, 1977), 121.

5. The Radical Linguistic Turn in De Man and Perloff

1. De Man, *Allegories of Reading*.

2. Ibid., 278–301.

3. Ibid., 20–56.

4. Here are just a couple of examples: "Reading is a praxis that thematizes its own thesis about the impossibility of thematization and this makes it unavoidable, though hardly legitimate, for allegories to be interpreted in thematic terms" (*Allegories,* 209); and "The readability of the first part is obscured by a more radical indeterminacy that projects its shadow backwards and forwards over the entire text. Deconstructions of figural texts engender lucid narratives which produce, in their turn and as it were within their own texture, a darkness more redoubtable than the error they dispel" (217).

5. De Man, *Allegories,* 13–19, 57–72.

6. G. P. Baker and P. M. S. Hacker, *Scepticism, Rules and Language* (Oxford: Basil Blackwell, 1984), 33. Kripke's account is in his *Wittgenstein on Rules and Private Language* (Cambridge: Harvard University Press, 1982).

7. Marjorie Perloff, *The Poetics of Indeterminacy* (Evanston, Ill.: Northwestern University Press, 1999).

8. Ibid., 4–18.

9. Ibid., 67–108.

10. Ibid., 72–77.

11. Charles Bernstein, *A Poetics* (Cambridge: Harvard University Press, 1992).

12. Consider the following statements in Bernstein's *Poetics: "Poetics is the continuation of poetry by other means.* Just as poetry is the continuation of politics by other means" (160); "Poets can operate as agents of resistance, poems can be sites of social struggle" (177); and "This [a phallocratic voice of truth and sincerity] is a constantly self-proclaimed public voice, implicitly if not explicitly deriding the inarticulations,

stutterings, inaudibilities, eccentricities, and linguistic deviance of specifically marked self-interest groups" (223).

6. John Ashbery and Samuel Beckett

1. Perloff, *Poetics of Indeterminacy*, 23.

2. Ibid., 29–30. The essay quoted from is James McFarlane, "The Mind of Modernism," in *Modernism 1840–1930*, ed. Malcolm Bradbury and McFarlane (New York: Penguin, 1976), 92.

3. John Ashbery, "And *Ut Pictura Poesis* Is Her Name," in his *Houseboat Days* (New York: Penguin, 1977), 45; copyright © 1972, 1973, 1974, 1975, 1976, 1977 by John Ashbery. The poems in *Houseboat Days* are reprinted by permission of Georges Borchardt, Inc., and Carcanet Press Limited.

4. John Ashbery, "Self-Portrait in a Convex Mirror," in his *Self-Portrait in a Convex Mirror* (New York: Penguin, 1976); copyright © 1972, 1973, 1974, 1975, 1976, 1977 by John Ashbery. The poems in *Self-Portrait in a Convex Mirror* are reprinted by permission of Viking Putnam, a division of Penguin Putnam Inc., and Carcanet Press Limited.

5. Altieri, *Painterly Abstraction*, 240–47.

6. Regarding poetry generally, Altieri is good at seeing how it remains phenomenological and not merely linguistic; how it allows for complex, shifting investments of the self. See his *Painterly Abstraction*.

7. Perloff, *Poetics of Indeterminacy*, 20.

8. Ibid., 200–247.

9. Perloff's quotation is from Samuel Beckett, "Ping," in Beckett, *First Love and Other Shorts* (New York: Grove Press, 1974).

10. Perloff, *Poetics of Indeterminacy*, 23.

11. Samuel Beckett, *Molloy*, in his *Three Novels by Samuel Beckett*, trans. Patrick Bowles (New York: Grove Press, 1965), 87.

12. Samuel Beckett, *How It Is* (New York: Grove Press, 1964), 7.

13. Perloff, *Poetics of Indeterminacy*, 208.

14. Ibid., 200.

15. Ibid., 241

16. Ibid., 245.

17. Ibid., 246–47.

7. New Historicism and Cultural Studies

1. Stephen Greenblatt, *Shakespearean Negotiations* (Berkeley: University of California Press, 1988). See also Greenblatt, *Marvelous Possessions* (Chicago: University of Chicago Press, 1991). I'm interested in certain arguments found in Greenblatt's texts, not in presenting the full range of his views.

2. Greenblatt, *Shakespearean Negotiations*, 94–128.

3. Ibid., 4.

4. See Karl Marx, *Economic and Philosophic Manuscripts of 1844* (Buffalo, N.Y.: Prometheus Books, 1988), 93–95.

5. Greenblatt, *Shakespearean Negotiations*, 12, 7. All further page references to Greenblatt within the text will be to this work.

6. Ibid., 21–65.

7. Ibid., 63.

8. Ibid., 121–22. On this theme see also Ian Wilson, *Shakespeare: The Evidence* (New York: St. Martin's Griffin, 1993), in which Wilson writes, "Davies left no explanation of why he made such a positive statement [that Shakespeare died a papist], yet the heavy air of Catholicism surrounding Shakespeare's two earliest patrons, his sentimental *Sonnet* harking to the Catholic past of 'bare ruin'd choirs,' his sending up of Protestants such as Sir John Oldcastle, his sympathetic portrayals of Catholic priests such as those in *Romeo and Juliet* and *Measure for Measure,* his father and elder daughter's featuring on recusancy rolls, not least, his careful avoidance of confronting a religious theme head on in his plays, all seem of a piece" (411–12).

9. The quote is from *King Lear* 3.4.

10. A simple but useful introduction to the model of cultural studies is Patrick Fuery and Nick Mansfield, *Cultural Studies and Critical Theory* (Oxford: Oxford University Press, 2000). As I am a professor of philosophy and not of literature, my remarks and generalizations emerge from an extensive and generous but perhaps not rigorously determined sampling of materials in bookstores, journals, anthologies of theory, and conference listings, and in one case from reading over two hundred applications for a recently offered teaching position in literature. A sampling of that sort is evidently not the same thing as seeing what goes on in graduate-school classrooms. I invite the reader to make a sampling similar to mine to see if my generalizations hold.

11. For Max Horkheimer and Theodor Adorno in *Dialectic of Enlightenment* the story of the *Odyssey* is already one of moving from myth to enlightenment, of feeling the burdens of a more rigorous individuation and the need to leave behind more archaic though still appealing experiences. That view, of course, guides their treatment of Odysseus and the Sirens, for example.

12. Stephen Greenblatt, "Psychoanalysis and Renaissance Culture," in his *Learning To Curse* (New York: Routledge, 1990), 131–45.

13. Thomas Nagel's *The View from Nowhere* (New York: Oxford University Press, 1986) gives a good description of the process of trying to move to such a point of view.

14. This is a large field, but the following texts are useful for thinking about issues in postcolonial studies: Bill Ashcroft, Gareth Griffiths, and Helen Tiffin, eds., *The Post-Colonial Studies Reader* (London: Routledge, 1995); Gayatri Chakravorty Spivak, *In Other Worlds: Essays in Cultural Politics* (New York: Methuen, 1987); Homi Bhabha, *The Location of Culture* (New York: Routledge, 1994); R. Radhakrishnan, "Postmodernism and the Rest of the World," in *The Pre-Occupation of Postcolonial Studies,* ed. Fawzig Afzal-Khan and Kalpana Seshadri-Crooks (Durham, N.C.: Duke University Press, 2000), 37–70.

15. See, for example, Kalpana Seshadri-Crooks, "At the Margins of Postcolonial Studies: Part 1," in *The Pre-Occupation of Postcolonial Studies,* ed. Fawzig Afzal-Khan and Kalpana Seshadri-Crooks (Durham, N.C.: Duke University Press, 2000), 5–12.

8. Literature and Regression, Benjamin, Derrida

1. James Merrill, "The House Fly," in his *Selected Poems,* 306.

2. For Hegel on the host in Luther and Catholicism, see G. W. F. Hegel, *The Phi-*

losophy of History, in his *The Philosophy of Hegel,* ed. Carl J. Friedrich (New York: Modern Library, 1953), 106.

3. James Merrill, "The Ring Cycle," in his *Scattering of Salts,* 28.

4. Herman Melville, *Moby-Dick* (1851; New York: Penguin Books, 1992), 53.

5. Thomas Mann, *Death in Venice and Seven Other Stories,* trans. H. T. Lowe-Porter (New York: Vintage International, 1989), 45–46.

6. Joel Whitebook, *Perversion and Utopia* (Cambridge: MIT Press, 1995), 165–215.

7. James Merrill, "Santo," in *Selected Poems,* 307.

8. My reading in Benjamin's work is largely from his *The Origin of German Tragic Drama,* trans. John Osborne (London: New Left Books, 1977); and his *Reflections: Essays, Aphorisms, Autobiographical Writings,* ed. Peter Demetz (New York: Harcourt, 1978). I came to that reading already much influenced by the treatments of Benjamin in Habermas, *Philosophical Discourse of Modernity,* 10–18; and Eagleton, *Ideology of the Aesthetic,* 316–40. An overview of Benjamin's work is given in John McCole, *Walter Benjamin and the Antinomies of Tradition* (Ithaca, N.Y.: Cornell University Press, 1993); I found this book helpful for my presentation here, especially regarding the wide range of Benjamin's writings that I am not familiar with. Reading widely in literary theory I found that references to Benjamin came up frequently, and I worry that I am reacting here more to a Benjamin who is an artifact of present discussions in the field than to Benjamin himself, for I certainly do not offer myself as an expert in his thought. My interest here, in fact, is less in the detail of that thought than in responding to an important argument that has become attached to his name.

9. See Habermas, *Philosophical Discourse of Modernity,* 92–105.

10. James Merrill, "Up and Down," in *Selected Poems,* 227–30.

11. Jacques Derrida, *Circumfession,* trans. Geoffrey Bennington, part of *Jacques Derrida* (Chicago: University of Chicago Press, 1993), the other part of which is *Derridabase* by Geoffrey Bennington. The page references in the text will be to this book.

12. Jacques Derrida, "Limited Inc abc," trans. Samuel Weber, *Glyph* vol. 2 (Baltimore, Md.: Johns Hopkins University Press, 1977), 2:162–254. See my treatment of this essay in Frank Farrell, "Iterability and Meaning: The Searle-Derrida Debate," *Metaphilosophy* 19 (1988): 53–64.

13. Habermas, *Philosophical Discourse of Modernity,* 164.

14. Merrill, "Book of Ephraim," 116.

15. I am considering here the view given in Jacques Derrida, "The Pit and the Pyramid: Introduction to Hegel's Semiology," in his *Margins of Philosophy,* trans. Alan Bass (Chicago: University of Chicago Press, 1982), 69–108.

16. Hegel's own treatment can be found in his *Lectures on Aesthetics,* trans. Bosanquet and Bryant, in *Philosophy of Hegel,* 333–42.

17. Derrida, "Pit and the Pyramid," 88, 105–8.

18. I've used the version of *The Waste Land* that appears, with Eliot's notes and the editor's notes, in the *Norton Anthology of World Masterpieces,* ed. Maynard Mack (New York: Norton, 1997), 2790–802.

19. Perloff, *Poetics of Indeterminacy,* 15.

20. Ibid., 14.

9. Literary Style and Transitional Space

1. Proust, *Swann's Way*, 35.
2. See Winnicott, "Location of Cultural Experience," 3–12.
3. Ibid., 5.
4. "Language succeeds the mother as a transformational object informed by one's personal aesthetic" (Peter Rudnytsky, "Introduction," in *Transitional Objects and Potential Spaces: Literary Uses of D. W. Winnicott,* ed. Rudnytsky [New York: Columbia University Press, 1993], xvi).
5. Colm Tóibín, *The Heather Blazing* (New York: Viking, 1992).
6. W. G. Sebald, *The Emigrants,* trans. Michael Hulse (New York: New Directions, 1997), 156–57.
7. W. G. Sebald, *The Rings of Saturn,* trans. Michael Hulse (New York: New Directions, 1998).
8. John Derbyshire, *Seeing Calvin Coolidge in a Dream* (New York: St. Martin's Press, 1996).
9. Mann, "Death in Venice," 45.
10. Friedrich Nietzsche, *The Case of Wagner,* in his *The Birth of Tragedy and The Case of Wagner,* trans. Walter Kaufmann (New York: Vintage Books, 1967), 157–74.
11. Marcel Proust, *The Fugitive,* vol. 5 of *In Search of Lost Time,* trans. C. K. Scott Moncrieff and Terence Kilmartin, rev. D. J. Enright (New York: Modern Library, 1993), 883.
12. See, for example, Chodorow, *Reproduction of Mothering;* Dinnerstein, *Mermaid and the Minotaur;* and Jane Flax, *Thinking Fragments* (Berkeley: University of California Press, 1990).
13. Alice Munro, "Differently," in *The Best American Short Stories, 1990,* ed. Richard Ford (Boston: Houghton Mifflin, 1990), 190–214.

10. John Updike and the Scene of Literature

1. John Updike, *The Centaur* (New York: Fawcett Columbine, 1996).
2. John Updike, "A Sandstone Farmhouse," in *The Afterlife and Other Stories* (New York: Fawcett Crest, 1994), 131.
3. Updike, "Sandstone Farmhouse," 140.
4. This passage from Proust, *Swann's Way,* 35, was quoted earlier.
5. Merrill, "The Book of Ephraim," *Divine Comedies,* 128.
6. John Updike, *Self-Consciousness: Memoirs* (New York: Alfred A. Knopf, 1989), 170.
7. John Updike, "The Happiest I've Been," in his *The Same Door* (New York: Alfred A. Knopf, 1963), 224.
8. John Updike, "Beautiful Husbands," in his *Trust Me* (New York: Fawcett Crest, 1988), 284.
9. John Updike, "Packed Dirt, Churchgoing, a Dying Cat, a Traded Car," in his *Pigeon Feathers and Other Stories* (Harmondsworth, U.K.: Penguin, 1965), 182.

10. John Updike, "The Rumor," in his *The Afterlife and Other Stories* (New York: Fawcett Crest, 1994), 214.

11. John Updike, "His Mother inside Him," in his *The Afterlife and Other Stories* (New York: Fawcett Crest, 1994), 246.

12. John Updike, "Museums and Women," in his *Museums and Women and Other Stories* (New York: Fawcett Crest, 1972), 9.

13. John Updike, "I Am Dying, Egypt, Dying," in his *Museums and Women and Other Stories* (New York: Fawcett Crest, 1972), 95–122.

14. Hegel seems to have been wrong, as apparently the Greeks often painted their statues, including the eyes.

15. See G. W. F. Hegel, "Selections from Lectures an Aesthetics," in *The Philosophy of Hegel,* ed. Carl J. Friedrich, 331–95.

BIBLIOGRAPHY

Altieri, Charles. *Painterly Abstraction in Modernist American Poetry.* University Park: Pennsylvania State University Press, 1995.
——. *Postmodernisms Now.* University Park: Pennsylvania State University Press, 1998.
Ashbery, John. *Houseboat Days.* New York: Penguin, 1977.
——. *Self-Portrait in a Convex Mirror.* New York: Penguin, 1976.
Ashcroft, Bill, Gareth Griffiths, and Helen Tiffin, eds. *The Post-Colonial Studies Reader.* London: Routledge, 1995.
Baker, G. P., and P. M. S. Hacker. *Scepticism, Rules and Language.* Oxford: Basil Blackwell, 1984.
Beckett, Samuel. *How It Is.* New York: Grove Press, 1964.
——. *Molloy.* In his *Three Novels,* 5–176. Translated by Patrick Bowles in collaboration with the author. New York: Grove Press, 1965.
——. "Ping." In *First Love and Other Shorts.* New York: Grove Press, 1974.
Benjamin, Walter. *The Origin of German Tragic Drama.* Translated by John Osborne. London: New Left Books, 1977.
——. *Reflections: Essays, Aphorisms, Autobiographical Writings.* Edited by Peter Demetz. New York: Harcourt, 1978.
Bennington, Geoffrey. *Derridabase.* In *Jacques Derrida.* Chicago: University of Chicago Press, 1993.
Bernstein, Charles. *A Poetics.* Cambridge: Harvard University Press, 1992.
Bhabha, Homi. *The Location of Culture.* New York: Routledge, 1994.
Block, Ned. "Troubles with Functionalism." In *Perception and Cognition: Issues in the Foundations of Psychology,* edited by C. W. Savage. Minneapolis: University of Minnesota Press, 1978.
Blumenberg, Hans. *The Legitimacy of the Modern Age.* Translated by Robert Wallace. Cambridge: MIT Press, 1983.

Borch-Jacobsen, Mikkel. *Lacan: The Absolute Master.* Translated by Douglas Brick. Stanford, Calif.: Stanford University Press, 1991.

Bowie, Malcolm. *Lacan.* Cambridge: Harvard University Press, 1991.

Bowlby, John. *Attachment and Loss.* Vol. 1: *Attachment.* New York: Basic Books, 1971. Vol. 2: *Separation: Anxiety and Anger.* New York: Basic Books, 1975. Vol. 3: *Loss: Sadness and Depression.* New York: Basic Books, 1980.

Boyd, Richard. "How To Be a Moral Realist." In *Essays on Moral Realism,* edited by Geoffrey Sayre-McCord, 188–99. Ithaca: Cornell University Press, 1988.

Bradbury, Malcolm, and James McFarlane, eds. *Modernism: A Guide to European Literature, 1890–1930.* London: Penguin Books, 1991.

Butler, Christopher. *Early Modernism: Literature, Music, and Painting in Europe 1900–1916.* Oxford: Clarendon Press, 1994.

———. "The Future of Theory: Saving the Reader." In *The Future of Literary Theory,* edited by Ralph Cohen, 229–49. New York: Routledge, 1989.

Chaitin, Gilbert. *Rhetoric and Culture in Lacan.* Cambridge: Cambridge University Press, 1996.

Chaudhuri, Amit. *Freedom Song.* New York: Alfred A. Knopf, 1999. Chaudhuri's work is a trilogy of novels: *A Strange and Sublime Address, Afternoon Raag,* and *Freedom Song.*

Chodorow, Nancy. *The Reproduction of Mothering: Psychoanalysis and the Sociology of Gender.* Berkeley: University of California Press, 1978.

Culler, Jonathan. "Paul de Man's Contribution to Literary Criticism and Theory." In *The Future of Literary Theory,* edited by Ralph Cohen, 268–79. New York: Routledge, 1989.

Davidson, Donald. "Belief and the Basis of Meaning." In his *Inquiries into Truth and Interpretation,* 141–54. Oxford: Clarendon Press, 1984.

———. "A Coherence Theory of Truth and Knowledge." In *Truth and Interpretation,* edited by Ernest LePore, 307–19. Oxford: Blackwell, 1986.

———. "Empirical Content." In *Truth and Interpretation,* edited by Ernest LePore, 320–32. Oxford: Blackwell, 1986.

———. "First Person Authority." *Dialectica* 38 (1984): 101–11.

———. *Inquiries into Truth and Interpretation.* Oxford: Clarendon Press, 1984.

———. "Knowing One's Own Mind." *Proceedings and Addresses of the American Philosophical Association* 60, no. 3 (1987): 441–58.

———. "On the Very Idea of a Conceptual Scheme." In his *Inquiries into Truth and Interpretation,* 183–98. Oxford: Clarendon Press, 1984.

———. "Radical Interpretation." In his *Inquiries into Truth and Interpretation,* 125–40. Oxford: Clarendon Press, 1984.

———. "Rational Animals." In *Actions and Events,* edited by Ernest LePore and Brian McLaughlin, 473–81. Oxford: Blackwell, 1985.

———. "Reality without Reference." In his *Inquiries into Truth and Interpretation,* 215–26. Oxford: Clarendon Press, 1984.

de Man, Paul. *Allegories of Reading.* New Haven, Conn.: Yale University Press, 1979.

Dennett, Daniel. *Consciousness Explained.* Boston: Little, Brown, 1991.

———. *Elbow Room.* Cambridge: MIT Press, 1984.

Derbyshire, John. *Seeing Calvin Coolidge in a Dream.* New York: St. Martin's Press, 1996.

Derrida, Jacques. *Circumfession.* Translated by Geoffrey Bennington. In Bennington and Derrida, *Jacques Derrida.* Chicago: University of Chicago Press, 1993.

———. "Limited Inc abc." In *Glyph,* vol. 2, 162–254. Translated by Samuel Weber. Baltimore: Johns Hopkins University Press, 1977.

———. "The Pit and the Pyramid: Introduction to Hegel's Semiology." In his *Margins of Philosophy,* 69–108. Translated by Alan Bass. Chicago: University of Chicago Press, 1982.

Dinnerstein, Dorothy. *The Mermaid and the Minotaur.* New York: Harper and Row, 1976.

Dupré, John. *The Disorder of Things.* Cambridge: Harvard University Press, 1993.

During, Simon, ed. *The Cultural Studies Reader,* 2d. ed. London: Routledge, 1999.

Eagleton, Terry. *The Ideology of the Aesthetic.* Oxford: Basil Blackwell, 1990.

Eliot, T. S. *The Waste Land.* In *Norton Anthology of World Masterpieces,* edited by Maynard Mack, 2790–802. New York: Norton, 1997.

Farrell, Frank B. "Iterability and Meaning: The Searle-Derrida Debate." *Metaphilosophy* 19 (1988): 53–64.

———. "Rorty and Antirealism." In *Rorty and Pragmatism: The Philosopher Responds to His Critics,* edited by Herman J. Saatkamp, 154–88. Nashville: Vanderbilt University Press, 1995.

———. *Subjectivity, Realism and Postmodernism.* Cambridge: Cambridge University Press, 1994.

Fish, Stanley. *Doing What Comes Naturally.* Durham, N.C.: Duke University Press, 1989.

———. *Is There a Text in This Class?* Cambridge: Harvard University Press, 1980.

Flax, Jane. *Thinking Fragments.* Berkeley: University of California Press, 1990.

Foucault, Michel. *The Order of Things: An Archaeology of the Human Sciences.* New York: Vintage Books, 1973.

———. *Power/Knowledge.* Edited by Colin Gordon. New York: Pantheon, 1980.

Fuery, Patrick, and Nick Mansfield. *Cultural Studies and Critical Theory.* Oxford: Oxford University Press, 2000.

Greenberg, Jay, and Stephen Mitchell. *Object Relations in Psychoanalytic Theory.* Cambridge: Harvard University Press, 1983.

Greenblatt, Stephen. *Marvelous Possessions.* Chicago: University of Chicago Press, 1991.

———. "Psychoanalysis and Renaissance Culture." In his *Learning To Curse,* 131–45. New York: Routledge, 1990.

———. *Shakespearean Negotiations.* Berkeley: University of California Press, 1988.

Greenblatt, Stephen, and Giles Gunn, eds. *Redrawing the Boundaries: The Transformation of English and American Literary Studies.* New York: Modern Language Association of America, 1992.

Habermas, Jürgen. *The Philosophical Discourse of Modernity.* Translated by Frederick Lawrence. Cambridge: MIT Press, 1987.

Hamilton, N. Gregory. *Self and Others: Object Relations Theory in Practice.* Northvale, N.J.: Jason Aronson, 1992.

Hegel, G. W. F. *The Philosophy of Hegel.* Edited by Carl J. Friedrich. New York: Modern Library, 1953.

Heidegger, Martin. "The Origin of the Work of Art." In his *Poetry, Language, Thought,* translated by Albert Hofstadter. New York: Harper and Row, 1971.

——. "What Are Poets For?" In his *Poetry, Language, Thought,* translated by Albert Hofstadter, 91–142. New York: Harper and Row, 1971.

Hemingway, Ernest. *A Farewell to Arms.* 1929. New York: Simon and Schuster, 1995.

Holmes, Jeremy. *John Bowlby and Attachment Theory.* London: Routledge, 1993.

Horkheimer, Max, and Theodor Adorno. *Dialectic of Enlightenment.* Translated by John Cumming. New York: Herder, 1972.

Husserl, Edmund. *The Crisis of European Sciences and Transcendental Phenomenology.* Translated by David Carr. Evanston, Ill.: Northwestern University Press, 1970.

Jameson, Fredric. *Postmodernism: or The Cultural Logic of Late Capitalism.* Durham, N.C.: Duke University Press, 1991.

Joyce, James. "The Dead." In his *Dubliners.* 175–224. New York: Viking, 1961.

Kripke, Saul. "Identity and Necessity." In *Naming, Necessity, and Natural Kinds,* edited by Stephen Schwartz, 66–101. Ithaca, N.Y.: Cornell University Press, 1977.

——. *Wittgenstein on Rules and Private Language.* Cambridge: Harvard University Press, 1982.

Lacan, Jacques. *Ecrits: A Selection.* Translated by Alan Sheridan. New York: Norton, 1977.

——. "Seminar on 'The Purloined Letter,'" Translated by Jeffrey Mehlman. *Yale French Studies* 48 (1972): 38–72.

Laudan, Larry. *Science and Relativism.* Chicago: University of Chicago Press, 1990.

Lehman, David. *The Last Avant-Garde: The Making of the New York School of Poets.* New York: Anchor Books, 1999.

Levenson, Michael H. *A Genealogy of Modernism.* Cambridge: Cambridge University Press, 1984.

Lipton, Peter. *Inference to the Best Explanation.* London: Routledge, 1991.

Mann, Thomas. *Death in Venice and Seven Other Stories.* Translated by H. T. Lowe-Porter. New York: Vintage International, 1989.

Marx, Karl. *Economic and Philosophic Manuscripts of 1844.* Translated by Martin Milligan. Buffalo, N.Y.: Prometheus Books, 1988.

McCarthy, Cormac. *All the Pretty Horses.* New York: Alfred A. Knopf, 1992.

——. *Blood Meridian.* New York: Vintage International, 1992.

McCole, John. *Walter Benjamin and the Antinomies of Tradition.* Ithaca. N.Y.: Cornell University Press, 1993.

McDowell, John. *Mind and World.* Cambridge: Harvard University Press, 1994.

McFarlane, James. "The Mind of Modernism." In *Modernism 1840–1930*, edited by Malcolm Bradbury and McFarlane, 71–93. New York: Penguin, 1976.

McGinn, Colin. *The Problem of Consciousness*. Oxford: Blackwell, 1991.

McHale, Brian. *Postmodernist Fiction*. London: Routledge, 1989.

Melville, Herman. *Moby-Dick*. 1851. New York: Penguin Books, 1992. First published by Northwestern University Press as Volume 6 of *The Writings of Herman Melville*, edited by Harrison Hayford, Hershel Parker, and B. Thomas Tanselle, 1988. This edition with an introduction by Andrew Delbanco and notes and glossary by Tom Quirk.

Menand, Louis. *Discovering Modernism: T. S. Eliot and His Context*. New York: Oxford University Press, 1987.

Merrill, James. "The Book of Ephraim." In his *Divine Comedies*, 47–136. New York: Atheneum, 1977.

——. *A Scattering of Salts*. New York: Alfred A. Knopf, 1995.

——. *Selected Poems 1946–1985*. New York: Alfred A. Knopf, 1995.

Munro, Alice. "Differently." In *The Best American Short Stories, 1990*, edited by Richard Ford, 190–214. Boston: Houghton Mifflin, 1990.

Murphey, Murray. "Charles Sanders Peirce." In *The Encyclopedia of Philosophy*, vol. 6, edited by Paul Edwards, 70–78. New York: Macmillan, 1967.

Nagel, Thomas. *The View from Nowhere*. New York: Oxford University Press, 1986.

Nietzsche, Friedrich. *The Case of Wagner*. In his *The Birth of Tragedy and The Case of Wagner*, translated by Walter Kaufmann, 157–74. New York: Vintage Books, 1967.

——. *The Genealogy of Morals*. Translated by F. Golffing. Garden City, N.Y.: Anchor Books, 1956.

Pears, David. *The False Prison*. Vol. 2. Oxford: Clarendon Press, 1988.

Perloff, Marjorie. *The Poetics of Indeterminacy*. Evanston, Ill.: Northwestern University Press, 1999.

Pinker, Steven. *How the Mind Works*. New York: W. W. Norton and Co., 1997.

Proust, Marcel. *The Fugitive*. Vol. 5 of *In Search of Lost Time*. Translated by C. K. Scott Moncrieff and Terence Kilmartin. Revised by D. J. Enright. New York: Modern Library, 1993.

——. *Swann's Way*. Translated by C. K. Scott Moncrieff. New York: Penguin, 1999.

Putnam, Hilary. *The Many Faces of Realism*. LaSalle, Ill.: Open Court, 1987.

——. "Meaning and Reference." In *Naming, Necessity, and Natural Kinds*, edited by Stephen Schwartz, 119–21. Ithaca, N.Y.: Cornell University Press, 1977.

——. *Realism and Reason*. Cambridge: Cambridge University Press, 1983.

——. *Reason, Truth, and History*. Cambridge: Cambridge University Press, 1981.

Pynchon, Thomas. *Gravity's Rainbow*. New York: Viking, 1973.

——. *Mason & Dixon*. New York: Henry Holt, 1997.

Quine, Willard V. O. "Existence and Quantification." In his *Ontological Relativity and Other Essays*, 91–113. New York: Columbia University Press, 1969.

———. "Ontological Relativity." In his *Ontological Relativity and Other Essays,* 26–68. New York: Columbia University Press, 1969.

Radhakrishnan, R. "Postmodernism and the Rest of the World." In *The Pre-Occupation of Postcolonial Studies,* edited by Fawzia Afzal-Khan and Kalpana Seshadri-Crooks, 37–70. Durham, N.C.: Duke University Press, 2000.

Rorty, Richard. *Consequences of Pragmatism.* Minneapolis: University of Minnesota Press, 1982.

———. *The Linguistic Turn.* Chicago: University of Chicago Press, 1967.

———. "Response to Frank Farrell." In *Rorty and Pragmatism: The Philosopher Responds to His Critics,* edited by Herman J. Saatkamp, 189–95. Nashville: Vanderbilt University Press, 1995.

———. "The World Well Lost." *Journal of Philosophy* 69 (1972): 649–65.

Rudnytsky, Peter. "Introduction." In *Transitional Objects and Potential Spaces: Literary Uses of D. W. Winnicott,* edited by Rudnytsky, xi–xxii. New York: Columbia University Press, 1993.

Rushdie, Salman. *Midnight's Children.* 1980. New York: Penguin, 1991.

Sartre, Jean-Paul. *Nausea.* Translated by Lloyd Alexander. New York: New Directions, 1969.

Schapiro, Barbara Ann. *Literature and the Relational Self.* New York: New York University Press, 1994.

Schwartz, Stephen, ed. *Naming, Necessity, and Natural Kinds.* Ithaca, N.Y.: Cornell University Press, 1977.

Sebald, W. G. *The Emigrants.* Translated by Michael Hulse. New York: New Directions, 1997.

———. *The Rings of Saturn.* Translated by Michael Hulse. New York: New Directions, 1998.

Seshadri-Crooks, Kalpana. "At the Margins of Postcolonial Studies: Part 1." In *The Pre-Occupation of Postcolonial Studies,* edited by Fawzia Afzal-Khan and Kalpana Seshadri-Crooks, 5–12. Durham, N.C.: Duke University Press, 2000.

Spivak, Gayatri Chakravorty. *In Other Worlds: Essays in Cultural Politics.* New York: Methuen, 1987.

Tóibín, Colm. *The Heather Blazing.* New York: Viking, 1992.

Tolchin, Neal L. *Mourning, Gender, and Creativity in the Art of Herman Melville.* New Haven, Conn.: Yale University Press, 1988.

Updike, John. "Beautiful Husbands." In his *Trust Me,* 280–88. New York: Fawcett Crest, 1988.

———. *The Centaur.* New York: Fawcett Columbine, 1996.

———. "The Happiest I've Been." In his *The Same Door,* 220–42. New York: Alfred A. Knopf, 1963.

———. "His Mother Inside Him." In his *The Afterlife and Other Stories,* 241–48. New York: Fawcett Crest, 1994.

———. "I Am Dying, Egypt, Dying." In his *Museums and Women and Other Stories,* 95–122. New York: Fawcett Crest, 1972.

———. "Museums and Women." In his *Museums and Women and Other Stories,* 9–20. New York: Fawcett Crest, 1972.

——. "Packed Dirt, Churchgoing, a Dying Cat, a Traded Car." In his *Pigeon Feathers and Other Stories,* 170–92. Harmondsworth, U.K.: Penguin, 1965.

——. "The Rumor." In his *The Afterlife and Other Stories,* 207–21. New York: Fawcett Crest, 1994.

——. "A Sandstone Farmhouse." In his *The Afterlife and Other Stories,* 107–40. New York: Fawcett Crest, 1994.

——. *Self-Consciousness: Memoirs.* New York: Alfred A. Knopf, 1989.

Whitebook, Joel. *Perversion and Utopia.* Cambridge: MIT Press, 1995.

Williams, Bernard. *Ethics and the Limits of Philosophy.* Cambridge: Harvard University Press, 1985.

——. *Shame and Necessity.* Berkeley: University of California Press, 1993.

Wilson, Ian. *Shakespeare: The Evidence.* New York: St. Martin's Griffin, 1993.

Winnicott, D. W. "The Location of Cultural Experience." In *Transitional Objects and Potential Spaces: Literary Uses of D. W. Winnicott,* edited by Peter Rudnytsky, 3–12. New York: Columbia University Press, 1993.

Wittgenstein, Ludwig. *Philosophical Investigations.* Oxford: Basil Blackwell, 1953.

Yenser, Stephen. *The Consuming Myth: The Work of James Merrill.* Cambridge: Harvard University Press, 1987.

INDEX